P9-AFB-441

We know now beyond any doubt what we suspected before—that Type A behavior can be treated effectively, that reduction or elimination of Type A behavior can reduce the incidence of heart attacks radically, and that Type A behavior can now be regarded alone among risk factors as a primary causal agent in the pathogenesis of coronary heart disease.

This book brings up to date what is now known about the nature and workings of Type A behavior in both men and women. What may be even more important in the long run—if only readers will take our findings to heart— is that it tells how Type A behavior can be treated.

Another Fawcett Crest Book
by Meyer Friedman, M.D.

TYPE A BEHAVIOR AND YOUR HEART
(with Ray H. Rosenman, M.D.)

TREATING TYPE A BEHAVIOR AND YOUR HEART

By Meyer Friedman, M.D., and
Diane Ulmer, R.N., M.S.

FAWCETT CREST • NEW YORK

We dedicate this book to James J. Gill, a devout Jesuit priest and a distinguished physician. We do so in appreciation of his making love a more meaningful spiritual power both to the counselors and to the participants he advised in the Recurrent Coronary Prevention Project.

A Fawcett Crest Book
Published by Ballantine Books

Library of Congress Catalog Card Number: 83-47939

ISBN 0-449-20826-5

This edition published by arrangement with
Alfred A. Knopf, Inc.

Manufactured in the United States of America

First Ballantine Books Edition: November 1985
Tenth Printing: May 1990

CONTENTS

FOREWORD

Early in May, 1971, America's most distinguished publisher, Alfred A. Knopf, then 79 years of age, sent me a short note. "I'm still enough of an eager beaver after more than fifty years in this business," he wrote, "to suggest that you have a book in you and that I would like to publish it." Two years later, *Type A Behavior and Your Heart,* by Meyer Friedman and Ray H. Rosenman, was published under the Knopf imprint. It alerted millions of men and women here and abroad to the possibility that a particular behavior pattern, which we called Type A behavior, might well be encouraging the development of coronary heart disease.

Now, after a further decade of study of both Type A behavior and coronary patients, Diane Ulmer and I have written this sequel. It presents new and quite specific information about how Type A behavior can be altered and the effect of such alteration on the progress of coronary heart disease in the susceptible individual.

This new information was largely obtained during the

course of a unique experimental project never attempted before. Beginning in 1977, we undertook to recruit over a thousand men and women, each of whom had suffered at least one heart attack, for a program designed to modify their Type A behavior. Our aim was to find out (1) whether such modification was indeed possible and (2) if it were, whether it would offer protection against another heart attack. This project gave us the rare opportunity of spending 60,000 patient-hours observing what does and what does not work in treating Type A behavior.

It was not at all easy to get this particular study underway or to see it through to the end, as we shall later explain. Certainly without a grant from the National Heart, Lung and Blood Institute and the moral and financial support of the officers of the Bank of America, Standard Oil of California, the Kaiser Hospital Foundation, the Zellerbach Family Foundation, and the Mary Lard Foundation, we would have had no hope of success.

There have been certain nonmedical friends of ours who, each in his own way, have since 1955 played indispensable roles in helping us to discover and publicize the fact that how a man or woman *feels* may have as much to do with causing coronary heart disease as what he or she eats, drinks, or inhales. These friends include S. Gale Herrick, James C. Nelson, Jr., the late Harold Zellerbach, Bayard Friedman, Lawrence Hoyt, James Vohs, Lieutenant General Elvy R. Roberts (ret.), Walter Morris, C. J. Bocchieri, and Judge Alfonso J. Zirpoli. To them, we shall always be deeply grateful.

We also wish to express our thanks to the cardiologists, psychiatrists, psychologists, nurses, biostatisticians, and administrators who manned the San Francisco Recurrent Coronary Prevention Project (RCPP). They include doctors James J. Gill, Carl E. Thoresen, Leonti H. Thompson, Gerald W. Piaget, Theodore R. Dixon, Edward F. Bourg, Virginia A. Price, Raphael B. Reider, Richard A. Levy, Paul M. Loftus, David D. Rabin, William S. Breall, Bernard de Hovitz, Berton H. Kaplan, Lynda Powell, Craig Wilson, and Peter Wolk; and nurses and administrators Deborah S. Casey, Nancy Fleischmann, Christine A. Melanson, and Elizabeth S. Mitchum. We owe particular thanks to the Superiors of the Society of Jesus and the administrators of the Harvard University Health Services for allowing Dr. Gill to commute monthly from Cambridge, Massachusetts, to San Francisco in order to lead and counsel 16 groups of participants in the RCPP study over a period of three years. We should also like to express now our tremendous debt to Dr. Sanford O. Byers, who for two decades furnished the biochemical expertise without which the fundamental pathophysiological effects of Type A behavior could not have been established.

Finally, if some of our research studies over this past quarter of a century do manage to help keep thousands of Americans from becoming premature victims of coronary heart disease, those Americans will also have to thank Jerome M. Rosefield of Los Gatos, California, because it was his advice and wisdom that made these studies possible.

One final note: Through much of this book we shall refer to the Type A person in masculine terms. It should be understood that this is done only in the interests of word economy; as will be seen in Chapter 4, Type A behavior is a disorder by no means limited exclusively to men.

MEYER FRIEDMAN, M.D.
San Francisco

PART ONE

THE TYPE A CONCEPT

CHAPTER 1

The History of an Idea

The classic anecdote regarding the discovery of the Type A behavior pattern has been told many times, among other places in a chapter contributed by Redford B. Williams, Jr., to a popular textbook on the heart. After crediting me and my colleague Ray Rosenman with first noting the pattern, Williams goes on to say that "at least partial credit belongs to their office receptionist, who initially called to their attention the curious fact that the upholstery on the chairs in their waiting room was worn only on the front edge of the seat." Well, it is true that an upholsterer (not a receptionist) did comment on the worn front edges of those chairs, but his remarks struck no chord in us at the time; we were still far from being able to recognize the significance of what had been called to our attention.

I (Meyer Friedman) am the sole author of this first chapter because my co-author, Diane Ulmer, did not arrive at the Harold Brunn Institute until 1977, and thus has no firsthand knowledge of how the Type A behavior—coronary heart disease concept originated and developed during the two decades prior to her arrival on the scene.

Actually, the discovery and subsequent development of the notion that a particular sort of behavior might be involved in the development of coronary heart disease (CHD) was the work of a team consisting of two cardiologists (Rosenman and myself) and a biochemist (Dr. Sanford O. Byers), working at the Harold Brunn Institute (HBI) of Mount Zion Hospital and Medical Center in San Francisco. Beginning three decades ago, we three researchers of the HBI team, each contributing his particular variety of expertise, sought evidence that might provide answers to two questions: First, can a person's feelings or thoughts have any influence upon the development of coronary heart disease? Second, if there is such a relationship, how does it work?

Our first vague suspicion that what a person feels or thinks might have something to do with the origin or development of CHD arose in 1954, when we were asked to write a review article concerning heart disease and cholesterol metabolism. In the course of reading the literature, we were struck with a new thought: As good a case could be made for nervous tension or excess competitive drive as a cause of CHD as too much cholesterol in the diet!

But suspicious as we increasingly became, it was not until 1956, when we studied precisely what 46 San Francisco Junior League women and their husbands ate over a period of two weeks, that we realized coronary heart disease could not be caused simply by what people eat or smoke. The women consumed just as much cholesterol and animal fat as their husbands did, but they were far less susceptible to heart disease. We knew that their relative immunity could not be laid to the female sex hormone, estrogen, because *black* females possess fully as much of this hormone as *white* females, yet black women have as much heart disease as their husbands do. There just had to be another factor at work.

The president of the Junior League thought she knew. "If you really want to know what is going to give our husbands heart attacks, I'll tell you," she said. I assured her that indeed I did wish to know. "It's stress," she said sadly, "the stress they have to face in their businesses, day in, day out. Why, when my husband comes home at night, it takes at least one martini just to unclench his jaws."

Unlike the upholsterer's remark, this comment did not fall upon "deaf minds." Coming as it did after the negative results of the dietary study and on top of our own suspicions about the possible role of emotional stress, it made us realize that we had to cease armchair philosophizing and start some serious investigative work.

The first step was a very tentative one. We sent out a questionnaire to several hundred industrialists and more than 100 physicians treating coronary patients, requesting their opinions of what they thought had caused a heart attack in a close friend or in their patients. Over 70 percent of the businessmen—and a similar percentage of the physicians—agreed completely with the Junior League president: that stress associated with meeting business and professional deadlines and *excessive* competitive drive had been the chief precipitating causes of the heart attacks. While we rather expected this sort of answer from the laymen, we were startled to find so many physicians ascribing lethality to a factor that was neither mentioned nor described in medical textbooks or professional journals of the day.* On the strength of this, Dr. Rosenman and I decided to take a long, close look at the coronary patients we ourselves were treating. This examination involved scrutinizing each patient as a *total* human being, not just a mobile exemplar of medical statistics such as blood pressure, pulse rate, electrocardiographic squiggles, and blood cholesterol, triglyceride, lipoprotein, uric acid, and sugar levels.†

---

*Matters are not greatly improved now. The most recent textbook devoted to heart disease has 1,943 pages, of which 215 are devoted to coronary heart disease, and only *four paragraphs* concern Type A behavior as a possible risk factor.

†Today, coronary patients also may receive vector cardiograms, treadmill electrocardiographic tests with and without radioactive thallium, plain or two dimensional echocardiograms, chest x-rays, and coronary angiograms.

As we looked at our patients in this new way, as individuals who possessed other organs besides their ailing hearts and also personalities, it became obvious that it was not simply their hearts that had gone awry. Something in the way they felt, thought, and acted was also in alarming disarray. Moreover, while only half of our patients smoked, and fewer than half possessed a high serum level of cholesterol or triglyceride, suffered from high blood pressure, or had been physically indolent prior to the advent of their heart attacks, they all exhibited various signs of a particular emotional complex. Noting this, it became even clearer to us that what people become excited or frustrated about, or struggle for or against might be playing a role, possibly a very important role, either in bringing on CHD or accelerating its progress. We decided to concentrate our research on the behavior pattern we soon began calling Type A behavior.*

Our first bona fide research effort in this field involved our studying 40 accountants, all volunteers. It was a smashing success. The blood cholesterol of these accountants and also the speed at which their blood clotted in January 1957 was completely normal and remained so when they were studied biweekly for the remainder of January and through February and March. During these same months the accountants did not alter either their eating or exercise habits. During the first two weeks of April, however, as the tax-filing deadline approached and

---

*I have often been asked how Type A behavior received its name. In 1958, when we had been refused funding twice for a study of "emotional stress" and its possible relation to coronary heart disease, I went to Washington to see whether I could find out what was going wrong. I spoke to Dr. C. J. Van Slyke of what was then called the National Heart Institute, who explained that because we used the term emotional stress in the title of our grant applications, they were always sent off to psychiatrists for review. These specialists apparently doubted that two cardiologists and a biochemist were equipped to study emotional matters, and refused funding. Dr. Van Slyke, who had himself examined our applications, suggested a small word change. "I believe you fellows are describing a behavior pattern, something that you've actually witnessed," he said. "Why don't you just label it Type A behavior pattern? That shouldn't upset the psychiatrists." We did so on our third grant application. It was favorably received and funded.

our subjects were desperately striving to finish their clients' tax forms and get them signed and in the mail, their average blood cholesterol level rose abruptly and their blood began clotting at a dangerously accelerated rate. In May and June, with no further deadlines to face, the blood cholesterol and clotting times of these men returned to normal levels. For the first time in medical history, a clear-cut demonstration of the power of the mind alone to alter man's blood cholesterol and clotting time had been achieved.

When one of us reported these findings to our colleagues assembled at the annual meeting of the American Heart Association, there was no applause following the presentation, only a dead silence. We felt very much as Lincoln must have felt at Gettysburg when a similar silence followed the delivery of his address. The news was no doubt shocking to those scientists who had spent almost their entire careers believing in the hypothesis that only what a person eats can affect his blood cholesterol level. Even today, more than a quarter of a century later, and after our findings had been repeatedly confirmed by other investigators throughout the world, the majority of scientists working in the cholesterol field, many doctors, and many researchers prefer to overlook the fact that the brain of a man may have as much to do with his blood cholesterol level as the ingestion of the yolk of a chicken's egg.

Our first experimental success was quickly followed by another, different sort of investigation. In 1958, we launched an epidemiological study involving 80 men who chronically exhibited Type A behavior, a second group of 80 men who exhibited no Type A behavior, and a third group of 40 subjects suffering a neurotic anxiety state. Although we found that the amount and nature of the food consumed by all three groups, as well as the amount of physical exercise, was basically the same, we again observed that the blood cholesterol was higher and the clotting time faster in the Type A subjects. Likewise the Type A subjects smoked twice as much as the other two groups. The 40 neurotic subjects were similar in all respects to the non-Type A group (a category we began calling Type B). The most surprising and terrifying finding was that the men in the Type A group *already* possessed a seven times greater incidence of coronary heart disease than those in the other groups. Yet all these men had been picked from the San Francisco Bay Area community solely on the basis of their behavior pattern.

We exultantly published these results in the *Journal of the American Medical Association* in 1959, fully expecting editorial praise from dozens of medical journals. Nothing of the sort happened. For all the attention our article received during the first few years after its appearance, it could just as well have been published in Swahili in some obscure Zanzibar newspaper. (The article was the first, incidentally, to use the terms Type A and Type B to designate the two different behavior patterns.)

For ourselves, however, the results of these studies completely erased any lingering doubts we still may have entertained about the importance of Type A behavior in the development of heart disease. Indeed, we were so bedazzled that we decided to go all out in further exploration, and proceeded to devise three new research approaches.

The first would be epidemiological. We would study large groups of human subjects in order to find out the possible prevalence of Type A behavior in men and women, in various races, in various socioeconomic classes, and in persons of various ages.

The second approach would be clinical. The aim would be to discover the precise biochemical and pathophysiological abnormalities that might be set in motion by the presence of Type A behavior in humans. For this sort of study, the HBI team planned to enroll normal volunteer Type A and B subjects whom we would study in much the same way as we previously had studied rats and rabbits in the course of other clinical research.

The third research approach would consist of attempts to replicate in a laboratory animal either the total Type A complex or some of its salient components. If we could find ways to do this, we would gain valuable opportunities to investigate not only the reactions of various organs in the body to Type A behavior, but also to find out which of these reactions played a part in the development of coronary artery disease.

These three approaches paid off wonderfully well in the ensuing 20 years. They led to the publication of more than 100 articles. The epidemiological researches demonstrated, for example, that women who exhibited Type A behavior possessed a much higher blood cholesterol, were subject far more frequently to hypertension, and already suffered more heart disease than Type B women (see Chapter 4). For the first time, the real cause for the *white* American female's relative immunity was thus exposed.

Probably the most important epidemiological research was our eight-and-a-half-year study of 3,500 healthy men.* At the start of the study, in 1960—1961, each man was classified according to three different techniques as being either relatively susceptible or relatively immune to a future heart attack, in hopes of finding out what predictive procedure was most accurate.

The first technique was the interview. Using this procedure, the HBI team determined that approximately half of the sample group appeared to be Type A and on that basis alone classified them as relatively susceptible to heart disease. The remaining half, appraised as Type B, were classified as relatively immune. The classification method, it should be noted, involved no complicated instruments or chemical analyses, only a 15-minute interview consisting of several dozen questions about habits of working, talking, eating, reading, and thinking.

The second classification was based on techniques developed by a group of researchers in San Antonio headed by Nicholas T. Werthessen, a distinguished physiologist.

*This study is now referred to in the medical literature as the Western Collaborative Group Study.

It employed a clotting test that the researchers believed could be used to identify heart-attack-prone individuals.

A third classification of the same 3,500 volunteers was made by a team based in Burbank, California, headed by an experienced pathologist named Reuben Straus. This group had devised a test involving the amount of cholesterol carried in the low- and high-density lipoproteins in the blood, which they felt could predict future susceptibility or immunity to heart disease.

Scarcely more than a year had passed before the HBI team had a strong hint of what the final results of the study would show. By that time we had discovered that, although only supposedly healthy men had been enrolled in the study, 113 men out of the total 3,500 in fact were suffering from coronary heart disease at the time of entry, as shown by electrocardiographic evidence. They did not know that they had it, and of course the HBI team's interviewer had no way of identifying them when the Type A/Type B classification was done. We realized that some indication of the accuracy of our predictions could be gained from finding out which of the 113 men had been identified as Type A's at the outset. The correlation was satisfyingly good: No fewer than 80 of the 113 (71 percent) already harboring coronary heart disease had been assessed as Type A. By the time the study was complete, the confirmation was even stronger: 178 of the 257 *new* heart attacks suffered by participants had befallen men initially assessed as exhibiting Type A behavior. In other words, Type A men were, over the course of the study, shown to be two to three times more prone to heart attacks than men classed as Type B. Moreover, not one of the men classed as "pure" Type B's in the initial 1960–1961 screening suffered a heart attack during the next 12 years!

Unfortunately, the blood clotting test of the San Antonio group failed to distinguish between those likely and those unlikely to have future heart attacks. But the predictive classifications of the Burbank group were essentially as good as ours. Persons who exhibited high blood cholesterol or triglyceride levels in 1960–1961 proved to be twice as prone to future heart attacks as those who showed normal values. The predictive study as a whole also affirmed what already had been known for a decade or so: Heavy cigarette smoking and high blood pressure were linked to future heart attacks.

From our point of view, this study was remarkable for another reason. Unlike all other epidemiological studies that had preceded it (and for that matter, that have followed it, to this day) it suggested the distinct possibility that Type A behavior *itself* might be producing the raised serum cholesterol, triglyceride, and low-density lipoprotein levels, to say nothing of high blood pressure and even the increased smoking of cigarettes. If this is ever finally proved to be true, it will mean that for decades cardiologists have been attributing *primary* causal importance to phenomena that are actually *secondary* to a phenomenon that they have completely overlooked.

By 1970, the major epidemiological research of the HBI team had been completed. The thousands of man-hours employed in these studies had uncovered just a few truths, but they were of transcendent importance. They were: (1) almost all coronary patients exhibit a certain sameness in facial and bodily gestures, voice tones, and biographical experiences, the complex which we term Type A behavior; (2) randomly selected persons exhibiting this behavior, whether male or female, are seven times more likely to have coronary heart disease (whether or not it has been diagnosed) as those persons exhibiting Type B behavior; they also usually possess a higher blood cholesterol content, their blood clots faster, and they smoke more; and (3) healthy Type A men are two to three times as likely to succumb to heart attacks as Type B men. In short, these results pointed to a simple relationship existing between coronary heart disease and Type A behavior: Where one finds coronary heart disease, one invariably finds Type A behavior and where one finds Type A behavior, sooner or later one will witness the advent of coronary heart disease.

But epidemiological studies can only do so much, and one thing they could not do was to establish the exact physiological linkage between Type A behavior and the development of coronary heart disease. Obviously other research techniques were needed. As we have already noted, the HBI team had launched two other investigations at the time the epidemiological studies began. One of these involved the clinical study of relatively small groups (50 to 60 persons) of Type A and Type B men. The volunteers—accountants, policemen, firemen, insurance agents, attorneys, media executives, architects, embalmers, municipal park gardeners, and garbage collectors*—were all "pure bred" in that each exhibited either Type A or Type B behavior in an extreme form. Year after year, these gentlemen cheerfully agreed to ingest or be injected with various drugs and hormones; to give blood or urine or both; to wear pulse-rate-counting apparatuses for weeks at a time; and to gorge or to starve themselves for up to 48 hours—all this so that the team could conduct metabolic, hormonal, and pharmacological experiments aimed at discovering the biochemical and pathophysiological changes caused by Type A behavior, in particular those changes possibly responsible for the coronary heart disease so often found in Type A persons.

Scores of studies began in high hopes; quite a few ended in crushing disappointment. We were almost certain, for example, that the hearts of Type A persons beat more rapidly during their working hours than the hearts of Type B persons, so Alvin Brown, our electronic engineering consultant, devised a beautifully precise electrocardiograph, approximately the size of a small domino tile. The volunteers wore it for a week. But the average pulse rate of the Type A proved to be no faster or slower than that of the Type B person. Also, our team was almost positive that various blood clotting elements of Type A

*For some unexplained reason, the HBI team was rarely able to induce a physician to serve as a volunteer in these studies. It was not that they disapproved of the studies; they always said that they were too busy to volunteer. Also, doctors as a group do not like to be bled for blood samples.

persons were being consumed at a more rapid rate than similar elements of Type B persons. Volunteers allowed huge amounts of blood to be withdrawn so that the clotting elements could be isolated, tagged with radioactive chemicals, and replaced. Despite the discomfort of the volunteers and the tedious, delicate labors of the chemists, the results were discouragingly negative.

But many of our clinical investigations did pay off. One of our most important findings was the relative inability of most healthy Type A persons to rid their blood of the fat absorbed from their food. This is a characteristic of most coronary patients. Thus, decades before Type A's show any sign of coronary heart disease, they already possess one of the more notable biochemical attributes of the disease in its active state. A further discovery was the tendency of this abnormal accumulation of fat in the blood to cause red blood cells to adhere or clump together. (This phenomenon and its dangerous significance are discussed in the next chapter.)

Possibly the most consequential discovery of all occurred in 1960 when we found that healthy Type A volunteers produced, and had circulating in their blood, far more of the so-called "struggle hormone," norepinephrine, than did Type B subjects. The possible role of this hormone in the development of coronary heart disease is described in the next chapter. Suffice it to say here that excess norepinephrine is now regarded by researchers throughout the world as playing an even greater role than dietary cholesterol in the development of coronary heart disease. It probably would have fallen under suspicion long before our findings if there had been a simple method of measuring it.

Very early in our investigation of the possible involvement of the brain in the development of coronary heart disease, we noted that the eyelids and the skin immediately above and below the eyes of coronary patients frequently appeared deeply tanned. The pigmentation was essentially similar to that seen in patients suffering from Addison's Disease, who lack functioning adrenal glands.

It has long been known that this pigmentation comes from an excess of a tanning hormone secreted together with the adrenal-stimulating hormone called ACTH. (The same cells in the pituitary gland simultaneously manufacture and discharge both hormones.) With the adrenal gland out of commission, the body wildly—and fruitlessly—increases the manufacture and discharge of ACTH, and along with it an oversupply of the pigmenting hormone. But this is not the only condition under which the pituitary delivers ACTH and its fellow hormone. It also does so when the person is involved in a struggle—physical or mental. It seemed likely to us that the same kind of thing was going on in coronary patients and healthy Type A subjects exhibiting pigmentation around the eyes: an excess secretion of ACTH, in connection with a continuous state of emotional struggle or perturbation.

With the indispensable help of the late Saul Berson and Rosalind Yalow (later a Nobel Prize recipient), whose New York laboratory was in 1970 the only place where the delicate process of assaying blood ACTH could be accomplished, we found that our suspicions were justified. Even when tested at 7 A.M., Type A's were already secreting more ACTH than Type B subjects. They continued to do throughout the day, indeed even at 9 P.M. In a way, they resembled those Columbia River salmon who in battling upstream to spawn and die also exhibit a marked rise in their ACTH blood level. It is now apparent that such excess ACTH production plays a leading role in a spawning salmon's cardiovascular exhaustion and death. The question remains to be answered whether the similar outpouring of ACTH into the bloodstream of a Type A as he or she struggles day after day, year after year, decade after decade, may not also hasten cardiovascular exhaustion and final collapse.

But the HBI team's clinical researches also revealed that more than cholesterol, triglycerides, norepinephrine, and ACTH were in chronic disarray in severely afflicted Type A persons. Many of them also exhibited inadequate amounts of pituitary growth hormone. Most laymen probably believe that growth hormone is responsible only for skeletal growth in youth, but recent studies indicate that it plays a significant role in various metabolic functions throughout life. We found, for example, that the normal secretion of growth hormone was absolutely essential for the maintenance of a normal blood cholesterol level. Yet more often than not, Type A persons appear to possess a low circulating level of this hormone. Whether this is due to inadequate supply or excessive destruction of growth hormone in Type A persons remains to be determined.

A final discovery was that most Type A persons experienced an excessive discharge of insulin into their bloodstream when they were fed a modest amount of pure sugar. Just what this abnormality might mean we still do not know. We do know, however, that the maturity-onset variety of diabetes is seen more frequently in Type A than in Type B subjects.

Like our epidemiological studies, these clinical studies also suggested the primacy of Type A behavior in the evolution of human coronary heart disease. They added indisputable evidence that this type of behavior and only this type of behavior is closely associated with blood elevations of cholesterol and triglyceride and with significant abnormalities of the hormones, norepinephrine, ACTH, growth hormone, and insulin. If possible mechanisms whereby Type A behavior might lead to CHD had to be demonstrated, the HBI team's clinical studies certainly provided such a demonstration. Nevertheless, the *cause* responsible for the development of CHD still remained to be identified with absolute certainty.

The HBI team's third research approach consisted of experimental studies carried on in the laboratory upon various species of animals, beginning in the late 1950s.

From the outset, it was dismally apparent that it would be difficult to replicate the chief components of Type A behavior in any experimental animal. How do you induce a sense of time urgency, or free-floating hostility, or a low sense of self-esteem in a chicken? We therefore decided that since it appeared impossible to present an *external* stimulus to any experimental animal that might evoke Type A-like emotional responses, perhaps it might be feasible to induce an *internal* stimulus (in the form of a tiny electrical current) directly to the hypothalamus, that part of the brain believed to be centrally involved in translating various emotional perturbations into physical responses on an unconscious level—making an angry person's heart beat faster, for example, or his face flush. If a tiny electrode could be implanted in the proper portion of the hypothalamus, then repeated electrical activation might be expected to produce an emotional state in the experimental animal similar in some respects to Type A behavior.

This was a big order, particularly in technical terms. The investigator had to have expert knowledge of the brain anatomy of the chosen animal, and also of electronics. We finally found the investigator we needed in Dr. C. G. Gunn, a brilliant young scientist working in the neurological research laboratories of the University of Oklahoma Medical School. Within a few months he had placed electrodes in the brains of 14 of 30 cholesterol-fed rabbits and was stimulating them four times a day for five minutes with a tiny amount of current. This continued for a period of three months. The remaining 16 rabbits served as controls. Both the stimulated and the control rabbits were fed exactly the same amount of cholesterol in their food.

Gunn noted emotional reactions ranging from dilation of the pupils to restlessness in the experimental rabbits every time the tiny current entered their hypothalamus. But the real payoff came at the end of the experiment, when autopsies revealed that the blood of those rabbits whose hypothalamus had been chronically irritated by electricity contained significantly more cholesterol than the blood of the control animals who were left alone. Moreover, the coronary arteries of the stimulated rabbits were two to three times more atherosclerotic or diseased than the coronary arteries of the control rabbits.

Here then was experimental evidence clearly indicating that electrical interference with the brain's emotional relay station could both elevate the blood cholesterol level and produce severe coronary disease. But there was one problem. It always was necessary to administer some dietary cholesterol to the rabbits. When Gunn stimulated the hypothalamus of a group of rabbits which had not been fed any cholesterol, their blood cholesterol level did not rise, nor did their coronary arteries show even a trace of atherosclerosis. These last facts, of course, suggested that electrical activation or stimulation of the hypothalamus had no effect on the animal's own manufacture of cholesterol but instead, in some still unknown manner, altered the animal's ability to get rid of the excess cholesterol in its food safely.

Excited as we were about these results, nevertheless several members of the HBI team expressed doubts about whether the electrical current administered to these rabbits four times daily *enhanced* or *inhibited* the normal functions of the hypothalamus. Also, they suspected that the electrical current might have destroyed portions of the hypothalamus. The blood cholesterol and coronary artery changes observed might be laid not to overactivity by the hypothalamus but to the fact that certain areas of it had been destroyed. Certainly these possibilities were worth exploring, because the hypothalamus participates in the regulation of norepinephrine synthesis and secretion, as well as controlling the rate of discharge of the pituitary hormones, ACTH, the tanning hormone (MSH), and growth hormone, In short, this part of the brain is uniquely involved in the control of the four hormones whose metabolism so often appeared to be in disarray in Type A persons.

Not until 1967 was the HBI team able to follow up this critical and revealing experiment. Dr. Gunn in Oklahoma was no longer available, and for a long while none of us was prepared to put aside his other clinical research and epidemiological surveys to learn the necessary techniques. When we finally did buckle down to the problem, we chose to work with rats, and to conduct all our experiments at the Harold Brunn Institute.

For many months, we studied monographs describing the rat's brain. Methods of chemically hardening the rat's brain so that sections of this organ could be cut, fixed, and stained had to be learned. The complicated apparatus for carrying a wire electrode into a rat's brain and bringing its tip into the several specific tiny areas of the hypothalamus had to be built. Then hours and hours had to be spent learning how to use this instrument. Our new approach called for deliberately destroying (rather than stimulating) a few square microns of the hypothalamus; it always had to be the same area. But what area should that be? What voltage and amperage should be employed? Which dyes would delineate most clearly the areas of the hypothalamus destroyed? These were just a few of the problems the HBI team had to solve if we were to induce in a rat something approximating Type A behavior.

Now, over 13 years later, it is difficult to remember how many hundreds of electrodes had to be inserted into various portions of the rat's hypothalamus and how many thousands of brain sections had to be fixed, stained, and microscopically examined before we knew the answers. It is easy to remember, however, our great satisfaction when in 1969, after two years spent in trial and error, we were finally able to convert rats that were previously timid and gentle, always huddling intimately and peacefully together, into frightening creatures that would lunge viciously at any animal—including a man—foolish enough to approach them. It required only a 20-second application of a two-milliampere current to a particular nucleus of cells lying quite deep in the hypothalamus, approximately 75 microns to the right and left of the midline and one millimeter below the surface of the rat's brain.

The behavior of these hypothalamus-injured rats was of course not identical to that of Type A men. There was no sign that they were obsessed by a sense of time urgency, and if they suffered from a loss of self-esteem or insecurity as do most Type A individuals, we had no way of finding out. They did, however, resemble the Type A man in one crucial respect: they exhibited a savage, free-floating hostility.

These maddened animals displayed almost all the physical problems of most severe Type A persons. Like those of Type A subjects, their blood cholesterol and triglyceride levels rose rapidly if just a little excess cholesterol and fat were added to their usual diet. Their blood pressure also rose, and their synthesis and discharge of the struggle hormone norepinephrine accelerated, just as it was seen to do in Type A individuals.

The remainder of this book could be filled with descriptions of the scores of experimental studies we did on these Type A rats. We obtained and analyzed thousands of blood and urine samples for possible changes in chemical and hormonal content; collected and analyzed hundreds of intestinal lymph samples for the amounts and the kinds of fat and cholesterol they contained; and performed scores of experiments in which the pituitary, the thyroid, and sex glands, as well as the adrenals and the pancreases, were tampered with. All of this was aimed primarily at solving one great mystery: how and why blood cholesterol and fat levels always rose in the Type A rats. We suspected (and probably rightly) that the same mechanism was at work in Type A humans.

Over the course of our ten years of work we published dozens of articles describing the results of our experiments, but not a single one of them was able to elucidate the key mechanism. The best we could do was to point out the organ and glands which were *not* involved or responsible. In 1979, when our research funds almost had run out, we stumbled upon the probable answer, one that had been staring us in the face, incidentally, ever since 1969. But just as much earlier we had been unprepared to register the signals our coronary patients were unconsciously transmitting to us about their Type A behavior, so again we had failed to take note of an obvious clue— the dull gray color of the digestive organs, including the livers, of the Type A rats. It should have been obvious to us that the change in color of these organs from their normal bright cherry red could be due to only one thing, a profound and chronic deprivation of blood supply, caused by the constriction of the blood vessels leading to them. It was only after we had devised and built some extraordinarily expensive electric equipment to measure the blood flow to various organs that we finally understood a message that we should have grasped ten years before: that the livers of these tense, hostile little beasts, once their hypothalamus had been damaged, ceased to receive their normal supply of blood. The hypothalamic injury converted our rats from amiable, nestling, peaceful creatures into taut fighting machines. And nature invariably redistributes the blood flow of any battle-ready animal from its intestines and liver to those parts of the body that will be called upon to win the expected combat: the heart, the brain, and the muscles. Many millions of years ago, nature apparently discovered that a belly well nourished with blood is not the best preparation for a struggle. As a consequence of this drastic reduction in blood supply, the liver can no longer remove and metabolize cholesterol and fat in the blood coming to it fast enough. The surplus stays in the blood, causing the observed increase in blood cholesterol (i.e., hypercholesterolemia) and triglyceride (i.e., hypertriglyceridemia).

Almost certainly this is the answer to the riddle, and one which we can be fairly sure explains why in most Type A individuals blood cholesterol and triglyceride levels are so often elevated, particularly during periods of stress. These people too are "in combat," as will be described in the next chapter. That in autopsy their livers are not in as bad shape as those of our rats may be due only to the difference in the *degree* of stress they suffer.

This important finding, however, still remains to be published in a first-rate scientific journal. Unfortunately, just when most of the experimental data had been obtained, our research funds ran out and the laboratory studies had to be discontinued. The notebooks containing the data now lie in the attic of Dr. Byers, our biochemist, who has since retired. As only he can decipher them, it seems probable that our findings may never be published, except for the brief account in these paragraphs. Perhaps one of these days some alert young mind reading this will be inspired to repeat the HBI team's experiments in his own and probably better way. But one hopes that in any event it will not be too long before it is generally recognized that much of the responsibility for a high blood cholesterol level in many persons is in their *chronic* battle or struggle against persons, things, or both.

Before we proceed further, it might perhaps be wise to summarize the various observations made by the HBI team during the 20 years after they had first begun to study the possible relationship between Type A behavior and coronary heart disease. They were as follows:

Observation 1: Persons suffering from coronary heart disease almost always also exhibit Type A behavior.

Observation 2: Persons who exhibit Type A behavior either already suffer from coronary heart disease, or eventually will, far more frequently and earlier in their lives than persons who exhibit Type B behavior.

Observation 3: Healthy Type A subjects usually display the same biochemical and pathophysiological stigmata noted in coronary patients.

Observation 4: The metabolism of several hormones (the struggle hormones, norepinephrine and ACTH) frequently appear to be deranged in Type A persons.

Observation 5: Experimental induction of a Type A-like behavior in rats produced many of the same biochemical and pathophysiological abnormalities observed in Type A humans.

Observation 6: The elevated level of blood cholesterol and fat observed in the experimental Type A animal was found to be due to a reduced blood flow to the animal's liver. This same mechanism could well be responsible for the raised levels of blood cholesterol and fat so often seen in Type A men and women.

No matter how long and arduously a group of medical investigators may labor and no matter how certain they may be of the importance and validity of their discoveries, their work will not be accepted either in the national or international medical marketplace until it has been closely inspected and duplicated not once but quite possibly dozens of times. This is particularly true when the principle involved is, like Type A behavior, one that does not initially lend itself to any of the measuring devices of orthodox medicine. Moreover, the introduction of a possible new causal factor for CHD, one which might compel a revolutionary change in treatment procedures, cannot help but stimulate intense (though not necessarily conscious) resistance among cardiologists possessing neither the personality nor the expertise to exploit its therapeutic potential.

Attempts at confirmation of our findings were understandably not quick in coming. No medical investigator in the 1950s, as far as we know, immediately dropped his own research studies to contend with ours. We had fair warning of this early indifference when only a handful of investigators requested reprints of our reports on the rise of blood cholesterol among the accountants at tax time, or on the fact that coronary heart disease was found seven times more frequently in Type A men than Type B men. This was somewhat disappointing: we had been accustomed to receiving hundreds of reprint requests for researches on other subjects. (Even our report explaining why the purebred Dalmation dog excreted uric acid—hardly a breathtakingly important piece of research—had elicited hundreds of queries.)

We did not despair, however; after all, I myself—the senior member of the team—saw and treated coronary patients for 25 years without recognizing the presence of Type A behavior. It was fortunate that we were prepared to be so forbearing. Apart from the quick confirmation of our 1958 observations that even the temporary advent of Type A behavior quickly alters the blood cholesterol level of human subjects, it was not until 1965 that other researchers even attempted to confirm or deny our other findings concerning the connection between Type A behavior and coronary heart disease. The first attempt, moreover, was jejune. A young psychologist knowing little about Type A behavior, and even less about coronary heart disease, teamed up with a Harvard cardiologist (who had ridiculed the Type A concept long before the two of them began this 1965 study), to see if Type A behavior was more commonly present in coronary patients than in noncoronary patients. Incredibly, they chose as their noncoronary "controls" persons suffering from another emotionally induced disorder, peptic ulcer. Worse, many if not most of the coronary patients they selected were so crippled by their heart disease as to be bedridden at the time they were interviewed. As the reader will learn when he reads the next chapter, Type A behavior is not commonly noticed in patients bedridden by their disease. And yet, despite this mixture of bias, medical naïveté, and sloppy experimental design, the results of the study nevertheless confirmed the HBI team's finding of a close relationship between the presence of Type A behavior and clinical coronary heart disease.

At about this same time, the HBI team was visited by two crack psychologists, each one of whom was willing and patient enough to learn thoroughly not only the technique necessary to detect the presence of Type A behavior, but also to consider seriously the nature of the emotional fire storm that fueled it.

Bernard Caffrey,* both a monk and a professor of psychology, was the first of them. He visited the Brunn Insti-

*Dr. Caffrey died of cancer in 1978.

tute in 1965, having earlier tried to find a reason why the incidence of coronary heart disease in American Benedictine monks was approximately three times greater than that of American Trappist monks, vegetarians living under a vow of silence. Dr. Caffrey recognized that diet alone could not be responsible; in Europe, although the same difference in diet prevailed, there was no difference in the incidence of coronary heart disease between the two orders. Caffrey also knew that in America (but not in Europe) another difference separates the Benedictines from the Trappists: The Benedictines dedicate their lives to teaching; the Trappists to agriculture. In Europe, both Benedictines and Trappists tilled the soil. As a professor himself, Caffrey was aware of the tensions associated with American secondary-school and collegiate teaching. He was also aware that the Type A behavior pattern was very much present in his Benedictine fellows.

Caffrey devised a research plan: He would visit Benedictine and Trappist monasteries throughout the country, trying to find out whether American Benedictines (particularly those already suffering from heart disease) exhibited Type A behavior more often than did the Trappists. The HBI team helped him devise a questionnaire (which omitted questions about car-driving habits, reactions to wives and children, and behavior while waiting in theater, restaurant, or bank lines, replacing them with questions on various aspects of the religious life), and off he went, having secured special permission from the leader of their order to interview Trappist monks.

For several years, Dr. Caffrey traveled the length and breadth of the North American continent, conducting interviews. He was never informed whether or not a particular monk was suffering from coronary heart disease until after he had decided whether or not the man exhibited Type A behavior. What he found was that the group of monks he classified as Type A (whether Benedictines or Trappists) harbored or suffered from coronary heart disease five times more frequently than the group of monks he considered Type B. As he had initially suspected, moreover, Trappist monks were far more likely to exhibit Type B behavior than were Benedictine monks.

These results, when published in detail in 1969, were the first unequivocal confirmation of the probable importance of Type A behavior in the course of clinical coronary heart disease. Dozens of other confirmations, both direct and indirect, would come later, but to us it was this energetic, brilliant, and intrepid monk-psychologist who deserves prime credit for retrieving the Type A concept from 10 years of total neglect. And Bernard Caffrey did more than publish the first confirmation of the Type A behavior concept. During the entire three years he traipsed back and forth the continent conducting his interviews, he never ceased preaching this simple message: Coronary heart disease cannot be due simply to what a person ingests or inhales; what he thinks and feels also must play a part.

Psychologist C. David Jenkins first visited the Harold Brunn Institute about the same time as Dr. Caffrey in 1965, but he did not arrive as a believer. He possessed the systematic intelligence of the trained biostatistician, and his questions to the HBI team reflected this mathematical sharpness. Within a week he, like Caffrey, had become totally convinced that the relationship of Type A behavior to clinical coronary heart disease was far too close to be coincidental. "You fellows have got something going for you," he told us more than once.

Most academic psychologists are quite susceptible to the fascination of questionnaires. Jenkins was no exception, and within a few weeks he was busily engaged in constructing a questionnaire based upon the oral interview we had used to identify Type A men in the Western Collaborative Group Study. Now copyrighted and widely known as the JAS Questionnaire (i.e., Jenkins Activity Survey), it is ingenious but, in our opinion, of dubious value. First, it was based upon a preliminary version of our oral interview, which has subsequently been expanded and improved. Second, the questionnaire tends to be regarded by those who use it as an objective diagnostic instrument when in fact it isn't; it depends for its accuracy upon the subject's own appraisal of himself, and most Type A subjects are notoriously poor observers of both their actions and their motives. Finally, it is not primarily what subjects think, say, or write about themselves that reveals the presence of Type A behavior, but the facial, vocal, and psychomotor manifestations they exhibit. (More about this in the next chapter.)

In spite of these basic flaws, Jenkins's questionnaire more often than not did allow the identification of *flagrant* Type A behavior. Moreover, it attracted scores of young psychologists enthusiastically eager to enter a field of medicine to which it seemed to offer a key. Beginning in the late 1960s and continuing to the present day, scores of heart studies employed this questionnaire (although frequently in various modified forms). Not always, but sufficiently often, these studies confirmed the HBI team's original epidemiological, clinical, and experimental observations. Enough of them had appeared by 1971 that Jenkins felt justified in writing a review for one of America's most conservative medical magazines, one particularly read by thousands of physicians who treated coronary patients. He did a first-rate job in assembling data from all over the world, and left little doubt in the minds of uncommitted cardiologists that in some way or other, Type A behavior was involved in the origins of heart disease. It probably also served to bring the subject at long last to the attention of agencies funding rearch activities in CHD, suggesting that here was a dark horse deserving of at least a bit of their consideration.

The publication of *Type A Behavior and Your Heart* by two members of the HBI team (Rosenman and Friedman) in 1974 made it awkward for any investigator or group of investigators to ignore the existence of Type A behavior completely. Readers all over the world read (and continue to read) this report, written for the layman. From 1974 on, no new research study aiming to uncover *all* the putative coronary risk factors could afford to omit from their design protocol a conscientious appraisal of the relevance of Type A behavior.

Unfortunately, however, dozens of multimillion-dollar epidemiological studies were already in progress. They had been designed to consider certain factors as *primary* coronary risk factors which, it is now apparent, may well not be primary at all. For example, high blood pressure, high levels of blood cholesterol, excessive cigarette smoking, and even maturity-onset diabetes, conditions heretofore thought of as *primary* coronary risk factors, very probably are the *result* of Type A behavior—and thus *secondary* to it. None of the many publications emanating from these long-term epidemiological studies makes any mention of this possible sequence. This is notably true of two recent monographs describing the famous multimillion-dollar epidemiological study of approximately 5,500 citizens of Framingham, Massachusetts, which has been going on for 30 years. Yet those citizens of Framingham must sometimes be sad or happy; sometimes hate or love; sometimes relax or struggle; and sometimes be afraid or exhibit courage. What they think and feel must affect their bodies, though you would not guess it from a perusal of these two monographs, or scores of other articles published by the Framingham researchers prior to 1980. Weight, blood chemistry, electrocardiographic findings, diseases, eating, exercise and smoking habits—these are factors that can be fed to computers and converted into graphs and tables, the substances of hundreds of publishable articles. Behavior is not like that.

Sometime in 1965, Dr. Suzanne Haynes, a young psychologist of the National Heart, Lung and Blood Institute, joined the Framingham project. She possessed a mind that was not content to feed data to a computer but intensely eager to learn how minds and hearts interacted. Moreover, she had a partner, Dr. Manning Feinleib, also a scientist at the National Heart, Lung and Blood Institute, who was no stranger to the Framingham project and who possessed as much statistical expertise as any of the old

Framingham stalwarts. They were a formidable pair indeed!

Dr. Haynes had read almost every article published by the HBI team. She also had long conversations with several of us. But she insisted on seeing for herself at Framingham whether our concepts made sense. Over a two-year period, she administered her own questionnaire to over 1,600 apparently healthy Framingham male and female volunteers. Her questionnaire attempted to place subjects on 20 different psychosocial scales, including one she called the Framingham Type A Behavior scale. Then, just as we were forced to do in our Western Collaborative Group Study, she and Dr. Feinleib had to wait eight more years. By that time a sufficiently large number of these initially healthy 1,600 men and women had suffered their first heart attack to permit statistically convincing conclusions to be drawn.

In 1980, approximately 31 years after the Framingham study had begun, and eight years after their work was completed, Haynes and Feinleib together with one of the Framingham old guard published their results. In the concluding paragraph of this publication the authors wrote as follows: "In conclusion, the present findings indicate that the Framingham Type A behavior pattern and suppressed hostility are important risk factors for CHD in both men and women. This study is the first to show a prospective relationship between Type A behavior and CHD in women and, in particular, working women." The authors also added that Type A behavior was a risk factor independent of the heretofore accepted coronary risk factors.

Just why Haynes and Feinleib considered hostility and Type A behavior as two separate things, when we had repeatedly stated for over a decade that one of the major components of Type A behavior is hostility, we never have been able to discover. But aside from this, their confirmation of the close association of Type A behavior and incidence of CHD represented a large step forward. The conservatism of the Framingham study leaders was everywhere evident, and an admission by them that a phenomenon they had not bothered even to investigate for over 20 years was indeed a coronary risk factor, was an admission indeed.

Even before the Framingham confirmation was published, other important support for the Type A behavior–coronary heart disease concept came from three separate groups of investigators, who reported that they found that almost all persons who possessed severely diseased coronary arteries, as shown by x-ray studies, also exhibited Type A behavior. Before this, no one knew at what stage in the development of heart disease Type A behavior pattern intervened. These results indicated that if Type A behavior *was* responsible, one way it worked was to make the atherosclerotic scarring of the heart's arteries worse. This of course did not rule out the probability that Type A behavior also might be involved in hastening the occurrence of a heart attack or a fatal irregularity of the heartbeat.

At the same time as this research was going on, a number of experimental psychologists and a few psychiatrists began trying to distinguish and isolate the emotional components making up the Type A behavior pattern in the hopes of discovering which were most dangerous. These included obsessive-compulsive disturbances; speed and impatience; excessive job involvement; hard-driving excessive ambition; anxiety; hysteria; cultural mobility; work dissatisfaction; hostility; and perhaps a half dozen other psychosocial abnormalities pulled out of the total Type A behavior syndrome as we initially defined it. We had our doubts about the timing and usefulness of these efforts, but could see that they indeed helped keep cardiac researchers aware, whether they liked it or not, of the Type A concept.

We are still not sure what it was that tipped the scale— the hundreds of publications by the HBI team, the continuing confirmations of the Type A behavior–CHD linkup by dozens of researchers here and abroad, the Framingham publication, the increasing demands from experimentally minded psychologists and psychiatrists for the creation of a national panel on the subject, or the persistent interest of Dr. Theodore Cooper, the distinguished cardiologist then serving as Assistant Secretary for Health, Education, and Welfare in the Ford Administration—but on June 1, 1977, Type A behavior received a new kind of recognition. A forum subsidized by the National Heart, Lung and Blood Institute brought together several dozens scientists to discuss "coronary prone behavior" at some length. At the close of the meeting, a summary report forwarded to the director of the Institute strongly recommended that a panel of leading scientists be assembled to study and discuss all the evidence available regarding Type A behavior and coronary heart disease.

This was done. Under the chairmanship of Dr. Cooper himself, the panel convened in December 1978 and spent several days examining the whole Type A issue. Then it divided into subcommittees to collate views and draw up final conclusions. These conclusions eventually appeared as a series of summary statements in the June 1981 issue of *Circulation*, the official journal of the American Heart Association.

From the start, the statements were gratifying, especially to those of us who had spent so much time and effort trying to establish the validity of the Type A concept. The opening paragraph declared:

The review panel accepts the available body of scientific evidence as demonstrating that Type A behavior as defined by the structured interview used in the Western Collaborative Group Study, the Jenkins Activity Survey, and the Framingham Type A behavior scale—is associated with an increased risk of clinically apparent CHD in employed, middle-aged U.S. citizens. This risk is greater than that imposed by age, elevated values of systolic blood pressure and serum cholesterol, and smoking, and appears to be of the same order of magnitude as the relative risk associated with the latter three of these other factors.*

Here then, a quarter of a century after the first presentation of the Type A behavior–CHD relationship by the HBI team, a panel of scientific peers officially certified its importance. No longer could textbooks on heart disease dispose of the role of the mind in the origin of CHD in a few sentences; no longer could cardiac epidemiological studies afford to disregard man's emotions; and no longer could committees of the American Heart Association fail to list Type A behavior as a potent coronary risk factor.

The HBI team unfortunately no longer existed when the panel's report was published. Its biochemist member, Dr. Sanford O. Byers, had retired to grow luscious tomatoes and read fine literature in his Marin County home. Dr. Ray H. Rosenman had transferred his research activities to the Stanford Research Institute. I, the remaining team member, was determined despite my fairly advanced age to begin and finish one more study—a study that would determine whether Type A behavior can be modified and if so, whether such modification would prevent or forestall the early advent or recurrence of a heart attack. Until such a study was done it would be impossible—no matter how many additional investigators might confirm our findings concerning the *association* of Type A behavior with CHD—to say for certain that Type A behavior played a direct *causal* role in the pathogenesis of human CHD.

I am happy to say that the study *was* accomplished. It is in fact the occasion for this book. Setting it up and carrying it out, a process that took all of seven years, was probably the most difficult work I have attempted in half a century of medical research and treating patients, and

---

*What this last, badly phrased sentence means to say, apparently, is that the risk of CHD associated with Type A behavior is *independent* of the risk associated with age, elevated values of systolic blood pressure and serum cholesterol, and smoking.

even given the same magnificent support I am not sure that I would undertake such a complex and demanding venture again. Later chapters will describe the study in detail; suffice it to say here only that it was a marked, even startling success. We *know* now beyond any doubt what we suspected before—that Type A behavior *can* be treated effectively, that reduction or elimination of Type A behavior *can* reduce the incidence of second heart attacks *radically*, and that Type A behavior can now be regarded, *alone among risk factors*, as a primary causal agent in the pathogenesis of coronary heart disease.

This book tells the story of the San Francisco Recurrent Coronary Prevention Project, and brings up to date what is now known about the nature and workings of Type A behavior in both men and women. What may be even more important in the long run—if only readers will take our findings to heart—it tells how Type A behavior *can be treated*. But first, let us consider what Type A behavior is.

CHAPTER 2

‚ ‑ ‑ ‑ ‑ ‑ ‑

The Nature of
Type A Behavior

What Type A Behavior Is

In *Type A Behavior and Your Heart*, we (Meyer Friedman and Ray Rosenman) described Type A behavior in some detail. Now, nine years later, much more is known about it, although the general outlines are basically the same. Thus, part but not all of the following description will be familiar to readers of the earlier book.

Type A behavior is above all a continuous struggle, an unremitting attempt to accomplish or achieve more and more things or participate in more and more events in less and less time, frequently in the face of opposition—real or imagined—from other persons. The Type A personality is dominated by covert insecurity of status or hyperaggressiveness, or both.

It is one or both of these two basic components that generally causes the struggle to begin. The struggle itself sooner or later fosters the emergence of a third personality ingredient, that sense of time urgency we have designated hurry sickness. As the struggle continues, the hyperaggressiveness (and also perhaps the status insecurity) usually shows itself in the easily aroused anger we term free-floating hostility. Finally if the struggle becomes severe enough and persists long enough, it may lead to a fifth component, a tendency toward self-destruction.

As the above description implies, Type A behavior erupts most frequently in a person already aggressive and unsure about his status when he encounters situations that he construes as either status-threatening or irritating and anger-provoking. It is only then that the struggle ensues, bringing in its wake a sense of time urgency or free-floating hostility, and, after the passage of many years, the tendency to self-destruct. Now let us look more closely at these various components of full-fledged Type A behavior.

INSECURITY OF STATUS. Why do Type A persons struggle so ceaselessly and so senselessly to accomplish more and more things or involve themselves in more and more events? Sometimes it is because their position truly demands superhuman efforts, but rarely. Usually they struggle because they suffer from a hidden lack of self-esteem. At first glance, one might not think this true of such Type A's as presidents of the United States (for example, John F. Kennedy and Lyndon B. Johnson), presidents of great banks or prestigious universities, heads of huge foundations and corporations, distinguished generals and admirals, famous opera and film stars (for instance, Maria Callas and Peter Sellers), even Nobel laureates. But we have found that many such persons *are* beset by various kinds of insecurities.

The Type A's doubts about his status are not as a rule based upon what friends or members of his family think or say, but rather on what he himself thinks of himself. This estimate often depends upon comparisons with others. For example, most Americans probably believed that President Johnson was a secure individual with a very high degree of self-esteem. Perhaps even his wife and children believed this too. But there is evidence that Mr. Johnson kept comparing his own historical standing with that of Abraham Lincoln, Franklin D. Roosevelt, and even President Kennedy, generally to his disadvantage. Similarly, General George Patton, triumphantly striding along with his aides, inspecting thousands of his soldiers as they stood at attention, was probably regarded by many as the epitome of personal confidence. But General Patton, obsessively measuring himself against the exploits of his rival Field Marshal Bernard Montgomery, seems to have suffered repeated blows to his self-esteem. By the same token, two distinguished rival cardiovascular surgeons may very well base their self-esteem not on the admiration of their junior medical staffs but on such competitive factors as the number of heart operations performed or the fame of each other's patients.

As William James pointed out almost a century ago, a person's self-esteem or sense of security depends upon the equation

$$\text{Self-Esteem} = \frac{\text{Achievements}}{\text{Expectations}}$$

Thus, regardless of the opinions of strangers or friends, if a person's expectations are in excess of his achievements, his self-esteem remains inadequate. As one of our Type A coronary participants recently said, "Our trouble is that our ratio of achievements over expectations always seems to be less than one." In subsequent sections, we shall further explore this all-important matter of inadequate self-esteem. It may in itself be largely responsible for other aspects of Type A behavior.

HYPERAGGRESSIVENESS. What is excessive aggressiveness? How does it differ from ordinary ambition, from a wish to achieve or to compete and win? The answer is that the hyperaggressiveness associated with Type A behavior involves not merely a desire to win but to *dominate*, with indifference to the feelings or fundamental rights of one's competitors or opponents. It may involve an active attempt to put down the other person and damage *his* self-esteem. Thus, Type A hyperaggressiveness is an emotional drive that carries in its train a certain bumptious ruthlessness. No one has expressed this more accurately than author Jess Lair when he wrote: "Before I had my heart attack, I didn't have any friends. When I played poker, I played to win from the bastards."

No matter whether hyperaggressiveness develops slowly out of a sense of insecurity or springs full-blown, it most often appears early in the life of a Type A. Indeed, a psychiatrist colleague of ours declared to us several decades ago that he was reasonably certain that he could visit a hospital nursery and pick out those infants who later would exhibit full-fledged Type A behavior. They would be more active and exhibit more aggression, he felt. Many dog fanciers also are certain that they can, out of an extremely young litter, pick those puppies that will show lifelong aggressiveness. Despite this, hyperaggressiveness is not always easy to discern; it often exists for decades in a hidden form in a Type A person.

FREE-FLOATING HOSTILITY. It is impossible to say whether free-floating hostility derives totally from thwarted hyperaggressiveness or whether it develops simultaneously and from the beginning forms part of the hyperaggressiveness syndrome. In any case, it undoubtedly would not emerge if status insecurity had not preceded it.

Free-floating hostility is a permanently indwelling anger that shows itself with ever-greater frequency in response to increasingly trivial happenings. Like status insecurity and hyperaggressiveness, it may remain undetected and unrecognized for a long time. The Type A is very good at hiding it by always finding excuses and rationalizations for his more or less permanent state of irritation. For example, when he becomes angry at another driver, as a rule the other driver has indeed committed a gaffe. Again, when he expresses displeasure at having to wait in a long line at a bank or a restaurant, he seems to have logic on his side, and others are likely to condone his outburst.

The rancor of a Type A toward young men carrying blaring radios on buses and into restaurants and shops makes perfect sense. And so on. But sooner or later, even the closest and most understanding friends of the hostile Type A begin to notice that he is finding far too many things to get upset about, and also getting angrier than the situation calls for. One of our hostile Type A patients, for example, having stopped for a red light, lit a cigarette just as the signal turned green. The female motorist behind him honked several times. Reacting, he slowly got out of his car, sneeringly smiled at her and then sauntered to the front of his car, opened the engine hood, and pretended to look for some mechanical breakdown. "I think the bitch got the message," he later remarked to a friend.

A Type B person might regard such behavior by anyone as most unusual. But he would be wrong. Horn-honking almost invariably arouses outrage in the hostile Type A. Dr. W. Gifford-Jones, writing recently in his nationally syndicated medical column, described a similar incident. He was driving with a hostile Type A surgeon, who was slow to step on the gas pedal of his car after the signal at the intersection had turned green. Dr. Gifford-Jones then described what happened:

> The result was a sudden and loud horn honk from the car behind us. Immediately the Irish temper flared. My friend jumped up, walked to the car behind us, opened the door, grabbed the keys out of the ignition, and with a mightly toss threw them into a snowbank.... Meyer Friedman and Ray Rosenman would have something to say about that scenario. These ... researchers would quickly classify my Irish friend as a Type A personality. The same label would probably apply to the horn-honking Bostonian behind us, and they might predict an early coronary for both.

Yes, Dr. Gifford-Jones, we would probably have classified these men precisely as you suggest.

Of course, the rancor of the hostile Type A person is by no means confined to the capers of motorists. It often reveals itself in the violence of his opinions about what he considers the unworthiness or fat-headed behavior of politicians (including presidents from Franklin D. Roosevelt to Ronald Reagan), television personalities (particularly Howard Cosell), and sports figures. Most people criticize public figures, but usually in a calm, detached manner; not so the hostile Type A. Obsessively, he appears to seek ways to bring the people he despises repeatedly back into the conversation. Moreover, he usually seethes with anger while doing so. In the same way, the Type A finds it difficult not to express irritation when he is delivering his opinions about the racial, sex-related, ethnic, and other problems of Western society.

Even ordinary family conversations of extreme Type A's may be marked by this sort of hostility. Offering contradictions, using such pejoratives as "stupid," "ridiculous," "idiotic," or "nonsensical" to belittle the comments of others, swearing—all these characterize the Type A's anger. An opposing opinion may make his face flush, cause him to speak more rapidly and loudly, and show obvious impatience and disgust. While playing a game such as tennis, golf, handball, or bridge, he is likely to react explosively to any error on the part of either an opponent or his own partner.

It should be easy to see why we have designated the Type A variety of hostility as free-floating. It is always present and always prepared to fasten on *something*, trivial or silly or wrong as that something may be. No disinterested physician, observing the number and kind of external stimuli that can arouse the anger of the hostile Type A person, can escape the conclusion that there is a large fund of hostility in such a person simply looking for excuses to vent itself.

This hostility, of course, makes it difficult for its possessor either to attract or to accept pure affection. It is because of the essential incompatibility of hostility and love that so many Type A's find it very difficult to receive or give love gracefully. Yes, the Type A can give loyalty, he can bring humor, he can feel concern, but he too often shies away from the *verbal* expression of love—or at least of *human* love, for he can love and freely receive the love of various animal pets. A strange paradox.

SENSE OF TIME URGENCY (HURRY SICKNESS). This component, which in *Type A Behavior and Your Heart* we designated hurry sickness, arises from an insatiable desire to accomplish too much or to take part in too many events in the amount of time available. The Type A resorts to two basic stratagems in response to this exorbitant desire: a speedup of almost all his daily activities and constant attempts to do or think more than one thing at a time.

SPEEDUP OF DAILY ACTIVITIES

To keep up with his overload of projects, the Type A is forced to accelerate the rate at which he thinks, plans, and executes almost all his daily functions. Thus he increases not only his own rate of speech but also forces others to speak more quickly to him; attempts to read and write faster; to walk and eat faster; to drive his car as fast and as cleverly as he can without actually violating traffic regulations (or getting caught at it). Even his minor activities will be accelerated. For example, the male Type A may seek to shave faster by discarding soap, brush, and blade for the most efficient electric razor he can find. One Type A physician friend of ours has already bought ten different electric razors, in a search for the one that shaves fastest. And we know of three Type A's who use two electric razors so that they can save time by shaving both sides of the face simultaneously!

The Type A often substitutes instant for regular coffee, preferring speed over flavor. He also brushes his teeth hurriedly, and (if a male) puts off getting his hair cut. If there is any way to avoid a line, whether it be a short one or long one, at a theater, a supermarket, a bank, post office, restaurant, airport, or on the highway, the Type A will strive desperately to do so. He chafes if he has to wait before teeing off at his golf club, or if he is kept waiting by his physician or dentist. Indeed many topflight Type A corporate executives, arriving at their office in the morning, cannot bear to wait the few minutes it takes their secretaries to serve up the morning mail. One of America's most distinguished industrialists, a man repeatedly given "cover treatment" by various business magazines, suffers so severely from a sense of time urgency that he customarily goes to his secretary's desk and extracts "the letters I really want to see" from the "junk mail." His secretary has been heard to ask him, "Are you doing this because you'd like to have my job?" but so far as we know she has not ventured to wonder (out loud at least) what the stockholders who pay him in excess of half a million dollars a year would think of his spending his time and their money this way.

POLYPHASIC THINKING AND PERFORMANCE

Despite incessantly striving to accelerate the pace at which he thinks, plans, and executes his daily activities, the Type A is still not satisfied that he is accomplishing enough every minute of his 16 waking hours. He therefore unconsciously attempts to gain more time (and accomplish more tasks) by trying to think about or to do two or more things simultaneously. Perhaps the most common form of polyphasic activity indulged in by the Type A is his habit of "doubling up" a conversation—thinking about or doing something else while ostensibly listening to another person. This activity particularly tempts the Type A when the conversation is by telephone. He can indulge in, say, writing and signing checks or previously dictated letters, or looking at a magazine or incoming correspondence, all the while pretending to pay attention to the unseen person on the other end of the line. He knows consciously that this is wrong or impolite, so he is usually careful to do it quietly. But not always. One of our friends complains that he invariably found speaking to his publisher in New York City upsetting. "I can always hear him crinkling up other telephone memos or turning the pages of something while we are supposedly communicating. I wouldn't mind if I heard him doing this when I was speaking, but hell, he shuffles that paper even when *he's* talking to *me*!"

Another favorite time for polyphasic activity is while driving a car. Besides trying to eat or drink his breakfast or lunch while driving, the Type A also may dictate letters or make reminder notes on index cards. If he is important enough to have a radiotelephone in his car, he will use it to talk to clients, customers, or patients (though seldom with friends). And if he is rich enough to command the services of a chauffeur, he is likely to have a miniature office on wheels, complete with telephone, dictating unit, a pad for writing, and a lamp sufficiently powerful to illuminate fine print. One of us has several times had the doubtful pleasure of riding with Type A executives in such limousines. It is a busy scene indeed—the executive dictating, scribbling, reading, and telephoning, the chauffeur also telephoning ahead to the corporate security office telling precisely where the car is, its rate of speed, the direction of the journey, and the fact that all is clear (at least for the moment).

The time-harassed Type A often practices polyphasic activities in the bathroom. For example, while using an electric razor and listening to a radio news broadcast, he also may try to read trade journals or other sorts of business or professional magazines. Indeed, some Type A persons take pride in their ability to defecate, shave, and scan a newspaper simultaneously. And more than few Type A men brush their teeth as they urinate or take a shower. To normal individuals (and certainly to Type B's) these activities may appear bizarre if not downright ludicrous, but the Type A person sees them simply as additional ways in which to make the best use of his time.

Television also offers an opportunity. Some Type A's may be found attempting to view television, read a newspaper or trade journal, and eat lunch or dinner, all at the same time. "When the commercials come on, I turn down the volume and read my newspaper," is a statement we hear repeatedly. It is not unusual for a Type A to view two football games on two different television sets as he irons a shirt or treads an exercycle. One of our post-coronary patients is proud of having built a desk onto his exercycle, which is in turn positioned so as to allow him to view television. He thus is able to get his daily exercise, sign checks, read trade journals, and also view television—quadriphasic activity. "My wife can always tell when some exciting football play is taking place. I pump the pedals so fast that she can hear it in the next room," he once proudly told us. Are these madmen? No, they are just time-harried Type A's like Lyndon Johnson, who was uncommonly proud of the fact that he had three-screen television consoles installed in his White House bedroom and in the Oval Office.

Many Type A persons carry small index cards with them in order to jot down ideas, plans, or memoranda even while attending committee meetings or listening to operas, symphonies, lectures, or sermons. The widow of one of our deceased coronary patients sadly commented that for a year after her husband's death she continued to find these note-loaded index cards in drawers, books, and cubbyholes. Another woman, the wife of a still-living Type A executive, wryly observed, "I really don't mind George writing on those darned index cards when we listen to an ordinary sermon at our church, but I don't think it's right for him to make notes at funerals."

THE DRIVE TO SELF-DESTRUCTION. Besides the covert insecurity, the hyperaggressiveness, and the sense of time urgency that all Type A subjects harbor, and the free-floating hostility that almost all Type A persons possess, there is a fifth element of the Type A syndrome to which many or most *severely* afflicted Type A individuals eventually fall prey: an unconscious drive toward self-destruction. This component was not described in *Type A Behavior and Your Heart*, because a decade ago none of us at the Harold Brunn Institute suspected that seemingly successful, good-humored, and even optimistic Type

A subjects might be harboring a covert instinct to destroy their careers or themselves. Even now, confronted by irrefutable evidence of this drive, including what amounts to an open admission of it in the comments of many of our Type A post-infarction patients, we still find it difficult at times to understand why it exists.

We first suspected its presence when we heard about two chief executives of major multinational corporations who deliberately failed to file their federal income tax returns year after year. Both were finally indicted, pleaded *nolo contendere*, and were forced to resign their positions. We are reliably informed that they were men of fine principle, healthy, and not in any financial difficulties. But both of them exhibited severe Type A behavior. "It may seem strange to you," the top administrative aide of one of these men told us, "but I am sure that my chief found the stresses and strains of his position so overwhelming that he tried to get out from under them by doing something that he knew would give him a release. When the federal prosecutor asked him why he hadn't filed for three consecutive years, he replied that he couldn't find the time to fill out the necessary forms. But hell, he knew he had dozens of accountants who would have been glad to fill out his forms. I would have done it for him myself."

Before any reader of this book concludes that this sort of career suicide is rare, he would do well to remember Henry Kissinger's comment about President Nixon: "It was hard to avoid the impression that Nixon, who thrived on crisis, also craved disasters." Similarly, Spike Milligan, an intimate friend of Peter Sellers, was quoted as saying to Sellers's son soon after the death of his father, "Your father was always searching for a bloody heart attack as if it were a letter he knew had been posted and hadn't arrived."

Actually, this aspect of Type A behavior was suggested to us several years ago by some Type A volunteers involved in our earlier biochemical studies. After reading *Type A Behavior and Your Heart*, they said that while they found the book interesting, they could not understand why we had not mentioned the urge of many Type A persons to destroy themselves. Do you mean to shoot or poison yourselves? we asked. They impatiently shook their heads, saying that they would never try to do away with themselves by any conscious act. Yet they all felt that sooner or later they would succumb to the stress they were bringing on themselves by living and working at such a killing pace. They would unconsciously seek some avenue of escape from the crushing load of trash events in their everyday lie.

Alerted by these comments—which at that point we had no reason to consider typical—we began to observe and question scores of Type A's who were in the process of recovering from heart attacks. To our surprise, we found that over half of these men had not only expected to have a heart attack before they actually had one, but had in fact yearned for it. As they lay on their beds in the coronary care unit, the pain of the acute attack having abated, they could be heard saying such things as:

"I'm glad it finally came. I just couldn't seem to find any other way to get out from under all the junky stuff loading me down."

"It may seem strange to you, but I knew I was going to get this attack and I sort of looked forward to it."

"It's so damned nice to lie here and have no responsibilities and to have such pretty nurses taking such good care of me. I really would like to stay here forever."

"I wouldn't ever admit this, not even to my wife, but I knew this was coming and so I wanted to get it over with, one way or the other. And frankly, I didn't care a damn which way it came out just as long as I didn't have to have someone wheeling me around for the rest of my life."

"Now I can retire from the company and begin to live like a real human being again. You know what? I wanted this to happen and I didn't care whether I lived or not. There's enough insurance for the wife and kids and they may have been a lot better off without me." (Compare

Proust's remark: "Every death is a simplification for the survivors.")

Why do so many severely afflicted Type A persons harbor an unconscious drive to destroy their careers or themselves? We shall expand on this matter later in this book. But note that the phenomenon was observed long before we came on the scene. Emily Dickinson's father had recovered fully from his heart attack by the year 1871, when Emily wrote: "I hope I am mistaken, but I think his physical life don't [sic] want to live any longer." Mr. Dickinson died three years later.

SECONDARY ASPECTS OF TYPE A BEHAVIOR. Several often observed characteristics of Type A behavior are not, we now believe, as basic as the five components described above. They apparently follow in the wake of the struggle that distinguishes Type A behavior, and hence may be considered secondary phenomena. We will not discuss them at length here, but simply list them:

- A tendency to use numbers and quantities when thinking and speaking
- A failure to use metaphors and similes in thought and speech
- A relative inability or unwillingness to develop various kinds of imagery

WHAT TYPE A BEHAVIOR IS NOT. There is still considerable confusion existing in some people's minds—particularly the minds of some physicians—about how Type A behavior differs from ordinary anxiety neurosis. We should like again to emphasize that when a person suffers fears, worries, or depression, finds them overwhelming and finds himself unable to cope with them and seeks medical help, whatever he may be suffering from, it is not Type A behavior. The Type A is invariably engaged in a very active *struggle* against the obstacles confronting him. The anxiety neurotic figuratively implores, "I need your aid, so please help me." In contrast, the Type A appears to say, "I'm O.K., Jack, what can I do for you?" Likewise, the stress and adaptation syndrome observed in rats by Hans Selye has nothing to do with the struggle involved in Type A behavior. Dr. Selye observed how various kinds of stress act upon the rat's adrenal gland, causing it eventually to become deranged. Type A behavior arises as easily in men without adrenal glands as in men with them. President John F. Kennedy reportedly suffered from insufficient adrenal gland function; yet he exhibited very well developed Type A behavior, as described to us by one of his physicians.

Where Type A Behavior Comes From

Insecurity of status (primarily arising from an inadequate or diminished sense of self-esteem), or hyperaggressiveness, or both, almost always serve as the initiating and core causes for the development of Type A personality. The Type A personality in turn, when exposed to the proper environmental stimuli or challenges, evokes in its possessor the struggle pattern we have designated Type A behavior.

At the present time it is not clear, as we have already pointed out, just how much status insecurity and hyperaggressiveness are due to genetic and how much to environmental influences. The study of identical twins who were raised in totally different environments seemed the most promising way to answer these questions, and at least two such studies have been done. Unfortunately, the results are contradictory.

The studies done so far on animals point clearly to the fact that environmental factors alone can induce marked aggression. Be it monkeys or mice, if as infants they are deprived of maternal care, they exhibit violent aggressive tendencies when they mature. These results also suggest that hyperaggressiveness may not be an independent phenomenon but may arise as a compensating factor for a sense of security that has not been allowed to develop properly.

Besides these animal studies, there are various epidemiological data suggesting that Type A behavior and hyperaggressiveness can be environmentally enhanced. For example, whereas *individual* aggressive behavior reportedly is rare in native Japanese,* many Japanese immigrating to the United States exhibit this characteristic of Type A behavior after living for several decades or less in this country. The increase in Type A behavior has been spectacular in Finland since 1945, when it began to urbanize and industrialize. In less than four decades, it changed from a primarily rural nation into one in which more than half of its citizens live in cities and towns. At the same time it has industrialized so rapidly that its per capita GNP now exceeds that of Great Britain and France. For these advances Finland has paid a price—the highest coronary death rate in the world.

Various epidemiologists committed to the idea that the consumption of animal fat is the chief cause of coronary heart disease swarmed into Finland hoping to prove their case by complex and often expensive survey studies. They felt that a change in diet had probably led to the rocketlike rise in coronary mortality. But no such change could be found. Nor could the rise be tied to any other generally accepted coronary risk factors. We remain convinced that the real reasons are the sociocultural changes leading to more Type A behavior; no terribly expensive epidemiological expeditions need be sent to Finland to see this. A glance at the section devoted to Finland in the most recent edition of the *Encyclopaedia Britannica* is quite enough.

But despite the importance of environmental factors in the development of Type A *behavior*, we cannot rule out the strong probability that the Type A *personality* is in part heritable. After all, we do expect tiger cubs to

---

*Of course, *group aggressiveness* is not at all rare in Japan.

exhibit a bit more aggressiveness than Easter bunnies. Similarly, while all guard dogs require training to become aggressive enough to attack man, trainers usually prefer to work with German shepherds or Dobermans rather than cocker spaniels. The differences in aggressiveness among these breeds are, we believe, heritable.

The other components of Type A behavior, namely a sense of time urgency, free-floating hostility, and at the end, a tendency to self-destruct probably are not heritable but grow out of the initial status insecurity and hyper-aggressiveness.

Let us then examine more closely where these components come from and how they develop.

Origins and Development of Type A Characteristics

STATUS INSECURITY

We now believe that one of the most important influences fostering status insecurity is the failure of the Type A person in his infancy and very early childhood to receive *unconditional* love, affection, and encouragement from one or both of his parents.*

We were not aware of this until we read Doris Kearns' *Lyndon Johnson and the American Dream.*† Doris Kearns, who was not a physician but a Harvard candidate for a Ph.D. in Government, after listening to Johnson tell of his unhappy boyhood—spent with a mother incapable of giving *unconditional* love and a father for whom he felt contempt—began to sense that for all his seeming power, Johnson had a most tenuous sense of personal status. Two paragraphs in the prologue of this beautifully percipient book opened our eyes. The first is the following:

---

*In the case of male Type A's, it is more specifically a shortage of unconditional *maternal* love and emotional support that seems to block full development of adequate self-esteem.
†Harper & Row, New York, 1976.

We talked mostly in the early hours of the morning.* Johnson slept poorly these days, waking up at 5:30. Terrified at lying alone in the dark, he came into my room to talk. Gradually, a curious ritual developed. I would awaken at five and get dressed. Half an hour later Johnson would knock on my door, dressed in his robe and pajamas. As I sat in a chair by the window, *he climbed into the bed, pulling the sheets up to his neck, looking like a cold and frightened child*. [Our italics]

The second, and far more important, paragraph is this one:

As I listened to him speak, I often wondered why I was his audience, why he permitted and apparently trusted me to hear all this. One day, a year and a half before he died, he took me on a long car ride. He wanted to tell me, he said, that all along he'd been hiding from me the fact that I reminded him of his dead mother. In talking with me, he had come to imagine he was also talking with her, unraveling the story of his life.

Of course, Ms. Kearns also observed and noted Lyndon Johnson's fascination with numbers, whether they represented Gallup Poll results, Viet Cong body counts, the number of eggs his Texas chickens laid each day, the number of people visiting his birthplace (2,828 in one week), the number of different license plates on their cars, the number of books and postcards sold, the admission receipts, and so forth. She also noted his sense of time urgency, his hyperaggressiveness, and his free-floating hostility—all the characteristics, in short, of the full-fledged Type A.

*The interviews took place in Texas following Johnson's retirement from the presidency. These two excerpts are from pp. 17–18 of *Lyndon Johnson and the American Dream*.

In 1979, when we read this account, we were in the process of studying more than 1,000 Type A's who had already suffered one heart attack (a full report on the study appears later in this book). We were struck by the possibility that the men and women we were working with may also have received just such a blow to their sense of personal security as did President Johnson in his early years. Therefore, to 120 participants (chosen at random) we distributed self-addressed cards carrying two questions: First, did you receive sufficient love and affection from (1) your mother and (2) your father? Second, at what age did your free-floating hostility begin? We asked our respondents not to sign these cards but simply to answer the questions and mail them to us, thus ensuring complete anonymity. We found that over 70 percent of them believed that they had not received sufficient love and affection from either of their parents. High as this percentage is, we believe that it might very well have been higher; almost all of our participants had by then lost their parents, and it is logical to suppose that many of them felt reluctant to admit, even anonymously, a defect in the deceased.

After we had received these results, we announced them to six groups containing a total of 60 Type A post-infarction patients, inviting anyone whose experiences had been markedly different to raise his or her hand. Almost never was a hand raised!*

It now seems in retrospect that in searching for the origins of Type A behavior we should have struck earlier on the phenomenon of parental deprivation of love and affection. We were aware of the fact that if newborn monkeys or mice are deprived of maternal care and affection, in maturity they will exhibit excessive insecurity and aggressiveness. We also were aware of the fact that many Type A men ceaselessly search for an ideal woman, but

---

*It is important to note, at least in passing, that the hypercritical nature of most Type A's might lead them to exaggerate the failures and imperfections of their parents. Nevertheless, their own perceptions of the situation may be held responsible for its effects on them, and there is no doubt in our minds that their memories all contained at least an element of truth.

we ascribed this to an overactive sexual drive or some poorly defined desire to find the ultimate in female beauty or social position. (Indeed, we even called such a search the Gatsby Drive, not realizing that these men were unconsciously seeking the unconditional mother love most of them never received.) Actress Liv Ullmann seems to have been speaking of this yearning when in discussing her love affair with the famous cinema director Ingmar Bergman, she wrote that "he sought the mother. Arms that would open to him, warm and without complications."

It was only after we had discovered this characteristic deprivation in the early childhood of the majority of our Type A coronary patients that we ran across Freud's statement: "If a man has been his mother's undisputed darling, he retains throughout life the triumphant feeling, the confidence in success, which not seldom brings actual success along with it," and Eric Erikson's observation that a child who does not receive *adequate* love from his parents may think he is at fault and experience a sense of diminished self-esteem. We might have been tipped off by what we knew of hostile, hyperaggressive, numbers-obsessed Ernest Hemingway, who seems to have spent much of his life searching for a wife who would supply him with what his severely disapproving mother never would. Or General U. S. Grant, alcoholic and strongly insecure, whose hatred of his mother for her earlier treatment of him vividly shows the importance of parental love.* In any case, our suspicions were confirmed when we questioned a number of Type B men about their childhood experience. Without exception, they all insisted that they had received *unconditional* maternal love, and almost all received paternal affection too.

Of course, it is conceivable that because of an inherited hyperaggressiveness, a coldness or deadness of spirit, some Type A persons even as small children are difficult

*This hatred was still strong enough after 46 years to prevent Grant from inviting his mother to attend his presidential inauguration.

if not impossible for either parent to love. If the distinguished psychiatrist Alfred Adler is correct, aggression can be an inherited trait; its presence in a child might indeed chill the heart of any mother initially eager to bestow unlimited amounts of affection.

Further, it appears that for a parent, particularly a mother, to be totally satisfying and sustaining to the Type A person in his early childhood, she must not only bestow love, she also must be pleasant enough in appearance and sufficiently intelligent and educated for him to be proud of. Apropos of this, one of us recently discussed the matter of parental love with the wife of a Type A distinguished scientist who had suffered a lethal heart attack. She at first insisted that her deceased husband had received unlimited quantities of affection from his mother. But suddenly she stopped talking, reflected a few seconds, and then blurted out, "But his mother was such a huge, ungainly person that I always suspected that he was rather ashamed of her."

Certainly Doris Kearns could not have served as a mother substitute for President Johnson had she been a pretty but illiterate showgirl. Nor would the wit, intelligence, and charm of Clare Boothe Luce have sufficed, were she physically repellent. With this in mind, we may understand why some of the sons and daughters of immigrants exhibit an extraordinary amount of aggression, which may be said to serve as a sort of Band-Aid on the unhealed emotional wound resulting from freely proffered but not adequately appreciated parental love.

Third, although the failure of a youngster to obtain the love and affection of his parents probably does seriously damage his sense of self-esteem, success in gaining it in no way guarantees that his self-esteem is firmly implanted and impregnable to future assaults. If there is one human trait that needs frequent reinforcement, it is self-esteem. All too often during late childhood and adolescence, one's self-esteem may well receive some terribly unsettling jolts. Such jolts, moreover, are almost certain to continue as life goes on.

All normal children desire very much to be liked by their peers. This desire of course is intensified if the child has failed to receive *unconditional* parental affection and support. But even if a child had and continues to receive unqualified parental affection, if he nevertheless is actively disliked or teased by his peers because of some physical defect (such as very short stature, the wearing of spectacles or orthodontic braces, impaired speech, cross-eyes, congenital skin blemishes, or marked ineptitude in playing ordinary games), or shunned because he belongs to a minority or even because he is poorer than his classmates, then his self-esteem, whatever its earlier status, is bound to deteriorate. The distinguished Harvard psychiatrist Dr. Robert Coles has strikingly emphasized how a majority can tear down the self-esteem of a child of a minority race. A 26-year-old black youth is speaking of his childhood:

> I remember learning that over and over again when I was five or six—how pretty white people are and how useless and hopeless it is for us to try to be pretty or good-looking or whatever. It's not the words, it's the feeling, you know. My parents never came out and told us that "white" meant beautiful or "black" meant "ugly" or "menial." They made us *feel* all that—and you never forget it that way....

But suppose the parents of this black boy had made him feel that black meant beautiful. Would he then have felt so unpretty or so useless? Possibly not. We say this because recently the distinguished black president of a great foundation related to us how his mother (and father too), from the very first, made him feel as loved and as important as any little white boy with whom he played. One day, after a white playmate's mother refused to let him enter their house, he asked his mother why.

"Oh, son, don't worry about Mrs. Smith, she's prejudiced," replied his mother.

"And do you know, I thought my mother meant Mrs.

Smith had some sort of illness. I certainly never worried or thought about this incident again because even then I knew that I wasn't sick, she was." Undoubtedly his self-esteem, already well fortified by parental affection, survived this potentially traumatic event. Nevertheless, he still remembered it half a century later, suggesting that environmental trauma may possess the potential for unsettling even the staunchest self-esteem.

Comparatively speaking, elementary school itself is unlikely to undermine a child's sense of security. Grades are not of great importance as yet, and there is no academic competition. This begins when a child enters secondary school and is forced to judge himself against others. "Why can't I get A's too?" such a child begins to ask, thus beginning a secret self-flagellation that may continue for the rest of his life. It is probable that this practice is the most common cause of damage to self-esteem that male Type A's can suffer at secondary school, college, or graduate school. As a rule, however, the Type A keeps his anguish secret from friends and even from family members; he finds it difficult, even in retrospect, to admit the slightest intellectual inferiority to himself, much less to anyone else. Of course many students can accept the intellectual or scholarly superiority of others without damage to their self-esteem. Perhaps the majority of children who have received unconditional parental love and affection will be able to do so. Nevertheless, it seems clear that relative inferiority in mental activities is far more damaging than relative inferiority in athletic matters. Socioeconomic inequalities leading to exclusion from clubs, societies, fraternities, and social events also can slash deeply at self-esteem, especially if the child is unable to explain his exclusion in terms of racial or ethnic prejudice.

It is in secondary school that the young person whose self-esteem has been previously damaged by a lack of parental love or some later trauma begins to try to compensate. Unfortunately he invariably tries to achieve too many things or participate in too many events in the time available to him. In short, he begins the *struggle against time* which marks the onset of Type A behavior. If it is not already present (and it may well be), *hyperaggressiveness* also will enter the picture at this time, and if this in turn gives rise to free-floating hostility (as it almost always does eventually), then the result—even at this early age—is fully developed Type A behavior.

College poses the very same problems and offers the very same dangers to the vulnerable youth. Too often the person whose self-esteem has survived secondary school intact finds it damaged by the competition of undergraduate work, with similar consequences. An identical crisis faces the university graduate student. Indeed, the confrontation may be even more intense, because at this point more than scholarly excellence may be demanded. That mysterious quality, original thinking, will single out those students who are destined to become truly distinguished scholars. For a brilliant young person to face up to the fact that a classmate, while perhaps far less brilliant than he is, nevertheless possesses the primaveral freshness of originality, is galling in the extreme. Any psychiatrist counseling university students knows that one of his most frequent and difficult tasks is shoring up the battered self-esteem of young scholars. Here again, if the compensation consists of attempted overachievement and hyperaggressiveness, Type A behavior begins.

Nor does graduation from college necessarily spell the end of the problem. Even in mid-career, one can be assailed by the same doubts that touched off Type A behavior in others earlier. At the memorial service for his friend Peter Sellers, who succumbed to a heart attack at the age of 55, David Niven described Sellers' condition of extreme insecurity, which he dated to the midpoint of his career. "It was only when Peter was well on his way to becoming what he had his heart set on, a big international success, that he looked down from halfway up the mountain and discovered that he had a bad case of vertigo." The result was an agony of wrecked self-esteem. Niven quoted a remark he said Sellers had made as the two of them had left a well-attended memorial service for Noel Coward a few years before: "I hope no one will arrange that sort of thing for me. I don't think anyone will show up."

Now it may well be that Peter Sellers' insecurity stemmed from sources deep in his childhood; we do not know. But it is nevertheless true that many millions of adults who have reached maturity and a position of comfortable stability in their work nevertheless suffer from increasing insecurity and respond to it by developing Type A behavior. Why? One reason is almost embarrassingly obvious—the conditions of modern life, in which technological advances have not only made everyday objects and practices virtually unintelligible, but threaten to change forever the socioeconomic structure we all live in and depend on. How secure can any person be, having gained a hard-earned skill, when he is informed by a futurist that within a few decades he will be rendered obsolete by a machine? And there are more general threats facing even the most sophisticated of us, well summarized by the late scholar-scientist Jacob Bronowski when he remarked: "We are all afraid that something is happening which we shall not be able to understand and which will shut us out from the fellowship of the brighter and younger people." In other words, the fear of being old and outmoded. Can anyone escape it?

And there is, of course, more. Western man is just now being threatened in a very specific way by a firestorm of inflation and unemployment that no one seems capable of bringing under control, and which seems altogether capable of destroying not only status but the means for bare sustenance. Even multimillionaires, aware of what happened in Germany after World War I, now express actual fear. To those of us whose resources are much more modest, their fears may seem ludicrous, but remember that fears usually do seem ludicrous to those not tormented by them. Certainly in these past few years of trying to alter Type A behavior we have found the fear of inflation to be one of our most obdurate obstacles. It is a threat people take very much to heart.

Oddly enough, most large dangers do not seem to play a part in creating individual insecurity and Type A behavior. War, nuclear bombs, earthquakes, hurricanes, and other natural disasters—while these may concern us collectively, they rarely bother us individually in the same way as inflation or job competition. This is probably because, as the great psychiatrist Karl Menninger pointed out years ago, a stressful event thrust indiscriminately and unavoidably on a large group of people seems to produce little individual stress. To illustrate this, he noted that during World War II, signs of individual stress such as alcoholism and suicide virtually disappeared among the blitzed population of London. The distinction seems to be between catastrophes that threaten only a few and can be taken personally, and those which threaten everyone impersonally. One final point: It is not the catastrophe itself that damages one's sense of security, but the *anticipation* of catastrophe.

HYPERAGGRESSIVENESS

We already have stated that it is uncertain just how much hyperaggressiveness is heritable and how much of it arises out of a loss of self-esteem or security in early childhood. Psychiatrist Alfred Adler believed that while aggression was a normal instinctual drive (and thus heritable), it could evolve into hyperaggressiveness when a child developed what he called feelings of inferiority. Freud, however, ridiculed Adler's insistence on the primacy of inferiority and hyperaggressiveness in the origins of neuroses, believing that childhood sexual disorders were mainly responsible. When two such giants in the field of psychology so sharply disagree, we—who are not psychiatrists—had best refrain from any arbitrary conclusions.

Nevertheless, we can report what we have frequently witnessed, which is hyperaggressiveness arising in the childhood of those who later developed full-fledged Type A personalities. These same persons were invariably deficient in self-esteem. Indeed, it is difficult to avoid the conclusion that regardless of whether hyperaggressiveness precedes, appears concomitantly with, or comes in the wake of a loss of self-esteem, its development represents the Type A person's way—probably his only way—of attempting to shore up his declining self-esteem. Perhaps the crucial difference between the anxiety neurotic who finds it difficult to perform even the ordinary chores of daily living without the aid of psychiatrists, psychologists, or psychotropic drugs, and a *seemingly* successful, superachieving Type A person is that while both have suffered a shattering blow to their ego or sense of self-esteem, the Type A alone compensates with hyperaggressiveness. As a psychologist told us several decades ago after she had interviewed a dozen Type A's we had sent to her: "They all have one common characteristic: They 'motorize' away their anxieties." She meant that they assuaged any possible feelings of anxiety or insecurity by resorting to an almost derring-do variety of actions.

FREE-FLOATING HOSTILITY

Hostility is usually slower to follow inadequate self-esteem and hyperaggressiveness than a sense of time urgency. It more gradually emerges as the irritations resulting from a sense of time urgency and the frustrations attending hyperaggressiveness begin to erode the individual's equanimity.

SENSE OF TIME URGENCY

The sense of time urgency, the most easily observable trait of Type A behavior, grows (as we have noted) from the hyperaggressiveness and insecurity felt by the Type A. It is these latter two feelings that impel their possessor to strive ever more intensely to achieve more and more things and to participate in more and more events in the necessarily less and less time available to him. Thus the Type A sense of time urgency arises very early. Asked when theirs began, most adult Type A's can usually recall having suffered from it even in secondary school. Still, it can appear for the first time during the middle or even late adulthood of an individual if such an individual only then suffers blows to his sense of security and resorts to compensatory hyperaggressive actions. But whenever it begins, it quickly involves its possessor in the self-created struggle which is the benchmark of Type A behavior.

TENDENCY TO SELF-DESTRUCT

What leads a Type A person to the point where he is ready to bring his career or even his life to an end? We suspect that it is the exhaustion of spirit caused by the Type A struggle itself, that ungovernable, senseless drive to achieve more and more, accompanied by a diminishing capacity to give or to receive affection. As this perilous drive continues, the Type A person no longer confines his disdain to those persons he is able to control; eventually he begins to entertain less and less regard for himself. It is when this latter process begins that his own spirit starts to wither, and the urge to self-destruct mounts. Much of this occurs in the unconscious, of course, which makes the tragedy no less profound.

As might be guessed, the self-destructive tendency is less likely to arise in the "green years" of youth than in the "gray years" of the Type A's midlife or beyond. Still, the more severe the free-floating hostility, the earlier it appears.

Diagnosing Type A Behavior

Type A behavor, as we have seen, usually consists of five components. The first three—hyperaggressiveness, free-floating hostility, and a sense of time urgency—are usually overt, and thus offer us a means of detecting and measuring the intensity of the syndrome. The other two components—inadequte self-esteem and/or insecurity and a drive toward self-destruction—are more than likely hidden, apparent only in the course of a very complete analysis of the total lifetime activities of the subject. For all practical purposes, the easiest and quickest way to detect the presence of Type A behavior in an individual is to look for psychomotor signs and biographical manifestations of a sense of time urgency and free-floating hostility. Some of these signs and manifestations were described in *Type A Behavior and Your Heart*, but we have uncovered a considerable number of additional indicators of the presence of Type A behavior since that book's publication.

IDENTIFYING AND ASSESSING HYPERAGGRESSIVENESS AND FREE-FLOATING HOSTILITY

Psychomotor Signs

a. Facial hostility (see Fig. 1) which usually reveals itself in the set of the jaw and mouth muscles and the belligerence of the eyes. On occasion, something approaching a chronic sneer is evident.
b. A *tic-like* grimace in which the corners of the mouth are twitched back, partially exposing the teeth. When this grimace is observed, it *invariably* indicates the presence of severe free-floating hostility.
c. A hostile, jarring laugh.
d. Fist-clenching during ordinary conversation.
e. Unpleasant, frequently irritating, grating speech.
f. Frequent use of Anglo-Saxon obscenities.*
g. Teeth-grinding.
h. A *tic-like* tendency to open the eyes widely, exposing the whites around the pupil.*

Biographical Manifestations

a. Eagerness to undertake all activities in a spirit of competition.

*Newly discovered indicator.

b. Intense compulsion to win at all costs, even when playing in minor contests or with pre-teen-age children.

c. Inclination to dominate in social as well as in business situations.

d. Easily aroused irritability, particularly in regard to the actions of other persons which do not conform to his sense of propriety or correctness.

e. Fixed and angrily defended opinions on various sociological, economic, and political matters.

f. Failure to be elated or joyful at the success of others.

DIAGNOSIS AND ASSESSMENT OF A SENSE OF TIME URGENCY

Psychomotor Signs (Voice and Body)

a. Facial tension and, often, a tense body posture.

b. Rapid blinking (over 30 times per minute).*

c. Rapid speech, with characteristic elision or telescoping of the terminal words of sentences.

d. Hurrying or interruption of the speech of others.

e. Sucking in one's breath during speech while continuing to speak.*

f. Rapid, vigorous finger-tapping or jiggling of knees.

g. Browning of skin of eyelids and of skin immediately below the eyelids. This tan pigmentation is due to a chronic excess discharge of a pigment-inducing hormone (melanocyte-stimulating hormone, MSH) by the pituitary gland. Unlike the tan coming after exposure to excess sunlight, this type of periorbital pigmentation never seems to disappear. Although it is by no means common to all persons exhibiting Type A behavior, its presence in Caucasians invariably indicates severe Type A behavior and usually a relatively high level of serum cholesterol.

h. Lip-clicking while speaking.* (If you compress your lips closely, bring the tip of your tongue to the back of your upper incisors and then open your mouth

*Newly discovered indicator.

quickly, you will make this sound.)

i. Expiratory sighing.* This brief sigh or muffled grunt occurs during breathing out. It is usually preceded by a slight lifting of the shoulders.

j. Head-nodding while speaking.* Normal persons often nod affirmatively while someone is speaking to them, to show their agreement with what is being said. Type A nodding occurs in the speaker while he himself is speaking.

k. Rapid body movements. The Type A tends to move and act rapidly.

l. Excessive perspiration on forehead and upper lip.*

Biographical Manifestations

a. Self-awareness of impatience.

b. Pace of activities so rapid as to attract frequent advice from others to slow down.

c. Difficulty in sitting and doing nothing.

d. Intense dislike of waiting in line.

e. Fast walking, fast eating, and unwillingness to dawdle at table after meals.

f. Habitual substitution of numbers for metaphors and nouns, even in casual conversations.

g. Polyphasic thought and actions. As already noted, the Type A has a strong tendency to attempt to think of or do more than one thing at a time.

Not all—indeed, very few—Type A's exhibit *all* the above psychomotor signs or biographical manifestations of hyperaggressiveness, free-floating hostility, and a sense of time urgency. Most of them will, however, exhibit four of the above listed six psychomotor signs of free-floating hostility: facial hostility, a jarring laugh, fist-clenching, and use of obscene words. Fewer than one out of ten Type A's exhibit tic-like grimaces or bulging of eyes.

Most Type A's also exhibit at least six of the above

*Newly discovered indicator.

listed 12 psychomotor signs indicative of the presence of a sense of time urgency: rapid speed with elision of the terminal words of sentences, hurrying or interrupting the speech of others, rapid finger-tapping or jiggling knees, lip-clicking, head-nodding when speaking, and rapid body movements. Most Type A persons will admit having all of the biographical manifestations associated with a sense of time urgency. On the other hand, fewer than 2 percent of Type A's exhibit profuse facial sweating.

THE RELUCTANT TYPE A

When *Type A Behavior and Your Heart* was published in 1974, it became a faddish game to tag one's friends and acquaintances as possessing either Type A or B behavior. Peculiarly, although many Type A individuals were extraordinarily proficient in detecting the presence of Type A behavior in others, most of them were quite unable to accept the fact that they themselves were obvious Type A's. While admitting that they possessed at least some of the indicators described above, they nevertheless insisted that they did not have all of them, so they were not Type A's. It is of course true that very few Type A's admit to harboring free-floating hostility, so magnificently well have they rationalized their need for its existence. Such self-delusion helps explain, incidentally, why paper-and-pencil questionnaires are of very little use in establishing the presence of Type A behavior.

We have repeatedly been asked questions like these:

"Can't a person be a mixture of Type B and Type A?"

"If a person acts like a Type A during some business deals or crises but is a totally relaxed person at home or on a vacation, isn't he really a Type B?"

"If I act as a Type B when I'm with my dog and my little daughter but sometimes not so B when someone is tailgating me, aren't I at heart a Type B man?"

"Doctor, doesn't a Type B guy ever lose his cool when

he has to meet so many sons of bitches as I do every day?"

When in our earlier research we had need of absolutely "pure" Type B's, we made a point of choosing people who did not possess a single one of the above-described Type A psychomotor and biographical manifestations. For "pure" Type A's, we selected those who manifested essentially all of the above-described traits. Now, while we are perfectly ready to accept the fact that not everyone has all of the characteristics, we still draw a sharp line between Type B's (those who do not have even one of the traits) and Type A's (who may have anywhere from one to the full complement of them). This means that if a person reveals only a single aspect of Type A behavior, we would still label him as a Type A, although possibly a very mild one. If a person possesses almost all the above-listed traits, then we would label him as possessing severe or fully developed Type A behavior. In short, we consider a spectrum of Type A behavior to exist, ranging from very mild to very severe.

The sharp division may seem quite arbitrary to many readers, but it has proven to have real meaning to us. First, this isolation of the Type B from all shades of Type A behavior has permitted us to assure him with almost absolute certainty that *he will never suffer a heart attack before the age of 60 or 65 years at the earliest.* We have found that *no such assurance can ever be given to a Type A, even if he manifests no more than one of the indicators.* Indeed, if profuse facial sweating or a tic-like grimace or pigmentation beneath the eyes is observed as the *sole* Type A symptom in a person, its presence nevertheless indicates his possession of *severe* Type A behavior.*

Second, drawing the distinction between Type A and

---

*We are aware of several cases in which persons died of heart attacks while maintaining that they were not Type A's because they showed only a few Type A traits. It seems altogether probable to us that their Type A status was not only real, but significantly accelerated the onset of their heart attacks. Their Type A behavior had been apparent to their widows.

Type B as we have done has enabled us to detect the biochemical and hormonal imbalances which we now believe are the causes of the tissue damage brought on by Type A behavior. We shall discuss these imbalances in a later section.

What Type A Behavior Can Do

THE THREAT TO CAREERS

In modern times we have succeeded in accomplishing miracles in our industrial, commercial, scientific, and professional activities. These miracles have been the work of individuals creating and following up ideas, working hard on their own and harmoniously with others, putting their energies to constructive purpose. What a tragedy it would now be if we were to credit such magnificent achievements as these to the hollow "virtues" of Type A behavior! For the fact is that Type A behavior, far from bringing about successes in the factory, office, laboratory, or marketplace, is actually responsible for repeated disasters—careers and lives wrecked, whole businesses and large enterprises threatened with ruin.

Is this hard to accept? Consider that Thoreau, Emerson, and Oliver Wendell Holmes more than a century ago were warning their fellow Americans of the perils of impatience, and then think how few corporate executives take the time even to read such purveyors of common sense—or for that matter practically any other printed words apart from trade journals, a few newspapers, and maybe a detective thriller before bed. We have interviewed more than 100 topflight American executives and can state that at least 90 percent of them rarely read more than one or two non-job-related books a year. How can these men and women be expected to create great ideas, or even to be aware of the trends and demands that will affect their businesses (and the country at large) in the future? Yet if they fail to do so, who will? Too many of them, expressing their Type A sickness by constantly worrying about the short term (more acquisitions, brighter quarterly earnings reports) are in fact charting courses which should lead their companies to collapse, and incidentally putting us all into jeopardy through their failure to appreciate the effects of their quick fixes.

In a few famous instances, Type A behavior has apparently caused certain high executives to destroy themselves, either literally through suicide or figuratively by deliberately ruining their careers. Far more common, we suspect, are the equally tragic but never publicized cases of Type A's who have simply burned themselves out in pointless struggle, impatience, and anger far down the executive ladder, or at the factory workbench, or in a large office somewhere.

THE THREAT TO PERSONALITY

The components of Type A behavior are responsible for damaging more than the careers of millions of people. They have also devastated—in at least as many cases—the relations between husbands and wives, and between parents and children. We have frequently had a widow of Type A man tell us that though she is sorry her husband died, she nevertheless felt relieved to be spared the tensions of living with such a man. As syndicated columnist Ellen Goodman writes, "The hard-driven, competitive people are seen nationally and emotionally as lousy spouses." Certainly few would deny that if the relations between men and women could be spared the easily aroused anger and impatience of Type A behavior, our present divorce rate of 50 percent would fall precipitously. There are thousands of counselors now working to save marriages and the gist of all their counseling may be contained in something a young Woodrow Wilson once wrote: "If you come at me with your fist doubled, I think I can promise you that mine will double as fast as yours, but if you come to me and say 'Let us sit down and take counsel together' ... we will presently find ... that the points on which we agree are many." This is also essentially the same message child psychiatrists urge upon parents and children.

We earlier referred to the tendency of the Type A to employ enumeration increasingly in all phases of his life. It turns up in everything. A businessman describes success in terms of how many objects he has sold or how many dollars he has accumulated; an attorney by the number of clients he has served, the number of cases he has won, and of course the amount of money he has made. We noted that President Johnson enjoyed almost anything that could be counted. A socially select but very Type A lady recently told us with considerable joy that since her divorce proceedings began a few months earlier, she had dated 33 different men. When we asked her about the quality of these 33 dates, she shrugged her shoulders.

Perhaps this fascination with enumeration would be a venial error at worst if it did not in some mysterious but definite way lead the Type A to cease using metaphors in his thought and speech. This is of course symptomatic of a reduced capacity to employ imagery. Because of the increasing tyranny exerted by enumeration, the Type A seems to lose interest progressively in those things and activities that cannot be counted. It is at this juncture that the erosion of his personality becomes obvious even to his friends. His egocentrism was bad enough, but when it is joined by a passion for universal enumeration, the result is irretrievably dull and boring. Even more tragic, nothing anyone else can say or do will make much difference; he is, almost by definition, oblivious. Because of familial, commercial, or professional relationships, other people too often cannot avoid him and must figuratively grit their teeth and put up with him. This conspiracy of enforced silence is enacted millions of times every day of every year.

Finally, Type A behavior can inflict another sort of

trauma. While we lack scientific data showing that Type A's are actually addicted to the excess norepinephrine they generate, this possibility must be kept in mind. Norepinephrine can and does influence brain functioning, and any drug which habitually either excites (as do norepinephrine and amphetamines) or depresses (as do the barbiturates) the brain or allays pain or induces pleasure (as do morphine and heroin, respectively) can be addictive, as any street drug dealer knows.

We do not mean that the Type A is likely to be tempted to inject himself with norepinephrine. But his addiction may very well lead him to create or involve himself in exciting or hate-filled situations that result in excess discharges of norepinephrine. It takes many Type A persons a long, long time to adjust to the opposite condition, the gentle pleasures of tranquillity.

If Type A behavior is capable of causing such damage to the careers and personalities of men and women, why do so many people persist in believing that it has played a constructive role in whatever successes they achieved? Why do they genuinely doubt that Western society will prosper if Type A behavior is eradicated? We have pondered these questions ourselves, and we have also made a point of asking the opinion of the chief executive officers of 15 of *Fortune* magazine's leading 500 industrial corporations (seven of whom, incidentally, exhibited not Type A but Type B behavior). Here are the provisional conclusions we have reached:

First, Western men (particularly Americans) have consistently regarded enthusiasm as an admirable virtue when it comes to tackling any task. We agree. In practice, however, the fine line that separates enthusiasm from impatience is frequently crossed. And impatience, particularly when it degenerates into a frenzied, greedy drive to accomplish more things more rapidly, sooner or later leads to disastrous mistakes in analysis, judgment, and action. Yet when such disasters occur, they are rarely attributed to Type A behavior.

Second, the hyperaggressiveness so often observed in Type A's does initially seem to bring them more victories in the marketplace than less aggressive individuals appear able to gain. If this hyperaggressiveness did not carry in its train a tendency to dominate other persons, perhaps it would continue to be useful. But as we already have emphasized, it invariably does involve domination, first wrecking friendships, then familial relationships, and in the end effecting career disasters.

Third, Type A's refuse to recognize that there are Type B's who—by working long hours, generating creative ideas, analyzing and solving problems correctly, and working harmoniously with their superiors, peers, or subordinates—achieve far greater successes. Repeatedly we have pointed out to severely afflicted Type A executives in our various studies that not only some of their immediate superiors, but in some cases the presidents of their companies, exhibit Type B behavior. Knowing these Type B's even better than we do, they quickly agree. But at our very next meeting these same Type A's will again ask defiantly: "Give us some examples of successful men who are Type B." What sort of willful blindness is this?

Finally, since childhood, American children are showered with such aphorisms as "the early bird gets the worm" and "the devil take the hindmost," while victory always goes to him who "gets thar fustest with the mostest."* Haste and competitive drive are thus presented to American children as glorious virtues to acquire and employ as soon as possible. How tragic it is that so few are told of the contrary virtues possessed by the kindly, unhurried Benjamin Franklin (who wrote how proud he was of the fact that he had not exhibited personal hostility for over 50 years), the calm, variously talented Thomas Jefferson (who having written the Declaration of Independence and served as our third president, requested that his tomb-

---

*Confederate General Nathan B. Forrest, to whom this apothegm is credited, died of "natural causes" at the age of 56.

stone mention only the fact that he founded a university), or the majestic Abraham Lincoln, whose patience vied with his humility. Certainly these Type B men did not wreck our country, they helped to form and preserve it. Their style and approach to life surely deserves greater praise and emulation than the witless ambition of Horatio Alger's heroes.

THE THREAT TO LIFE

We already have pointed out in Chapter I how Type A behavior, by causing emotional changes in the limbic system of the brain, sets in motion a complex series of reactions in the midbrain which in turn activates far-flung responses from the endocrine and sympathetic nervous systems. Such responses result in the excess production of at least two hormones (norepinephrine and ACTH) and possibly the excessive consumption of a third hormone, the pituitary growth hormone.

We believe that it is the *excess* discharge of norepinephrine—the hormone manufactured by the sympathetic nervous system, and employed as its messenger agent to control the correct functioning of the heart and the degree of constriction or dilatation of the body's large and small arteries—that is chiefly responsible for the development of arterial diseases. The exact role of ACTH, and the possible excess consumption of pituitary growth hormone in worsening these arterial diseases, remains to be determined. We may discover that they play a very important role. But we have no doubt at this time that the excess norepinephrine generated by Type A behavior must bear the greatest share of blame.

The three arterial diseases that we believe Type A behavior initiates or worsens are: (1) migraine (owing to an initial narrowing and a later excess dilatation of the small arterial vessels supplying blood to the tough covering of the brain); (2) high blood pressure (due to possible overenergetic heart contractions and the narrowing of very small arteries, called arterioles, throughout the body); and (3) coronary heart disease (due in great part to the deterioration of the atherosclerotic plaques in the coronary arteries). The third of these is obviously the most critical, and the way it seems to work is this: The tumor-like atherosclerotic plaques present in one or more of the three major coronary arteries gradually break down and finally rupture, exposing the blood flowing through the vessel to the dead debris. Such exposure causes the blood to clot— i.e., form a thrombus—and this thrombus then *totally* obstructs the previously narrowed interior of the blood vessel. The blockage in turn cuts off the blood supply to a portion of the heart's muscle, causing it to die. This is what we call a myocardial infarction, or heart attack. It is of course life-threatening. (This sequence of clot or thrombus formation was demonstrated in studies performed and published by the Harold Brunn Institute team 15 years ago.)

We are not absolutely sure how Type A behavior undermines the internal structure of an atherosclerotic plaque, causing it to decay, rupture, and touch off a life-threatening thrombus. But we suspect that the excess norepinephrine, generated by Type A behavior and carried in the bloodstream, seriously interferes with the nourishment and metabolism of the mishmash of muscle, scar, cholesterol, fat, and calcified masses making up a typical coronary atherosclerotic plaque. Norepinephrine probably does this in several ways, perhaps the most important being to induce chronic narrowing of the tiny blood vessels which supply and nourish a plaque. This eventually leads to the decay and death of large portions of the plaque.

Another way in which excess norepinephrine may accelerate the decay of a plaque is its tendency, when present in excess, to promote the deposit of various thrombotic elements upon the plaque surface. This process of course makes the plaque bigger and more difficult to nourish.

But infarctions or heart attacks are not always due to

a thrombosis; at least 15 percent of them take place without any clotting in advance. These occur, we believe, because in the wake of a heavy meal containing excess fat, the excess norepinephrine generated by the Type A behavior cuts down the blood supply to the liver, interfering with that organ's usual ability to rid the blood of the extra fat it is carrying. Too much fat in the blood encourages red blood cells to stick together in a process called sludging, and this in turn slows the flow of blood for hours through the very small blood vessels of the body. Unfortunately, there are many such small blood vessels in the heart. Many of them have been newly formed in an attempt by the body to bypass large atherosclerotic plaques obstructing blood flow. If these aggregations of red blood cells plug up the new small heart vessels (called collateral vessels), the heart muscle may be dangerously deprived of its usual blood supply. The result may be either an infarction or—even worse—a fatal arrhythmia or irregular heartbeat. We suspect that scores of thousands of Americans die yearly because of this sludging, which even a single fatty meal can bring on. *And remember, vegetable or fish fat can be just as lethal in this regard as the fat of the cow, pig, or lamb*. William Osler, the father of American medicine, understood this very well when he cautioned in 1899 that "there is death in the pot" for coronary patients.

Excess norepinephrine is also capable of producing, in persons who harbor scars in their heart (of which they may be completely unaware), the deadly irregularity of heartbeat called ventricular fibrillation. When this occurs, the patient in effect drops dead and will probably not recover unless cardiopulmonary resuscitation is begun immediately, followed by the use of a defibrillator able to shock him back to life with several hundred joules of direct electric current.

Finally, Type A behavior is associated with cigarette smoking and excessive inhalation. We have rarely encountered a person who smoked more than 20 cigarettes a day who did not exhibit Type A behavior. Indeed, most Type B persons do not smoke cigarettes at all, although a number of them are pipe smokers. Many medical researchers now believe that it is excess carbon monoxide generated by cigarette smoking rather than the absorbed nicotine which may be leading to premature disease of the major arteries of the body. Certainly when an excess of this gas is dissolved in the blood, thrombotic elements tend to be deposited in the arteries. But as we have already emphasized, cigarette smoking cannot be the sole or even the principal mechanism by which Type A behavior accelerates the onset of clinical coronary heart disease. We are certain of this because, of a group of coronary patients under 64 years of age whom we recently examined, fully 95 percent exhibited Type A behavior, yet a quarter of them had never smoked cigarettes.

HOW TYPE A COMPONENTS INTERACT

Type A components are interdependent. An increase in the severity of one component (such as hurry sickness) increases the severity of one or more of the others. Chronologically, insecurity or inadequate self-esteem, or both, appear first. This suggests that either one or both of these components may be fundamentally responsible for the emergence and maintenance of the full-fledged Type A behavior. We believe this is so because we have yet to see a Type A who does not suffer from one or both of these defects, try as he may to hide them not only from others but even from himself.

The diagram below shows the sequence as we understand it. Note that the processes which are responsible for the emergence of clinical coronary heart disease may be set in motion either directly, through a sense of time urgency, hyperaggressiveness, and free-floating hostility, or indirectly, by the emotional exhaustion those components tend to promote. Also note that both deterioration of personality and emotional exhaustion are implicated in the drive toward self-destruction.

Diagram Illustrating Interrelationships of Type A Components and Pathophysiological Processes

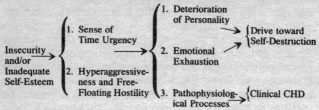

CHAPTER 3

The Type B Man

Although millions of words and thousands of pages have been spent describing Type A behavior and Type A men, relatively little attention has been given to men exhibiting Type B behavior. Like almost all the researchers writing on this subject in the past, we have tended to describe the male Type B negatively—as an individual who *lacks* the traits of a Type A man. Such a description is unfortunate because in a very real sense, it is the Type A who should be said to lack valuable Type B qualities. The Type A's prominence may be laid primarily to the spectacle he has made of himself, adopting traits that are sometimes dramatic, sometimes ludicrous, and always self-destructive, to make up for the Type B qualities he lost, gave away, or possibly never possessed. A Type A is unfortunately more interesting to a physician than a Type B, for the same reason that a child with scarlet fever is more interesting to a physician than a completely healthy youngster.

It is important to us that no one get the idea that all Type B's lead sane but dull lives or that their main excitement in life comes from changing the brand of cereal they eat at breakfast, the route they drive to work, or the television programs they view in the evening. Actually, as we hope most readers will gather by the time they have finished this book, many Type B's live magnificent lives, lives in which their capacity to appreciate beauty, affection, and creative novelty offers them the chance to experience a myriad wonderful events—the first flowering of a cattleya orchid they have been nurturing, their grandchild stutter-mumbling his first sentence, the shy smile of thanks of an old lady on the street, granted because they took the time to notice her existence by smiling at her. Some Type A men *talk* with more spice and zing, but Type B's often *do* far more satisfying things.

NO SENSE OF TIME URGENCY

The second, the minute, even the hour hand of a watch are neither the masters nor the enemies of Type B's. Most Type B's do wear a wristwatch, but look at it infrequently. Unlike severely afflicted Type A's, they do not believe that the passage of time requires their constant attention. They almost never convey the impression, during social or professional activities, that those with whom they are involved are being boring or tedious, or that they themselves have other (and presumably better) things to do with their time. Which is not to say that the Type B cannot keep appointments or catch planes or trains. On the contrary. It's just that he seems able to do these things without the Type A's overtones of frenzy and rage.

Over the years we have asked a number of Type B's why they appear to be on such gracious terms with time. They usually respond vaguely, with a comment like, "Why get bothered about something one can't do anything about?" or "I think it isn't healthy for a person to be too concerned about the passing of time." One Type B quoted

Jonathan Swift: "Whoever is out of patience is out of possession of his soul."

For our part, we suspect that Type B's possess patience because they have the capacity to take what a Type B corporate chief executive recently described to us as "the long view" of their activities. "Looking at a watch," he said, "encourages haste, and in my opinion, nothing leads to mistakes more certainly than hasty thinking." Pointing to a monthly calendar sitting on his desk, he continued, "I admit I do have to look at that calendar sometimes, but even so I'm not sure that substituting months for minutes gives me enough time to make the kind of decisions that will affect this corporation during the next several decades." During this interview we pointed out that his wristwatch was running about four minutes slow. He smiled, looked at the watch for a few seconds, and then said, "Yes, my wife has noticed that too. I guess I'll get it cleaned or regulated or something one of these days." We are virtually certain that he has still not done so.

Besides their tendency to take "the long view," Type B's feel secure enough not to have to rush to complete every task on a deadline basis. (We shall discuss their security a little later in this chapter.) They rarely try to accomplish too many objectives or participate in too many events for the time available; they know that time is not an infinitely expandable container into which they can go on stuffing endless activities. To attempt to do so, they know, simply evokes a feeling of compression in themselves.

Type B's usually differ from Type A's in the way they delegate authority. Type A men can and do sometimes delegate authority, but always with some trepidation and an air of irritability and impatience. Only if his appointed surrogate manages to go at a task *precisely* as he would and with a speed equal to or exceeding his own, will he allow his surrogate to continue. But if the surrogate fails to do so, working too slowly or in a different way, the impatience of the Type A will force him to step in and take over.

Type B's *expect* their subordinates or associates to perform tasks differently. Speed, too, is less of an issue, unless slowness would lead to actual disaster.* Even more important, a Type B—unlike a Type A—can stand quietly by, without taking over, even as it becomes obvious that his surrogate will fail. Needless to say, a truly consequential failure won't be permitted; but anything less may well be viewed by the self-confident and secure Type B as a valuable learning experience for the subordinate. (The basic insecurity of the Type A man is such that no delegated task *ever* appears to be of minor significance.) Rightly or wrongly, a Type B tends to regard his socioeconomic status as totally secure, as immutable as a pyramid of Giza that can withstand severe shocks and still endure. Type A's, on the other hand, unconsciously regard their status as something utterly fragile, ready to collapse following a slight jolt, or perhaps none at all!

If former President Lyndon B. Johnson showed every sign of being a virulent Type A, it's worth noting that former President Harry S Truman was just as obviously a Type B. From the evidence, he certainly would have agreed with Thoreau's remark that "Nothing can be more useful to a man than a determination not to be hurried." Margaret Truman was well aware of her father's refusal to treat time as his enemy. "The pace of the farm was reflected in the pace of the era," she wrote in *Harry S Truman.** "There was no sense of frantic urgency, no burning need to hurry; as Cousin Ethel said, 'Harry was always a deliberate man.'" He was even deliberate about courting his wife-to-be. "Sometimes I think that if World War I hadn't come along, he might not have married until

---

*As Harry Truman once said, "If a fella can't be patient and considerate of people who are actually doin' the work for him, then he's not any good, and I don't like him." From *Plain Speaking* by Merle Miller (Berkley Pub., 1974).

*William Morrow and Co., New York, 1973.

he was forty or fifty, and I might never have gotten here,"
writes his daughter.

Was Truman a Type B man because he had matured
in a slower-paced era? Some Type A's might be tempted
to claim this. They should, however, keep in mind that
presidents Gerald Ford and Ronald Reagan also exhibit
Type B behavior, and these gentlemen were born at just
about the same time as most of the older readers of this
book.

Type B's generally indulge in periods of contemplation.
This may range from sheer cerebration to spiritual musing
or meditation. They are always aware of the fact that
compulsive thinking about one's immediate affairs,
untempered by a recollection of past happiness or
achievements, is very little different from worrying, and
is thus likely to induce anxiety and impatience. *The Type
B person has learned to value and enjoy himself as much
or more for what he has already done or experienced as
for what he may accomplish in the future.*

A locally distinguished Type B architect of our
acquaintance, for example, rarely allows a month to pass
by that he does not visit all the structures (small or large)
he has designed, sometimes admiring them, occasionally
finding fault, but always with the awareness that "these
visits to my past tell me who I was and what I was like."
This life-enhancing habit is markedly different from the
practice of a Type A architect we know, who enjoys a
national reputation for having designed huge urban structures. He never finds the time even to look over photographs of his glamorous, gaudy, yet vaguely meretricious
structures, much less visit them. "He talks of artistic purpose and all that sort of stuff, but his ears are always
ready to hear the sounds of jingling coins," says one of
his clients.

We have always admired the first architect for his willingness to take the time to enjoy and gain spiritual sustenance from his creations. We have likewise always felt
pity for the second, who seems to feel little regard or

tenderness for the dazzling but vulgar piles of concrete and steel he has put on earth. How little sparkle still remained in his eyes, how little charm in his voice, when last we saw him!

To a certain extent the Type B uses his periods of contemplation to reflect on the things he likes about himself. This is not a matter of immodesty; it is simply a natural and honest assessment of reasons why he has a right to feel comfortable with himself (as in fact most people do, if they would only admit it). The process has the incidental advantage of making it almost automatically unnecessary for him to become obsessed by the inadequacies of others. Type B's have the capacity for appreciating what they *are* as much or more than what they can *do*. As John Locke pointed out long ago, one's personal identity is actually a process. At any given moment of a man's life, he remembers other moments and fuses them, building a sense of who and what he is out of a mixture of past and present. Type B's are fully aware that if either the present or the past consists of no more than the bleakness of numbers, of digits, ciphers, and decimals, the fusion of past and present events required for the *sustenance of personal identity* cannot occur.

NO FREE-FLOATING HOSTILITY

Type B men are not necessarily warmhearted, completely altruistic models of Arthurian chivalry. We have known Type B's who are quite coldhearted, calculating, even self-centered. But most Type B men are not like this, and none harbors free-floating hostility. This absence of hostility chiefly stems from their high degree of self-esteem. They do not find it necessary, as do hostile Type A's, to engage in a ceaseless struggle to bolster their own low self-esteem by finding fault with others.

Because of their high self-esteem, Type B's generally have no wish to take control of the *total* environment in which they find themselves. They can live in mixed circumstances, because they have learned the art of knowing what to overlook. For example, the errors or the belligerence of other motorists may make them cautious but rarely angry or irritated, just as they can accept with equanimity the occasional or even frequent trivial errors of subordinates. To them, life is a matter of proportion—they practice the art of being wise by knowing what to disregard!*

Type B's rarely feel tense or induce tension in their families. Again, this is chiefly due to their ability to overlook small mistakes and shortcomings in the speech, manners, or behavior of their wives and children. Their self-confidence lets them be objective when faced with the problem of, say, dealing with a teen-age child's minor behavioral failings. They can even do what is almost impossible for the Type A—put themselves in the other person's shoes. Yet such appropriate tolerance of minor errors by a Type B parent does not mean that he is likely to acquiesce in or condone *serious* bad behavior (for instance, theft, the use of drugs, dangerous driving, persistent truancy, or some act of sheer brutality). In such situations, a Type B parent seems much better able than the Type A to provide punishment that is fair and well-suited to prevent similar future transgressions. He is unlikely to harangue, lecture, or sermonize. Unsurprisingly, the children of Type B fathers only infrequently require punishment.

Type B's escape from the tyranny of free-floating hostility because of their sense of security and self-esteem. In addition, most of them appear capable of giving and receiving praise and affection, which makes them less vulnerable to irritations. "How can I become angry if I'm

---

*In recent years, we have run into a curious illustration of the way Type A men, in marked contrast to Type B's, are likely to take the silliest things seriously. More than half of them seem to be prepared to argue heatedly about the manner in which a toilet paper roll is placed in its receptacle: so that the paper unrolls over the top, or comes out underneath. It may be hard to believe, but we have witnessed grown men very nearly come to blows over this issue. The medieval churchmen who fought over how many angels can dance on the head of a pin must have been Type A's.

complimenting someone or if someone is complimenting me?" one of our Type B men jokingly asked.

Type B's also understand that simply *feeling* affection is not enough (many Type A men are capable of doing that) but that affection must also be *expressed*, both verbally and through touching. Most Type A subjects find this very difficult. Phrases such as "I love you," "I so appreciate you," "I missed you dreadfully," or "How fortunate I am to have you," are not difficult for Type B's to utter, while as much as a Type A might wish to do the same, some sort of inexplicable shyness appears to prevent him. Similarly, Type B's find physical displays of affection—a kiss, a stroking of an arm, shoulder, or face, or tender holding of a hand—relatively easy, natural, and delightful ways of expressing love for wife, child, or friend. Type A men again find it difficult to communicate in this fashion, except as a prelude to sex.

Oddly, neither Type A's nor Type B's seem to have any trouble showing affection for pets. We once heard a Type A unconsciously point out this contradiction when he said, "If all the people I have to deal with were as nice as my dog, I'd be able to treat them with affection, but too many of them act like rats or skunks. Who wants to pet a rat or a skunk?" It is too bad that so many Type A men regard other human beings as inferior to dogs.

A SENSE OF SELF-ESTEEM

If we were to describe the one attribute that most distinguishes the Type B from the Type A, it would be the Type B's possession of adequate self-esteem. A person's self-esteem, as we have said, is not determined solely by his achievements, no matter how many or how brilliant these may seem to other people. What matters is that those achievements match or exceed his own expectations.

From early infancy on, Type B's—unlike most Type A's—have received the parental affection and love they want and need on an unconditional basis. It does not come as a reward for achievement, it is simply and naturally *there*. As a result, Type B boys never develop the Type A's burning need to achieve endlessly in order to *wring* approval and affection out of their mothers (and possibly their fathers). This, of course, should not be taken to mean that Type B boys do not wish to achieve goals; on the contrary. But it does mean that the range of their expectations is in a healthy balance with their perceived capacities. For example, a Type B physician friend of ours likes to remark that when he sees himself in the mirror he knows he is looking at a physician who "always was second rate and always will be." Our friend smiles when he makes this remark, but he means it; he knows and accepts the fact that he will never be another Osler or Mayo. But since his expectations remain in bounds, his actual achievements (a fine private practice, a loving and lovely wife, several children successfully raised, and a modest fortune) have surpassed his expectations, creating a very secure sense of self-esteem.

Our friend Dr. Albert Goggans of Fort Worth has told us of an ancient man, well over 90 years of age, whom he considers not only a perfect Type B but also a truly fine gentleman. The man's secret of long and happy life, according to Dr. Goggans, is expressed this way: "My mother told me to always do the best I could and be satisfied with the result. I've tried to do just that." That is the Type B essence—and a model for us all.

Type B men can and do work as hard or even harder than Type A men, but if they fail at something, their self-esteem does not collapse. They recognize that they have not stinted in their efforts and, realistically aware of their intrinsic shortcomings, they feel no pointless shame. When a Type B friend of ours was passed over as president and chief executive officer of his bank, he went home and told his wife, "The directors have always been good friends of mine so I know that they acted in good faith in selecting Bill instead of me." His self-esteem was not even scratched. Indeed, six months later, convinced that the board had acted wisely, he went to Bill and told him that, after seeing how he had taken over, it was obvious that the board had made the right decision. (It would be nice if we could report that our man's friend Bill also possessed sufficient self-esteem. But Bill is a Type A, and his expectations even today exceed whatever he has managed to achieve, including the bank presidency. If he were asked point-blank what his greatest expectation was, he would mumble that he would like to be considered as great a banker as a particular chief executive officer of a New York bank, who also is a Type A. But even if he were to be so considered, and he never will be, his expectations would drive him to create new and still more difficult goals. And the reason for this insensate agitation? Probably the residue of the tortured longing of the little boy he once was for the unconditional love and attention his mother either could not or would not bestow. Unfortunately, in his own selfish preoccupation to find self-esteem, Bill has succeeded, in turn, in emotionally crippling his own children. Such chain reactions do not subside easily.)

We should note in passing that the self-esteem of many (though not all) Type B men is safeguarded, even enhanced, by their capacity to give and receive love and affection from parents, wife, children, or friends.

AN INTACT PERSONALITY

All of us wish to find the means to support ourselves and to achieve some degree of status among our peers and our superiors. At one time, particularly when we attended secondary schools and universities, most of us actively sought to capture and enjoy those things generally considered beautiful and worthwhile. But Type A's, in their monomaniacal drive for status enhancement, tend as they grow older to desist from this last quest, increasingly substituting the numerative for the numinous. Type B's never do this.

Many Type B's nourish and enhance various aspects of their personalities by their continued reading of literature of the most diverse kinds. They may augment their personalities by playing or listening to various works of music. Others find satisfaction in viewing and appreciating paintings and sculpture, or in attending the theater, the stadium, the arena, or by watching the more significant television productions. Indeed, some Type B's find the time to indulge in all these activities.

But whatever the aesthetic and intellectual needs of Type B's may be, they are never satisfied by the mere accumulation of numbers. George Steiner may have been correct in believing that the language of modern business is no longer words but graphs, tables, and numbers, but Type B's know, with Samuel Johnson, that language, not numbers, is the "dress of thought." Type B's still retain and employ a good store of metaphors. They use them to enrich their relations with other men and, yes, with animals and plants too. Even their daily speech reveals the liveliness and richness metaphors provide them with.

NO TYPE A TICS

Because Type B's do not suffer from a sense of time urgency, they exhibit none of the psychomotor manifestations associated with it. They speak at a moderate, unharried rate. They almost never try to hurry the speech of others by gasping, "uh huh, uh huh" or nodding their heads quickly. They walk and eat at a moderate speed, one that never embarrasses a fellow walker or diner. They are unlikely to jiggle their knees nervously. The skin beneath their eyes shows no sign of being darkened by melanin.

This typical Type B manner tends to evoke a very pleasant feeling of relaxation and serenity in others, unless, of course, the other person suffers from a very severe Type A syndrome. In the latter case, the result may well be irritation, and an attempt on the part of the Type A to hasten the speech rhythms of the Type B—almost never successfully.

The Type B man never shows the psychomotor signs

of free-floating hostility. His voice and laugh carry no overtones of anger or irritation; his voice consequently seems pleasant and his laughter delightful. He almost never utters obscenities. Nor does he ever clench his fists in emphasis or to show exasperation. Finally, unlike Type A's, Type B's absolutely never show covert hostility in their facial expression, or suffer from the common Type A tic that involves drawing back the lips spasmodically as if to bare the teeth.

TYPE B'S AS LEADERS

Perhaps the most vivid illustration of the fact that it is by no means necessary to be Type A to be an important leader in American society is the following table showing the results of interviews we have conducted within the last eight years with men and women holding a variety of distinguished positions:

The Presence of Type A and Type B Behavior in 106 National Leaders

Type of Leaders	Total Number	Type A Behavior	Type B Behavior
1) University Presidents	11	6 (55%)	5 (45%)
2) Bank Presidents	5	3 (60%)	2 (40%)
3) Corporation Chairmen	30	21 (70%)	9 (30%)
4) Generals, Admirals	11	6 (55%)	5 (45%)
5) Archbishops, Bishops, Rabbis	4	2 (50%)	2 (50%)
6) Journalists, Publishers	22	16 (73%)	6 (27%)
7) Nobel Laureates	11	6 (55%)	5 (45%)
8) Congressmen, Senators	7	3 (43%)	4 (57%)
9) Federal Judges	5	2 (40%)	3 (60%)
Total	106	65 (62%)	41 (39%)

While it is true that Type A's predominate here, it must be recognized that Type A men are actually in the great majority in this country. Not long ago we completed a survey of approximately 1,100 male federal postal employees; it revealed Type A behavior in no less than 75 percent of them. In other words, about three out of four urban men, regardless of their economic or professional status, exhibit Type A behavior. Moreover, if one excludes the journalists and publishers from this table, then 42 percent of the remaining leaders were Type B's. In other words, among our most prestigious national leaders the Type B person is by no means a rarity. Incidentally, we have yet to come across a single top Type B corporate executive who suffered a heart attack prior to his 65th birthday.

CHAPTER 4

The Type A Woman and the Type B Woman

Until fairly recent times, very few women exhibited Type A behavior. In part, this was due to the fact that human females (like sub-human primate females) do not possess the aggressiveness, typical of males, that is generally associated with the male hormone testosterone.*

At least as important as the hormonal differences, however, was the relative isolation of women from the economic and professional pressures that so often drive a Type A personality into Type A behavior. While women like Susan B. Anthony and Carrie Nation no doubt possessed and displayed tremendous amounts of free-floating hostility, they were the exceptions; and whatever the admiration their activities attracted, relatively few women went so far as to emulate them. Traditionally, most women took pride in who they were, even though such identity

---

*Recently we have observed that the level of this hormone is increased in Type A men.

was often necessarily expressed in terms of their dependent relation to others—their husbands or their families. One has only to look at photographs or portraits of women prior to World War I to note the complete absence of a sense of time urgency, or hostility.

But the apparent lack of Type A behavior does not mean that all of these women necessarily felt secure or possessed adequate self-esteem. On the contrary. Women of the lower economic classes, working long hours performing dreary, monotonous, personality-destroying tasks for starvation wages suffered from insecurity in its most acute form. The lot of thousands of middle- and upper-class women was scarcely better. Unmarried, they had little education or professional training to fall back on, while law and custom specifically favored men in almost every socioeconomic situation. Married, they were entirely at the mercy of their husbands' abilities, and if these were inadequate the only alternatives were to find work themselves or get a divorce; neither choice was attractive, or, in most cases, even practical.

In short, until very recently, an aura of intractable hopelessness attended whatever insecurities women possessed. For every one woman who chose struggle as a means of relieving her insecurities, 99 others submissively and hopelessly accepted their lot. Type A behavior cannot flourish in the absence of struggle. Indeed, an attitude of hopelessness and Type A behavior are antithetical.

Beginning in the 1970s, however, women have achieved an ever-increasing number of victories in their fight to attain parity with men in all phases of human activity. They have successfully entered the professions, commerce, and industry. No one now finds it strange that we have policewomen and female penitentiary guards, female military officers, female astronauts, female university presidents, and female cabinet officers, governors, judges, and mayors.

Under the circumstances, it is hardly surprising that many women would begin discarding their former shrouds of hopelessness in favor of a variety of struggles aimed at ridding themselves of their old insecurities and gaining new levels of self-esteem. Type A behavior has of course followed, and now presents itself as a growing danger. And, as might be expected, the incidence of coronary heart disease is increasing rapidly among women.

As we earlier noted, severely afflicted Type A professional and business women not only were found to be suffering from coronary heart disease approximately seven times more frequently than Type B women remaining in their homes as housewives,* they also suffered from this disorder just as frequently as Type A professionals and businessmen. This study marked the beginning of the end for the old assumption that females were protected against coronary heart disease by the female sex hormone, estrogen.

How Type A Behavior Develops in Women

Type A women are similar to Type A men in that they are prone to insecurity and a lack of self-esteem.

Unlike Type A men, however, whose problems with security and self-esteem so often originate in their failure to obtain the unconditional love and affection of their mothers, the critical relationship for most Type A women was with their fathers. Moreover, just as Type A men generally lacked the love and affection of a mother of whom they could be proud and with whom there could be two-way communication, so the Type A woman in her childhood was denied the same things from her father. If he was a failure in his own career, if he was an alcoholic, or if he was dominated by his wife, then no matter how

---

*Dr. Suzanne Haynes and her associates in the Framingham Study recently reported that they found CHD four times more prevalent in Type A employed females than in Type B employed females.

intense his love may have been for his daughter, she was unable to accept his affection as totally satisfactory. She may have felt pity for such a failed "hero," but not the kind of spirit-enhancing admiration that was necessary if his love was to provide her with a firm sense of security.

How valid are these generalizations about the origin of insecurity and inadequate self-esteem in Type A women? They derive from our own repeated observations and interviews, in which we often heard such women either expressing a bitter contempt for an inadequate or non-loving father, or a wistful desire to find a husband who may serve as the sort of loving father they would have liked to have had or had lost early in their childhood through death or divorce. Here are a few examples from a variety of severe Type A women:

1. The unhappy wife of a bank executive, mother of a six-year-old boy: "I hated my father. He never complimented me but always told me that I'd never be worth a damn as a wife or mother. God, how I would like to have had a real father."

2. A top folk singer, a divorcée: "I didn't have much use for my father. He thought I didn't have much of a mind compared to my brother's. When I asked him a question, I'd always add, 'just give me an answer in a few words, don't give me a lecture.' He lived in his tiny academic world of medieval history."

3. A restless but fairly successful housewife: "I never really knew my father. He was a gambler and deserted my mother and me when I was just a baby."

4. A prominent novelist, now divorced: "I've fallen in love with a man who has my father's same expressions. A few days ago I passed him in my car and he shrugged his shoulders and lifted his arms exactly as my father used to do. I trembled all over."

5. A single woman, cynical, an active feminist:

"Let's face it, my father was a dope. When I got my Phi Beta Kappa key from Smith, he got the idea that I should round up a few other Phi Betas and then he'd bill us in a night club act as the 'Dancing Phi Betes.'"

6. A young divorcée and topflight corporate executive: "I was 34 years old and already married to Jack for 10 years before I had my first climax and I had to do it for myself." When asked who was the erotic image during this episode, she replied: "My boss, who is as old as my father would have been."

7. A young, recently divorced socialite: "I really couldn't bear to have Bill touch me because he wasn't anything like my father, nor was he ever able to displace my father. Of course I never had any sort of relationship with my father, but I always tried to win his affection and admiration by trying to get ahead in the things I thought he would like, but somehow I never really quite pleased him."

8. A middle-aged, highly successful businesswoman: "When Dad died last year, I tried to cry but couldn't. After all, he was dominated completely by my mother and had been a business failure. Yet, when I was promoted a few weeks ago, I cried all day because he wasn't here to exult in my success." She showed his photograph, commenting cynically as she did so, "He probably was potted when he had it taken."

The nagging desire of so many Type A women for a satisfactory relationship with their fathers is poignantly illustrated by the pathetic attempt Maria Callas made to establish a filial relationship with her godfather. "I wish you were my father," she wrote him. "My people have given me nothing but unhappiness. You have always been a source of pleasure and happiness." This same fury-ridden Type A woman ("Only my dogs will not betray me") also once blurted out, "Only when I was singing did I feel loved."

Like a boy, a girl also requires more than parental affection to sustain her security and enhance her self-esteem. She too requires the acceptance of her peers. If she is teased because of some physical defect (glasses or braces, for example, or a pimply face) or shunned because she belongs to a minority or comes from a markedly poorer family, her self-esteem can deteriorate.

"I was a mess in high school, with my teeth in braces, my freckles, and my mousy brown dull hair," we were told by one Type A public relations executive who is now quite glamorous. "I did have pretty blue eyes but my spectacles hid them. I didn't have a single date, even in my senior year. Sure, I know I look good now, but I feel as though I'm a cosmetician's creation—bleached hair, contact lenses, false eyelashes, dental crowns, powders, ointments, and polishes. Sometimes I have so much make-up on that I'm afraid to laugh for fear I'll break out in facial fissures. And even if men do tell me I'm glamorous, I still feel the true me is that high school mess."

Unlike secondary-school boys who later become Type A men, grades and sports are not necessarily of paramount importance to girls destined to become Type A women. But friendship and popularity with other girls are vital. If a girl is excluded from a sorority, a club, or some sort of social group, or if, most important of all, she fails to find another girl who will regard her as her best friend, then her self-esteem is likely to diminish drastically. And like a boy with bad marks, she will probably avoid telling her parents about it.

Type A behavior usually becomes overt in boys during secondary school, as they attempt to achieve too much in too little time and begin to compete bitterly. Some girls show the same tendencies in their early teens, but most do not. Nor do most girls in their college years succumb completely to Type A behavior, unless they fall into a habit of "pushing" time. Such an exception was a Type A lady we recently interviewed. She finished a four-year college course in three years, meanwhile serving as president of her sorority, working in a cleaning establishment, and selling semiprecious jewelry to fellow students. "I didn't see any reason why I shouldn't get out of college as fast as I could and also make some money too," she explained. Still, it is uncommon for women to show or feel the telltale signs of Type A behavior until they begin their professional or business careers.

One reason may be that most girls from a very early age are discouraged from being aggressive or even assertive. This kind of social training seems to shield women from the grosser aspects of Type A behavior until the beginning of the third decade of their lives—and sometimes, thank goodness, far past the third decade!

Just as with their mothers or grandmothers, low self-esteem or insecurity does not necessarily induce young women to become Type A's. Some, perhaps most, such emotionally scarred women accept their lot and fall back into a kind of hopelessness. But particularly among women in business and the professions, low self-esteem can and frequently does lead to fully developed Type A behavior.

A sense of time urgency usually is the first overt manifestation. Such potential Type A women invariably create a staggering schedule for themselves. Fired up to beat men at their own game, many of these women may work a 50-hour week in junior or middle management positions. In addition, they have to market and cook for themselves (and often for their boyfriends or husbands), do their own housekeeping, laundering, and ironing, visit their hairdressers, shop for clothes, and—certainly not least—appear ebullient and attractive.

These feminine chores and duties become no easier with the passage of time, and seem in many cases to become a focus for hostility and frustration that persists no matter what position the woman attains. We once spoke, for example, to a woman who, as a cabinet officer in a recent administration and the mother of grown children, still resented the time she had to take from her career to devote to her husband, her home, and her children. "Justice Holmes could find the time to write a famous series of letters to Harold Laski, because he had a wife who did all the scut work. I didn't have a wife, I had to do the scut work myself."

The sense of time urgency tends to be soon followed by signs of free-floating hostility. In many young women pursuing careers, this may first develop along with the realization that in competitive situations men are likely to forget their commitment to courtesy and chivalry, and bear down hard—and perhaps unfairly—on their female colleagues. Then, as the young woman finds (often to her shock and surprise) that she cannot necessarily count on members of her own sex for support in the office wars, her free-floating hostility may really start to bloom. The fact that women can be competitive *with other women* is one aspect of the modern scene that feminists have regrettably played down;* the discovery that an older Type A female superior is prepared to hold her down as pitilessly as any man might do can be traumatic to a rising young woman executive, and certainly exacerbates whatever insecurities and anger she may already feel. Further anger is bound to stem from the recognition that pay scales are not the same for men and women in many professions; while professions more commonly occupied by women (such as teaching and nursing) are as a matter of course poorly paid in comparison to those occupied by men (such as medicine and the law).

The social pressures on the young Type A business and professional woman create special difficulties. To maintain her status she feels she must dress well, but dressing well frequently makes her sexually attractive to the men with whom she works. This may well happen whether she wants it to or not, and often sets the stage for more hostility—anger and repugnance if she perceives the man approaching her as her inferior, insecurity and

---

*The far from lovely legal confrontation now proceeding between such literary feminists as Lillian Hellman and Mary McCarthy should serve notice that conflicts between human beings may have intrasexual as well as intersexual origins.

emotional conflict if the man is a professional superior with some control over her position and future. The latter case is particularly painful because the woman knows that if she handles things clumsily, she may be fired or blocked from advancement. The hostility cannot be vented, but must be silently turned inward.

We have known few Type A women, regardless of how high a position they have reached, who have never wished at least once in their lives to get married. Moreover, most of them have a very clear idea of the sort of man they would like to marry—one whose intelligence, education, and drive not only equal but exceed their own. Having failed to receive unconditional paternal support, they seem unconsciously to be seeking a man who can serve as a surrogate father. It is this attitude that makes successful 55- to 60-year old business executives so attractive to 30- or 35-year old Type A women. In the event, most Type A women marry men no more than 10 years their senior. Nevertheless, we have repeatedly observed that when Type A women do marry men within 5 or 10 years of their own age, divorce is quite common, whereas it is much less common when husbands have a high position and are 15 to 25 years older than their Type A wives. Flattered by the attention of women so much younger than themselves, such older husbands are apparently more inclined to treat their wives as talented children instead of rivals. Often they are Type B's. Because of her husband's seniority, the Type A wife more easily accepts advice and opinions from him, unconsciously comforted by the father role the husband's age permits him to assume. Yet such a Type A wife may take satisfaction in the thought that in the end she will be the strong one, if only because she will still be active when old age catches up with her husband. As one such Type A wife said, "He's running interference for me now, but in a few years, I'll probably be pushing his wheelchair."

Still, relatively few young Type A women find successful 55- to 60-year-old men to marry. And quite a few Type A women, still athletically active and eager to hike, ski, jog, and play tennis, would rather not marry much older men. If they do marry someone closer to their own age, that person is almost invariably a Type A. The aggressiveness, the quickness, the apparent drive, and the outright machismo of so many young Type A men make them quite attractive to their female counterparts.

Quite a few, perhaps as many as half, of these marriages prove unsatisfactory and end in divorce. Type A husbands, unconsciously looking for surrogate mothers who will love and encourage them, too often find in their Type A wives only a competitor and critic. The Type A wives, unconsciously seeking ideal father figures to whom they can open their hearts in utter confidence and trust, confront in Type A husbands egocentric, demanding persons who—after the initial glow cools—resent any sort of superiority they may possess in breeding, intelligence, education, or training.

Such marriages, in which communication sickens and affections wither, are not rare. Often, however, because of shared housekeeping and sex, they stagger on. The advent of children may prevent total disintegration because the needs and the doings of growing children interest, capture, and sometimes hold the attention of both Type A wives and husbands, perhaps for a lifetime. Of course, children do create new pressures as well. The sense of time urgency of the Type A wife—particularly if she returns to work a few months after the birth of her child—becomes more intense. Domestic chores multiply. Back on the job, she finds that her superiors are prepared to afford her sympathy and consideration for about as long as they would for a man returning after a coronary bypass or some other equally serious operation—that is, for about two weeks! After this period of grace, the Type A working mother is expected to pull her own weight as enthusiastically as she did before, meanwhile being haunted by suspicions (encouraged by her basic insecurity) that pregnancy and motherhood have damaged her standing in the continuous race for career advancement. Most such Type A women are astute enough to suspect that male

executives can condone the marriage of their female subordinates but will never again have complete faith in their
devotion to a career once they have their first child.

Faced with this sort of situation, the majority of Type
A working mothers do in fact ultimately sacrifice whatever chances they once may have had for a brilliant career
and take up child care, sometimes along with less consuming—and less fulfilling—employment. This choice
further intensifies their frustrations and their hostility,
although most still succeed in keeping the turbulence covert. The destruction of their career hopes, needless to say,
does not ease the day-to-day burdens of those Type A
mothers who go back to work. As one of them told us,
"My area manager wanted sales increases, my husband
wanted food and sex in that order, and my children needed,
and probably didn't get enough of, my attention and affection. When wasn't I harassed? If I had it to do over again,
I would—" she paused, meditated a few seconds, then
shook her head in a bewildered way. "I guess I don't know
what I would have done."

Precisely how many of the 50 percent of American
women who work and the 90 percent of American wives
who have one or more children feel like this woman we
do not know, but we suspect there are more than a few.
Certainly the egocentrism of children and the need to deal
with their urgent demands are not likely to appease the
sense of time urgency or the free-floating hostility of harassed Type A mothers, whether or not they have employment outside the home. An almost predictable consequence
is a deep sense of frustration and disappointment. "Just
name me a mother who isn't taken for granted," we have
heard more than one Type A mother say ruefully, having
spent years contending with household duties (and very
probably listening to a Type A husband lecture her on
the proper way to perform them).

Perhaps in compensation for such disappointments and
sacrifices, many Type A mothers have a tendency to project distinguished careers for their children. As might be
expected, given our strongly meritocratic society, these

hopes are seldom fulfilled; the boys don't necessarily get into Yale or the girls into Radcliffe, and very few show even the promise of an exceptional career or a splendid marriage. This is not to say, of course, that *all* Type A mothers are disappointed in their own marriages or in their children. So far as we know, there may be many of them boasting wonderfully happy marriages and brilliantly successful children who appreciate everything their mothers have done for them. There may be ... but we have to say that in all our years of practice and research we have encountered very few.

Much more common, alas, are those Type A wives and mothers who, as they enter their fifties and sixties, suffer from a still greater loss of self-esteem as a feeling grows of no longer being needed by their children or their husband. Stimulated by this sense of failure, an unconscious yearning for self-destruction may take root and begin to develop.

It has not been easy for the two of us, a Type A physician and a Type A nurse, to write the preceding pages. We are intimately acquainted with the dismal foibles and faults described here, and not just as observers. Our only consolation—fortunately a large one—is that most women are still not severely afflicted by Type A behavior, and even those that are still have hope of ameliorating it, as we have done.

Diagnosing Type A Behavior in Women

As we already have mentioned, Type A women, like all other women, are trained from early childhood to refrain from many of the aggressive acts, gestures, and words that their brothers are permitted, if not directly encouraged, to indulge in. Social custom later reinforces these restrictions. As a result, most Type A women are inhibited from displaying the verbal and physical signs of their sense of time urgency and free-floating hostility. Thus even the most experienced diagnostician of the presence of Type A behavior can and frequently does fail to note its presence in women who are in fact quite markedly Type A.

In Type A women the psychomotor manifestations of the sense of time urgency are identical to those of Type A men, but less obvious:

- While Type A women generally speak more rapidly than Type B women, they rarely do so to the extent that the listener is irritated. Like Type A men, they rarely pause once they begin to utter a sentence. Unlike men, they do not often telescope or elide the terminal words of their sentences. Again unlike Type A men, they almost never stutter.

- Type A women do show a tendency to try to hurry the speech of others. Sometimes they will do so by repeatedly saying, "uh huh, uh huh" rapidly. If someone else begins to relate an anecdote, a Type A woman may well interrupt and attempt to deliver the ending.

- While a Type A woman's face rarely shows outright impatience, a close inspection of her eyes often reveals that while she is pretending to listen, she is actually thinking of something else. "I feel like taking out my pocket handkerchief and waving it in front of her face to get her attention back to what I'm talking about," a Texas banker once told us in describing how he felt talking to a Type A woman.

- Unlike Type A men, Type A women usually do not tap their fingers vigorously on tables, desks, or sides of armchairs, nor do they often jiggle their knees.

- Type A women do exhibit lip-clicking as frequently as Type A men, except that it is done in a quieter and less obvious fashion.

- Though they frequently blink their eyes, Type A women are much less likely than Type A men to nod their heads while delivering an opinion or making a statement.
- They are much less likely than their male counterparts to suck in their breath while speaking. They are, however, just as apt to display expiratory sighing, although the sighs are briefer than those of Type A men.
- Type A women are as apt as Type A men to move quickly and to sit in an expectant manner (that is, as if they were waiting for the starter's pistol to begin a race).
- They are just as likely as men to exhibit the pigmentation around the eyes described in Chapter 2. But it is more apt to involve only the lower eyelid. Clever Type A women who are aware of this pigmentation tan their whole face in the summer to obscure the brown eyelid.
- The excessive forehead and upper-lip perspiration mentioned in Chapter 2 does not seem to be present in Type A women.

The biographical manifestations of a Type A woman's sense of time urgency are almost identical to those of a Type A man. Type A women are frequently conscious of their own impatience, having been advised by their husbands or boyfriends (less often by their children) to slow down; they admit to having great difficulty in sitting and doing nothing; they dislike waiting in lines; they prefer to walk and east fast (but strangely, do not mind dawdling at the table); they frequently use numbers in their speech; and they habitually attempt to think about and do several things at once.

The psychomotor signs and biographical manifestations of free-floating hostility are similarly kept under far greater restraint by Type A women than by Type A men.

Thus the signs of facial hostility so often seen in Type A men are not frequently detected in Type A women.* In fact, we have observed such facial hostility only in a few Type A women whose attitude was marked by a generalized fury and bitterness.

Nor do Type A women usually reveal hostility in their voices, even when their anger is profound. Missing is the irritating, grating, frankly unpleasant tone of voice of so many hostile Type A men. Here again, the cause is probably earlier training to speak softly and gently. More often than not, however, particularly when the memory of a past unpleasant event irritates them and they are no longer on strict social guard, many Type A women will unapologetically blurt out obscene Anglo-Saxon four-letter words. "I know that when I speak filth a lot of women and some men too think I'm vulgar, but there come times when no other words will do to express how I feel about something," once growled a very hostile Type A woman writer.

Type A women harboring considerable hostility do clench their fists occasionally in the middle of a conversation, although not as frequently as their male counterparts do. They rarely pound on hard surfaces with their hands, but often exhibit the tic-like grimace of pulling back the corners of their lips. In women, this grimace does not manifest itself with the frequency or force shown in male Type A's; as in men, it is most likely to appear when the woman is upset about some immediate matter.

The biographical aspects of free-floating hostility in Type A women also are more muted than those of their male counterparts. Type A women probably feel more frustration than outright hostility in their daily lives. Accordingly, they do not generally rant about the erratic driving habits of other motorists, nor do they react furiously to opposing sociological, economic, and political opinions. If they are observed closely, however, a slight tightening of the lips and a hint of a glare sometimes can be seen when they encounter views with which they reso-

---

*If hostility is present, it can be detected best by observation of the profile.

lutely disagree. Again, social custom has conditioned them to mute their responses. So strong may such conditioning be that some Type A women will describe events that the observer knows have to be intensely frustrating in a seemingly emotionless, singsong voice, as if they have distanced themselves totally.

Teeth-grinding, which almost always is a sign of frustration coupled with hostility, is practiced more frequently by Type A women than by Type A men. Allowed by society to vent their frustrations only during their sleep, thousands of Type A women suffer from this tooth-destroying disorder.

In writing this description of Type A women, we have necessarily generalized, but our generalizations are based on fact: on the very close observation of 14 Type A women. These women, ranging in age from 30 to 58 years, come from various parts of the United States. Their professions and the positions they occupy also represent a wide range—university executive, major corporate executive, folk singer, socialite, presidential cabinet member, federal judge, nurse, attorney, young housewife without children, older housewife with grandchildren, even nun. Looking at these women as a group, we are struck by the following characteristics:

First, all of them are beset by a sense of insecurity varying from slight to so severe that it is crippling their lives.

Second, with the exception of the nun, none of them expresses true confidence that there is any Supreme Being who is watching over them *as a loving, totally forgiving, and accepting Father*, even though several of them have actively tried to believe. Even the nun recently told us, "I pray every day, of course, but I still can't escape the feeling that He is keeping a score on my actions."

Third, all 14 women suffer from a sense of time urgency. It ranges in intensity from a mild variety of impatience to a pitch of restlessness that evokes pity from their friends.

Fourth, of those women who are married, almost every

one appears capable of loving her husband and children and of exhibiting altruism and goodheartedness, yet only a few appear capable of tenderness. That is to say, most of these women do not outwardly manifest *gentle and warm* feelings for someone or something besides themselves. Apparently the presence of insecurity, frustration, and hostility is sufficient to stifle such an open, frank form of love.

It must be said in conclusion once again that even though the incidence of Type A behavior is increasing in women at an alarming rate, nevertheless it still occurs far less frequently in women than in men. Moreover, while the sense of time urgency in Type A women often is as severe as in Type A men, they are much more likely to be frustrated than openly hostile. If ever the phrase "more sinned against than sinning" applied, it applies to Type A women. The sinner of course is our flawed society.

Coronary Heart Disease in Type A Women

While Type A women appear to suffer from coronary heart disease about as frequently as Type A men, and certainly much more than Type B women, nevertheless they are far more likely to suffer from angina pectoris than an actual heart attack (an infarction). In other words, clinical coronary heart disease emerges most often in them in the form of angina pectoris, whereas in Type A men clinical coronary heart disease emerges as an infarction or some combination of angina and infarction.

This *relative* protection against heart attack still remains to be explained. It cannot be due to any female immunity to clots in blood vessels because women suffer from blood clots in the veins even more often than men. Nor have women evolved any type of more efficient bypass circulation that enables them to get blood to the heart in spite of increasing obstruction of the main original coronary arteries. Women's arteries are the same as men's. We ourselves suspect that the answer may lie in the smaller size of most female coronary atherosclerotic plaques. Such plaques thus may less often outgrow their blood supply, hence do not decay, rupture, and produce a clot which then totally obstructs the coronary artery, leading to an infarction.

All plaques begin as muscle cells which have entered the areas of arterial injury and started to multiply. Such multiplication probably proceeds more slowly in Type A females than in Type A males, hence smaller plaques. A similar disparity in the multiplication of muscle cells between the sexes explains the difference in musculature; just compare the biceps of the flexed forearm of a young girl with that of a young boy. A similar disparity in muscle cell development may explain why heavily muscled men have far more infarctions than lightly muscled men.

The Type B Woman

The Type B woman is similar to the Type B man in that she too, from early childhood on, always felt adequately loved and appreciated by her parents, particularly by her father. From the very beginning of her life she possessed a sense of security and self-esteem. Almost all Type B women whom we have encountered express satisfaction and pride in this parental love and devotion. Here are samples of the feelings of just a few of them:

1. A 43-year-old wife of an attorney, the mother of four children: "I was the seventh child of my parents. I received so much love and affection from my father that I feel guilty now because I sometimes think that I'm not giving enough of it to our kids. Dad always found the time to play, even ski with us. You asked me if I always have felt secure. Yes, as far back as I can remember."

2. A 57-year-old wife of a distinguished university

president, the mother of two grown and quite successful sons: "Let's put it this way: My father made me feel like a princess. I can't ever remember his having given me a single reprimand, and believe me, I sometimes needed it."

3. An 80-year-old retired professor of Spanish: "My father was a postman and he worked very hard to put me, my two sisters, and my brother through college. Sometimes he looked at me with such pride and love that I would run to the bathroom and burst into tears. I didn't know of any other way to express the intense joy that particular look of his gave me. I can still see that look, even after seventy years."

4. A 52-year-old, divorced but successful mother of four attractive girls: "I always knew that my father loved me even if he was so absorbed in his teaching chores at the university that he sometimes forgot which house to enter when he came home. On the day I left to go to Smith, just before he kissed me good-bye, he began to cry. I never had seen him cry before, but somehow I knew that he was going to cry when it came time for me to leave. That's why I know that he loved me. Does this sound silly to you?"

5. A 54-year-old, married president of a college: "My father was a distinguished academician but he always made me feel that someday I'd surpass him. Do you know that he never revealed to me that he had won a Phi Beta Kappa key until I had received mine? But above all, he made me feel that he would have loved me even if I were a moron."

Besides the support gained from her parents, the typical Type B woman is fortunate in having been able to escape or otherwise contend successfully with the sort of assaults on her self-esteem so common in the lives of girls and young women. After graduation from secondary school or university, the Type B women, like their Type A counterparts, may enter the marketplace or continue at university graduate schools. They may wish to compete and to get married. But they are likely to differ from Type A women in several important ways. First, much as they would like to obtain a good position and advance in business or one of the professions, they only infrequently display the ruthless, hyperaggressive drive of so many Type A women. (The fact is that although we have interviewed scores of business and professional women, we have found only Type A women occupying or strongly intent on obtaining truly high positions in industry and in the professions.)

It is our impression that most young Type B women consider their business or professional positions as a sort of holding pattern until they can attain the same aims that were sought by their great-grandmothers: a husband, a home, and a child, in this order. If this sounds like a sexist statement, it is not; we also believe that the *primary* aim of most Type B men is the same—for a wife, a home, and a family. For that matter, Western society would be a lot unhealthier than it presently is if a considerable number of its inhabitants—men and women alike—did not share these goals.

Primary aims or not, the facts make clear that most young Type B women do marry, do make a home of one sort or another, and do have a child. Most of them continue to work after their marriage, and often after they give birth to one or more children. But it is usually easy to see where the true interests of the married Type B women lie; regardless of how conscientiously she performs her duties outside the house, we have known very few Type B mothers who hesitated to leave a job (or a profession) when the family's economic circumstances made retirement possible. "When the children go to college, I'll probably go back to work again," they say, and perhaps they will.

Most Type B women marry Type B men. This is not because Type B women particularly prefer Type B men but because most Type A men do not find Type B women exciting enough. When a Type A woman and a Type B woman are in a group together, the Type A woman usually does the talking, the Type B woman the listening. The young Type A girl bubbles with enthusiasm and excitement; the Type B girl radiates composure. The Type A girl at best dazzles; the Type B girl at best glows.

Because she likes her home and loves her husband and children, the Type B woman finds her life essentially satisfying and worthwhile. She does not appear to find oppressive the chores and activities involved in rearing her children and satisfying the spiritual, intellectual, and emotional needs of her husband. Confessor of her children, confidante of her husband, she manages to give her charges what her father and mother gave her, love and affection.

Some children of Type B mothers fall victim to the same disasters that damage and destroy so many hundreds of thousands of young people; this is only to be expected. But it is remarkable to us how very few seriously flawed children we know of whose mothers and fathers were Type B's. Similarly, among scores of female patients, friends, and acquaintances who are divorced, we are not able to recall more than a few Type B divorcées.

Because the Type B woman is secure and does possess adequate self-esteem, exactly like the Type B man, she neither feels nor exhibits signs of time urgency or free-floating hostility. On the contrary, in her presence one notes an aura of tranquility. She seems to harbor few if any bitternesses, even if she has been ill used; her basic assumption is that most people under most circumstances are fundamentally decent.

This last trait is striking in her relations with her husband (or lover) and her children. Having herself experienced unconditional love and affection, she knows quite well the value these feelings have to those close to her. She is willing to communicate her love and affection not only by the spoken word but also by nonverbal language—a kiss, an embrace, a gentle stroke of the hand.

She is usually wise enough—and self-confident enough—to know when to overlook their *venial* sins, and to discipline children effectively when it is called for.

If this description of Type B women leads the reader to believe that they are extraordinarily without exception intelligent, life-enhancing, or even saintly, let us emphasize that this is not true. Many authentic Type B women are dull, uneducated, uninspiring. But no matter what the nature of their personality, we can be sure that it has never been damaged by the Type A frenzy to achieve more and more things and to participate in more and more events in less and less time. Regardless of their intellectual, educational, social, or financial status, Type B women never lose sight of the things worth being, a precious goal we briefly described in Chapter 2. In all, the world would be a happier place if there were more Type B women in it.

CHAPTER 5

—————

Can Type A Behavior Be Modified?

We have already described in Chapter 1 how a long time elapsed between our discovery of the Type A concept and its acceptance as a probable major risk factor in the development of coronary heart disease. We know enough about the way cardiovascular investigators think and work, and about the nature of their research projects, to understand why the delay was so protracted. No medical researcher, no matter how saintly, is prepared to yield easily on points that may well make all or much of his own hard work obsolete.

It therefore comes as no surprise to us that very few of the cardiovascular researchers who have finally brought themselves to accept the validity of Type A behavior as a coronary risk factor are now *also* willing to believe that Type A behavior can be modified. It is as if, having so painfully and so slowly reached the point where the connection between a particular behavior pattern and coronary heart disease made sense to them, they are now trying to avoid yet another revision in their thinking by labeling Type A behavior purely genetic and immutable. All too many of them have been insisting, in press interviews or articles, that "you can't change an individual's personality." And to them, Type A behavior *is* the personality.

This is wrong, of course. In our view, Type A behavior—however induced and however deep-seated—is neither purely genetic nor inaccessible. It *can* be changed by the individual himself or herself, and we have proved it. Much of the remainder of this book is devoted to describing just how. But before we proceed, it may be useful to survey the opinions and practices of the three different categories of medical practitioners involved in dealing with heart disease and Type A behavior. Such a survey says a lot about the extreme difficulty any new idea has in making its way when it cuts across formal boundaries between the professions.

CLINICAL CARDIOLOGISTS

Most practicing cardiologists have long suspected that emotional factors play a part in the development of coronary heart disease. It is probably fair to say that the majority of them today believe that Type A behavior is playing a role in the condition of their cardiac patients and possibly inflicting severe cardiac damage. Nevertheless, scarcely any of them are trying to deal with this behavior pattern themselves or referring patients to psychiatrists or psychologists. In fact, as of this date, while we know scores of cardiologists who now accept Type A behavior as a major coronary risk factor, we know of only one[*] who is seriously attempting in his private practice to modify the Type A behavior of patients who have already suffered a heart attack. (For over four years this cardiologist has been conducting group therapy sessions for postinfarction patients on a voluntary basis, and has

---

[*]Dr. Albert Goggans of Fort Worth, Texas.

achieved amazingly low recurrence rates. In spite of this, not a single patient has been referred to the group therapy by any of the doctor's four younger associates.)

There are several reasons, we believe, for this remarkable split between belief and therapeutic practice. The first has to do with the traditional reluctance of physicians other than psychiatrists to deal directly with those functions of the body that resist physical measurement. Ever since Claude Bernard (1813–1878) in physiology and Louis Pasteur (1822–1895) in bacteriology, physicians have been striving to substitute "science" for the "art" in medicine. Sir William Osler, for example, who may fairly be regarded as the father of American medicine, knew quite well that emotional factors play a role in the development of heart disease,* but when he published his classic *Principles and Practice in Medicine* in 1892 he never mentioned such factors in this connection at all.

Early in their training, medical students must decide whether they wish to enter psychiatry. Those who choose other specialties tend to conduct themselves thereafter as if psychiatry were not even a part of medicine. Few nonpsychiatrist physicians read psychiatric journals; they avoid psychiatric conferences and, if the truth be told, seldom go out of their way to mingle with psychiatrists. Deep down, most of them are unconvinced that psychiatrists deserve to be regarded as scientists in any sense of the word. As a result of this attitude, most cardiologists are less knowledgeable about, and certainly less interested in, psychiatry than are most novelists or journalists, and inherently suspicious of any theory that links the body and the mind like Type A behavior.

While it may be excusable for cardiovascular researchers to dismiss the value of attempting to modify the Type A behavior pattern, it is far less excusable for *practicing* cardiologists to feel this way. Most of them know the

---

*Osler maintained that he could always diagnose the presence of coronary heart disease simply by watching the way the patient entered his office. The vulnerable person was, he said, "a keen and ambitious man, the indicator of whose engine is always at 'full speed ahead.'"

truth. Nevertheless, in the long run the practicing cardiologists may be the ones lagging behind, and for very specific reasons. First, cardiologists in private practice now see about four patients per hour. Any real effort to modify Type A behavior requires far more than 15 minutes; it may require dozens of visits ranging each from an hour to an hour and a half. Second, the cardiologist himself lacks the expertise necessary to undertake modification procedures. And third, cardiologists—almost without exception—are themselves profoundly unreconstructed Type A's, a condition that virtually disqualifies them from guiding their patients out of the Type A trap. For them to find the desire, patience, and willpower to modify their own behavior first seems improbable, to say the least.

PSYCHIATRISTS

A large number of psychiatrists (perhaps a majority of all psychoanalytic psychiatrists) doubt the possibility of altering Type A behavior. As one well-known psychoanalyst told us, most psychiatrists have shied away from trying to treat organic disorders for quite a long time now, ever since attempts to link such disorders as hypertension and peptic ulcer with psychiatric maladies failed to come to anything. (Psychiatric treatment of patients with ulcerative colitis actually seemed to make their conditions worse.) Nowadays, this psychoanalyst said, "We confine ourselves on the whole to neuroses."

Yet such conservatism is not universal. Dr. James J. Gill is a Jesuit priest and America's most distinguished Catholic psychiatrist. His base is Harvard University, where he counsels graduate students, and in addition he travels 300,000 miles around our country and elsewhere in the world each year conducting teaching seminars for nuns, priests, and other members of the clergy. Dr. Gill reports that his psychiatrist colleagues at Harvard and Massachusetts General Hospital without exception find the key overt components of Type A behavior—hurry sickness, hyperaggressiveness, free-floating hostility—in patients suffering from coronary heart disease. All of them also consider the precursor characteristics (described in Chapter 2) to be present and most likely responsible for the full-blown Type A behavior. But they doubt that the behavior pattern can be modified. Dr. Gill is exceptional in believing that it can, a state of affairs probably explained by the fact that as a participant in our study, the San Francisco Recurrent Coronary Prevention Project, he knows at firsthand what can be done.

Nevertheless, psychiatrists are not likely to be invited soon by cardiologists and internists to see and help treat their coronary patients. Psychiatrists today, despite their initial training as general physicians, tend to isolate themselves from other fields of medicine. Few carry a stethoscope or wear a white coat in their offices, or indeed would feel comfortable attempting to treat a nonpsychiatric case in a hospital emergency room or in the wilderness. Their world is a closed one of *nonmedical* conceptual and therapeutic ideas. Until psychiatrists begin to interest themselves again in the physical disorders that demanded so much of their time as medical students, they cannot be entrusted with the care of coronary patients who are, incidentally, just as reluctant to visit psychiatrists as the latter are to treat them. We understand that there is a gentle movement toward "remedicalization" among psychiatrists and can only say that it is much to be desired as well as long overdue. We wish we could detect a similar movement in the opposite direction, by internists determined to establish a rapprochement with psychiatry.

CLINICAL PSYCHOLOGISTS

Unlike the majority of psychiatrists, there are hundreds of clinical psychologists very well versed in the psychodynamics of Type A behavior. It is from these professionals that most new knowledge concerning the causes, the modes of diagnosis and assessment, and the methods of coping with the disorder will come in the future. Indeed, if it were not for the work of such investigators we doubt very much if the association of coronary heart disease with Type A behavior would have been accepted as universally as it now is.

Most of these clinical psychologists are young, teeming with new ideas, and supercharged with energy. (Unfortunately, they too are mostly Type A's.) They would be likely to vote almost unanimously that Type A behavior is capable of modification. The problem is that they rarely have the experience to say this with certainty, or the background to deal adequately with the difficult mixture of the physical and mental that coronary heart disease so clearly is. Not many psychologists possess a solid basic knowledge of the pathological and clinical aspects of clinical CHD, or, for that matter, of the anatomy or the physiology of the human nervous system. Unlike the majority of psychiatrists, few of them are well grounded in the humanities, and most of them lack the literary and philosophical resources needed to deal with Type A behavior in a sophisticated way. In short, while we applaud their eagerness and of course welcome their enthusiastic support for the idea that Type A behavior is amenable to modification, we must also deplore their present dearth of means to do the job.

We would not have written this book if we were not certain of two facts: First, that Type A behavior not only can be modified, it can be greatly modified; and second, that such modification can and does (as we shall show in the next chapter) forestall the recurrence of another heart attack or sudden cardiac death in persons who have survived an earlier heart attack.

The reader should note that we speak only of persons who have already suffered and survived one or more heart attacks. Our study dealt only with such people, for technical reasons. But this should not be taken to suggest any belief on our part that Type A behavior in an individual who has *never* had a heart attack can't be changed, or that such change won't delay or even cancel out the possibility of a heart attack in the future.

In theory, since such persons are usually younger, modification of Type A behavior ought even to be easier than for heart-attack survivors. In actual fact, however, it well may not be, because most seemingly healthy Type A's tend to be convinced that whatever success they have achieved is basically due to their hard-driving Type A behavior. Believing this, the fact that only one out of ten Type A's get a heart attack before the age of 60 is to them a matter for optimism. Never mind that these statistics are about as grim as those for cigarette smokers, who stand roughly the same chance of succumbing to tongue, throat, or lung cancer as well. In a very real sense, smokers who die of lung cancer are unlucky people who wrongly assumed decades earlier that they would be lucky. Unreconstructed Type A's have their heads stuck in the same sand.

Consequently, we do not know many still-healthy Type A's who have altered their behavior significantly. Some no doubt exist; the publication of *Type A Behavior and Your Heart*, we sincerely hope, led a certain number to turn over a new leaf and in the process reduce their vulnerability to heart disease. This book may lead more to do so. Yet we possess no data on these people, and in terms of sheer time and numbers, a study focusing on them presents serious logistical difficulties.* We cannot therefore state flatly that modification of Type A behavior in men and women who are apparently well will forestall a *first* heart attack, but common sense says that it probably will. After all, if such modification can bring measurable safety to a heart already brutally damaged by one or more coronary attacks, why should it not also help protect a heart still ostensibly free of clinical heart disease?

*We are happy to report that we have recently begun a study in which modification of Type A behavior is being attempted with totally healthy Type A men and women in early middle age.

PART TWO

THE SAN FRANCISCO RECURRENT CORONARY PREVENTION PROJECT

CHAPTER 6

The Beginnings of a Therapeutic Revolution

Mere *association* does not prove *causality*. If it did, then Cadillacs and Mercedes-Benzes might be suspected of causing heart disease, since far more people who drive them suffer from heart disease than do drivers of Volkswagen Beetles. Similarly, wearers of spectacles suffer more from heart disease than those who don't wear spectacles. The reason, of course, is that Cadillac drivers and spectacle-wearers are as a group significantly older, and hence more susceptible to heart disease. The cars and spectacles have nothing to do with it.

Conversely, *immunity* to the onset of clinical CHD must not be attributed to any factor simply on associative evidence. An example of this bad reasoning would be to conclude that because farmers living in the area southeast of Lancaster, Pennsylvania, infrequently suffer heart attacks before their seventies, life in and near the villages of Bird in Hand, Intercourse, and Paradise somehow or other affords protection. This assumption would be total nonsense. The fact is that a large number of the farmers in this area are Amish. As we discovered in our own field trip there in 1978, they are relatively isolated from many of the pressures of our contemporary urban society. Not only do they manage to do without radios, television sets, novels, cameras, automobiles, telephones, electricity, watches, clothes buttons, patterned dresses, cigarettes, insurance policies, and high school educations, they also manage to do without Type A behavior. We believe that it is their style of life that protects them against clinical CHD. But still caution must be observed, because even the Amish life-style is only *associated* with the observed coronary immunity. No proof of *causation* is available. (By the way, the Amish diet, rich in foods heavy with cholesterol and animal fats, should make some of our colleagues a little hesitant to blame most of contemporary coronary problems upon what we chew, swallow, and digest!)

We have gone into some detail about this sort of false reasoning because it appears to be typical of most initial investigative approaches to the causes and cures of various diseases. Today we shake our heads over the innocence of our predecessors who believed that the night air was pestilential (because so many people exposed to it in certain areas later came down with malaria or yellow fever), that severe bleeding of sick patients is uniformly beneficial (because in some disorders, bleeding is occasionally beneficial), and that exposure to the sun is beneficial for nearly all sick patients (because the resting associated with sunbathing sometimes did help tubercular patients).

But are we all that much wiser today? It has only been in the last decade that we realized our error in attributing adult diabetes solely to a lack of insulin, because we were able to relieve diabetes symptoms by administering insulin. Until just a year or two ago, we believed that attacks of migraine were due to dilation of the blood vessels in tissues covering the brain solely because we could relieve migraine by giving drugs that intensely constricted these head arteries. Now we know that a migraine attack actually *begins* with constriction. We modern physicians and nurses still have much to learn, and much to be modest about.

This same logic suggested to us, as we explained in Chapter 1, that we stood in danger of assuming that Type A behavior was a *causative* factor in coronary heart disease, when all we really knew was that Type A behavior was closely *associated* with CHD. If we were not to be accused of making the same mistake as our colleagues who had been laying the primary blame on such factors as hypertension and smoking, we needed to perform a new study—a major study.

THE RECURRENT CORONARY PREVENTION PROJECT (RCPP)

As early as 1972, we began to think about an experimental study whose results would either indict or exonerate Type A behavior as a direct *causative* factor of clinical CHD. Producing a reasonable facsimile of Type A behavior in a laboratory animal would not, we knew, be enough. We had already done that. What would be enough would be to divide a large number of Type A persons into two groups—at random—and to try to alter the behavior pattern *and nothing else* in one of these two groups. If the Type A behavior pattern alone could be significantly altered, and statistically linked to a significant resistance to the early onset of clinical CHD, then we would have accomplished three important things. First, we would have demonstrated that Type A behavior can be changed. Second, we would have shown that persons who do alter their Type A behavior pattern will be less vulnerable to coronary heart disease. Third (and probably most important to us as medical scientists), we would have demonstrated that Type A behavior is not just *associated* with coronary tragedies, but also plays an important part in *causing* them. *Such proof, we stress again, has yet to be shown for any other of the presently accepted coronary risk factors.*

We were well aware of the difficulties involved even in starting such a study. For example, we knew from the beginning that we could not focus on individuals who exhibited Type A behavior but were still free of clinical CHD. Such persons, as we have pointed out, would be unlikely to cooperate in a study extending over a number of years that required them to attempt to change an emotional complex that most of them regarded as beneficial— at least to the extent that it appeared to be responsible for whatever successes they had achieved. Second, only 10 of 1,000 Type A individuals between 35 and 65 succumb each year to a heart attack. With 1,000 Type A's as participants, in order to obtain a statistically significant number of heart attack cases (at least 75 to 100) we would have had to carry on our study for at least 10 years. Since an additional 1,000 Type A's also would have had to be included as controls, we would therefore have been obliged to follow 2,000 people for at least 10 years. We now estimate that such a study would require more than 40 million dollars.* We were realistic enough to know that no funding agency would have ever hazarded even a tenth of that sum on the possible application of a concept that in the mid-seventies still had received neither general recognition nor confirmation. The best we could hope for was to find and enroll for a limited number of years a relatively small number of participants who might be amenable to behavioral counseling and yet suffer enough heart attacks to supply the statistical data we needed to prove or disprove our concepts and their therapeutic implications. Therefore we decided to confine our planned study to males and females who already had suffered one or more heart attacks (but not within the previous six months), who were under 65 years of age, who did not suffer from diabetes, and who had quite smoking tobacco in any form at least six months before.

---

*This estimate is based on the fact that in its 3.5-year study (ending in 1981) of 3,800 postinfarction patients of whom half received propranolol and no other type of medical intervention, the National Heart, Lung and Blood Institute spent over 20 million dollars. What this study would have cost if, in addition to propranolol, it had also involved thousands of hours of psychological counseling exceeds our imagination.

Our reasoning was as follows: Because susceptibility of postinfarction persons to future heart attacks was five to ten times greater than that of still healthy persons of their age, we would be able in a five-year study of 1,000 of them to observe at least 75 to 100 new heart attacks. This number was sufficient for statistically meaningful results. From our earlier experiences in private practice with postinfarction patients, we knew that many if not most of such persons would be willing and able to modify their Type A behavior. To some degree, they no longer deluded themselves with fantasies of personal immunity.

We chose not to enroll persons over 64 years of age because modification of one's behavior is difficult for even the middle-aged and we naturally thought the elderly would find change still harder. (Later we found that this initial assumption was not necessarily true at all.) Also, the elderly person is more likely to fall prey to various other diseases, thus confusing our findings.

We were fortunate indeed in our decision to enroll only nonsmokers or reformed smokers. The idea had been to avoid the possibility that smoking participants in the counseling group would be more likely to quit smoking than those in the control group. Further, we did not relish the prospect of spending thousands of hours trying to change Type A behavior—and in doing so reduce the cardiac recurrence rate—only to have our colleagues attribute the reduction to a decline in smoking. By choosing only nonsmokers and those who had given it up, we found that we had unwittingly enrolled a group of coronary patients eminently capable of altering deep-seated habits. Three-quarters of them had previously smoked and quit. And as we shall later make clear, a good deal of Type A behavior is composed of learned habits.

FUNDING, RECRUITMENT, AND STAFFING

It is tempting for us to describe at length the difficulties involved in getting the funds we needed to conduct the RCPP study. Suffice it to say that it was harder than we expected. The senior author of this book has been in the business of seeking funding for medical research at the Harold Brunn Institute for half a century, and during this period had been successful in obtaining, with relative ease, more than 80 grants totaling millions of dollars. This time, the National Heart, Lung and Blood Institute turned down our first application flatly in 1974. Our second, revised application was also rejected six months later. It was not until May 1977 that a third committee finally approved yet another application. There was one problem, however—the award covered only two-thirds of what we had asked for. As we had not padded our figures (unlike, we suspect, many other grant applicants), the shortfall appeared to spell disaster.

At this stage the goddess of chance (perhaps as a reward for our honesty) brought us help in the form of additional funds from the Bank of America, Standard Oil of California, the Kaiser Hospital Foundation, the Zellerbach Family Foundation, and the Mary Lard Foundation of Fort Worth, Texas. This money made up enough of the shortage to enable us to begin recruiting and organizing the staff and rounding up participants. On August 1, 1977, we got underway—five years after we started planning the study, three years after we first applied for funds.

The heads of large corporations of the San Francisco Bay Area did more than donate funds. Together with various union executives, they helped us recruit the majority of the men and women who took part in the project. The directors of personnel and medical directors of many large Bay Area corporations not only gave their approval to the RCPP study, but also—by repeatedly issuing memoranda, posting bulletins, and even inserting announcements in pay envelopes—actively encouraged their postinfarction employees to volunteer. Similarly, unions repeatedly carried announcements in their monthly newsletters that our study welcomed suitable volunteers. Bay Area Easter Seal Societies—though not, oddly, the half dozen local American Heart Association affiliates—also aided us in recruiting members. Newspapers, magazines, and radio and television stations gave us considerable publicity. Finally, we were tremendously helped by the formation of a Lay Collaborative Committee chaired by Benjamin F. Biaggini, Chairman of the Board of the Southern Pacific Company. Mr. Biaggini and his corporate associate, Lawrence Hoyt, not only helped us recruit participants but also played an indispensable role in obtaining conference rooms where we could conduct the hundreds of group sessions the study required. Bay Area hospitals also willingly furnished us with conference rooms.

Our first step in securing the necessary thousand or more participants involved conducting orientation sessions every few weeks for potential candidates. At these sessions, we explained the purposes of the study, introduced our staff of cardiologists, psychiatrists, psychologists, nurses, and members of the administrative staff, and perhaps most important of all, allowed prospective participants—all of whom had, remember, suffered one or more heart attacks—to hear postinfarction patients from our own private practice who a decade earlier had learned to modify their Type A behavior. Those attending the sessions were asked to volunteer to enter a pool of participants who would then be randomly assigned to one of two sections, Section I or Section II. Section I, the control section, would receive group cardiovascular counseling from first-rate cardiologists. Section II would receive the same cardiovascular counseling, but would in addition receive Type A behavior counseling from specially trained psychiatrists, psychologists, and cardiologists. A third section, Section III, was made up of those persons who did not wish to receive either type of group counseling, but were willing to serve as a comparison group and be subjected only to an annual examination.

In August 1978, a full year after we had begun recruiting, we had signed up 1012 postinfarction persons. Eight hundred and sixty-two of them agreed to be randomly enrolled either in Section I, whose members would be counseled by cardiologists solely concerning their drug, eating, and exercise habits, or in Section II, whose members would be similarly counseled and in addition receive Type A behavior counseling. The remaining 150 recruits were enrolled in Section III, the comparison group.

We often have been asked why it took us a year to recruit 1000 postinfarction subjects from an area that contained a least 10,000 eligible persons. The answer is plain enough, and it has to do with Type A behavior. (Note that we were not deliberately trying to recruit Type A's, but—this came as no surprise to us—more than *90 percent* of those ending up in the study were identified later as Type A. Very few Type B's would even have been eligible, because very few Type B heart attack victims under the age of 65 exist!) One of the components or characteristics of the Type A is that of denying the existence or occurrence of any important or crippling mishap to his or her body. Such denial apparently led many post-infarction patients to believe that it would be a waste of their time to attend even one of our orientation meetings. After all, they figured, their heart attack had been quite slight and was unlikely to happen again. Then too, most cardiologists in the area looked on our study with a mixture of slight amusement and bored disinterest. Only two cardiologists actively encouraged their patients to attend one of our orientation meetings.

From the very beginning of the RCPP study, the four of us initially in charge (the authors, psychologist Carl E. Thoresen of Stanford, and psychiatrist Leonti Thompson) occasionally differed in our views of how to manage certain details, but we always were in complete agreement about one matter: If we were to have even a chance of modifying or ameliorating the intensity of Type A behavior in our postinfarction participants, we had to select counselors possessing certain special qualities.

They would have to be sincere and believe in the truth and validity of every statement they made to the participants of their groups. Type A persons have a nose for hypocrisy. Even when they are themselves somewhat hypocritical, they nevertheless instantly reject anyone else tainted by it.

Our counselors also would have to look and act like mature, sensible, respectable, and well-mannered adults. These qualities we were particularly anxious to have them possess and project, in view of the fact that in the course of their counseling they would find it necessary to make some recommendations that their group members would at first glance regard as fantastic. (Common sense frequently appears fantastic to those who have lost their own.) They would moreover require a good sense of humor. They did not have to be raconteurs or comedians, but they should be able to laugh at their own foibles and sillinesses as easily as they could laugh at those of others.

We wanted counselors who not only were intelligent and learned in psychology but also possessed a good awareness of the humanities. Although they pride themselves on keeping abreast of their field, psychologists are as a group not famously cultivated people. We wanted counselors capable of receiving instruction, advice, and wisdom from the truly great psychologists and philosophers of the past, and with some knowledge of the more important resources of our culture beyond their technical specialties. They particularly had to be able to talk without falling into jargon; recourse to psychological jargon is disastrous when counseling Type A's. They have difficulty enough understanding and retaining principles described even in the simplest English words, much less jargon.

The dismal fact is that most psychologists and psychiatrists themselves are afflicted with Type A behavior. Such affliction, however, does not prevent them from being effective as counselors for Type A persons as long as (1) their Type A behavior is not too severe, (2) they are *aware* of its presence and are attempting to modify or hold it in check, and (3) they freely admit that they are victims of a disorder whose intensity they hope to ameliorate in others. If they fail in any of these respects, they cannot be successful counselors in altering Type A behavior.

It was important that counselors be able to communicate their messages effectively to the members of their groups. We had no magic scalpel or miraculous medicine. We had available to us only words, phrases, tones of voice, and a few simple blackboard diagrams. How these elements are combined and conveyed usually makes the difference between successful and ineffective counseling. If counselors have the power to inspire others, and can communicate well too, then they are more than simply effective, they are superb. We were fortunate in that we had more than one such counselor.

Finally, we wanted counselors who cared about the individual fate of each member of their groups. Unlike bypass heart surgery, this new tactic for preventing cardiac recurrence requires more than technical expertise. It requires something approximating love. This caring cannot be glibly explained in a sentence or two; it is a feeling of a leader for his followers which they in turn sense and trust. The phenomenon is nothing new—caring was a medical virtue known, we suspect, to Hippocrates. But it has always been rare.

The cardiovascular counselors we selected to lead the Section I groups (those who received no behavioral counseling) were well versed in all phases of cardiovascular pathophysiology, diagnosis, and therapy. Their job was to communicate their own knowledge about coronary heart disease and also to inspire their group members to comply with the regimen their own personal cardiologists had prescribed for them. In the RCPP study, the prime duty of the cardiovascular counselors was to complement, not replace, the participants' own cardiologists.

Diane Ulmer served as the field director of the RCPP study.* Her duties initially consisted of supervising the

*Note by Meyer Friedman: In addition, without any deliberate effort on her part, Diane Ulmer became a sort of surrogate mother to hundreds of our male Section II participants. Possibly the fact that she was the first person to interview and examine them for the study had something to do with it; in any

random assignment of the 862 volunteer participants to Section I or Section II; their initial and subsequent physical, electrocardiographic, and biochemical studies; the detection and assessment of the intensity of Type A behavior in all participants; the arrangement of places and schedules for all group meetings; and the collection and filing of all data obtained.

Besides counselors and a field director, we needed a contingent of nurses with experience in coronary care. They were to perform the physical examinations, admin-

case, they quickly sensed both her professional competence and her feminine gentleness—stiffened as it was with just a hint of maternal discipline—and adopted her as their own. She of course did just the same in reverse—she still knows both the surname and the given name of each and every one of our participants.

When a participant suffered a new heart attack or any sort of illness, it was always Diane and not his group counselor whom he asked to be informed. In the same way, many participants brought to her their medical, business, and family problems for discussion. In the course of all these visits and telephone calls, she never once became impatient or angry. This obviously meant a great deal to our participants. Caught up in a world that seemed perfectly uninterested in their problems, they could always count on Diane's unconditional willingness to hear them out, counsel them, if necessary console them. I shall never forget the time she spent several hours she could ill spare listening quietly and lovingly to a participant who knew he was going to die within weeks, as he spoke to her about his life, a life that would soon be over.

It is a tribute to the way she handled herself in these circumstances that never once did a participant attempt any sort of sexual overture. The wives of our participants admired and trusted her implicitly.

I believe that Diane's quasi-maternal role in the study, though unplanned, was of considerable importance to our eventual success. (It did not go unnoticed; in fact when Dr. Stephen Weiss of the National Heart, Lung and Blood Institute, who had visited us several times, read our first-year report, he asked why it had not mentioned Diane and her "maternal" function.) At the very least, she kept dozens of men from dropping out in the early stages, when their pride made it especially difficult for them to accept the criticism leveled at them by their group leaders and other participants. She was there to listen and, if necessary, to mediate on behalf of her "children." While we had been aware of the importance of inadequate maternal love and affection in the formation of Type A behavior in men, we did not realize until we were well along in the study that such deprivation could be to some degree compensated for in adult life. Diane Ulmer was able to do this. Presumably someone else as warm and dedicated could do the same. We must note in passing, however, that the wives of our male participants were rarely able to fill the role, one reason being that many of them were themselves Type A, and thus busy searching for (and not finding) the unconditional parental love missing in their own childhoods.

ister and interpret the electrocardiograms, and obtain blood samples. We had no trouble at all in recruiting nurses—and good ones, too. One explanation of this, we think, lies in the fact that many coronary care nurses become disenchanted after a few years in coronary care units. Only too often they find it difficult to admire or even respect the cardiologists from whom they are supposed to take orders and instructions. The nurses tend to spend much more time with coronary patients than the cardiologists do, listening to them and sensing the nature of the emotional stresses and strains that afflict them. Most of the nurses cannot help noting, first with dismay and later with suppressed contempt, how little interest cardiologists take in these emotional phenomena. In addition, the nurses find it increasingly difficult to maintain their own enthusiasm under circumstances of such pressure and complexity, where at any second during their eight-hour tour of duty the jolting alarm of an electronic monitor may scream out the message that the heart of one of their patients has stopped.

From the outset we required the services of statisticians and data processing specialists able to organize, store, and retrieve the myriad bits of information we expected to accumulate. We obtained personnel eminently qualified to perform these tasks. We made sure they understood, however, that we regarded numbers as of distinctly subsidiary importance. No data processing expert or statistician would have the opportunity to influence any medical tactic or strategy. They would serve solely to keep our scores and to advise us whether and when a score became statistically significant.

Finally, we secured an office manager to service the files, mediate all communications, and prepare all manuscripts that might be published.

CHAPTER 7

The Study Begins

We already knew from our own experience in the late sixties and seventies that Type A behavior could be, and in fact had been, modified in dozens of persons. What we were anxious to find out now was whether such modification prevented recurrent heart attacks. If such prevention did occur, then Type A behavior would have to be considered one of the causal factors in the pathogenesis of clinical CHD.

But to determine these possibilities, it was absolutely necessary that our volunteer postinfarction participants be divided into two large groups with essentially the same range of socioeconomic, historical, and cardiovascular qualities and characteristics. These two contingents would be counseled and handled in essentially the same manner, except that one would in addition receive counseling designed to alter their Type A behavior. We achieved this randomization by drawing names from a large container, ending up with 270 names assigned to Section I (cardiovascular counseling only) and 592 to Section II (cardio-vascular counseling plus Type A behavior counseling). If the laws of chance could be depended upon, the members of these sections should have approximately the same age, height, and weight, the same prevalence of Type A behavior, even the same number of future heart attacks.

The 150 postinfarction participants of our project study who had not volunteered to be enrolled in one of the two counseling sections but had agreed to be examined yearly of course could not be randomized. We had to assume that their socioeconomic and medical histories as well as the signs and symptoms of their CHD were essentially the same as those of our two randomized sections. Fortunately, as we later learned, this did turn out to be true.

We set up four intake procedures. These had to be performed as rapidly and efficiently as possible because our federal grant* covered only five years; if our initial examinations took too long, we would not have enough time to accomplish behavior modification or observe a sufficiently large number of coronary recurrences to provide statistically secure conclusions. It nevertheless took us over a year to do the necessary initial processing and enroll all volunteers into their respective sections.

We first obtained an adequate medical and socioeconomic history by means of a personal interview. This covered such data as age, height, weight, marital status, education, economic position, and income, then went on to include past illnesses, family history of diseases, the date at which the participant's first (and subsequent) heart attacks occurred, the presence of angina or shortness of breath, cigarette smoking, coronary bypass surgery (if any), and additional medical items.

Next, each volunteer was subjected to a physical examination, an electrocardiogram, the removal of a small amount of blood for blood cholesterol analysis, and a urinalysis.

*Grant 21427, obtained from the National Heart, Lung and Blood Institute.

The third procedure required the participant to complete a questionnaire especially designed to detect Type A behavior and assess the intensity of it. Each of the 592 postinfarction volunteers assigned to Section II, whose members were to receive Type A behavior counseling, was in addition asked to have his or her spouse and a business associate or close friend (i.e., a monitor) meet with us separately and also answer questionnaires intended to gauge the participant's Type A behavior from different perspectives.

Our plan was to repeat the questionnaires in subsequent years. In the case of our Section II participants, we would not only have their own judgment on their progress in changing their behavior, we would also have second and third opinions from spouses and monitors. This plan worked well for us, so well that we venture to suggest that psychiatrists treating their patients for miscellaneous personality disorders adopt a similar scheme. Certainly we made it clear to our Section II participants that if their spouses or monitors did not observe behavioral changes as time went on, probably none really did occur, despite their own possibly optimistic reports.

The fourth procedure involved a videotaped interview conducted by Nancy Fleischmann to determine whether Type A behavior was present and, if so, to what degree. With her two decades of experience in eliciting answers and observing psychomotor activities (that is, the vocal, facial, and body signs indicative of the presence of Type A behavior) Nancy could ferret out Type A behavior in even the most guarded volunteer. After so many years of listening and comparing Type A voices with those of Type B, she was as acutely sensitive to the subtle rasp of a Type A as George Szell, the late great conductor of the Cleveland Symphony, reputedly was to an off tone in his violin section. To avoid any charges of bias, we interspersed the 1012 postinfarction volunteers with a goodly number of unidentified Type B's who were free of coronary heart disease. The interviewer then could never be certain whether she was interviewing a coronary participant or a healthy Type B volunteer.

The interviews were videotaped for several reasons. First, the videotape allowed the interviewer to review the session if she was in doubt about any of her initial observations. Second, the tapes could be compared with later videotaped interviews to note changes achieved by our counseling. Third, they could be used for instructional purposes by other medical personnel who wished to learn our techniques for the detection and assessment of Type A behavior.

What sort of person is the typical urban American who has suffered one or more heart attacks before the age of 65? From the results of these studies at intake, we would describe this average person as male, approximately 53 years of age, weighing between 170 and 179 pounds, 69 inches tall, married, and at least a high school graduate. His average serum cholesterol is 259 mg/100 ml (about the American average); his chances of having had a mother or father who had suffered a heart attack were one in two; he probably once smoked cigarettes (three-fourths of all participants had); he had a close to fifty-fifty chance of high blood pressure and/or angina pectoris (pain in the chest due to insufficient flow of blood to the heart); and a one in four chance of having already undergone open-heart bypass surgery. As we have already noted, this typical heart attack survivor is almost certainly Type A. While over one-fourth to one-half of our 1012 crippled-heart folks had never had high blood pressure, an elevated blood cholesterol, a positive family history, or had smoked cigarettes, over 90 percent of them exhibited Type A behavior as detected by the videotaped interview technique.

Because most of our participants were recruited from the businesses and corporations of the San Francisco area, there probably were fewer females (only about 100) and certainly fewer blacks (only 13) and Oriental subjects (three) than in a comparable cross-section of the San Francisco population. But certainly we had a goodly number of taxicab and truck drivers, auto mechanics, plumbers, and utility repairmen mixed in with our engineers, attorneys, ministers, brokers, rabbis, professors, veterinarians, bankers, company presidents, and one physician.

We had no board chairmen of large corporations among our participants, because few if any board chairmen of large corporations in the San Francisco Bay Area had suffered a heart attack when this study began in 1977. We enrolled no more than one physician for a different reason. There is no shortage of postinfarction physicians in the Bay Area, but most of them apparently felt that they could not spare the time that involvement in the study demanded. We are sorry to report that we did ourselves have to find the time later to attend the funerals of two of these overbusy physicians.

These then were the general characteristics of our participants as they bravely, and with great expectations, were processed.

Upon completion of the entry procedures, the members of Section I were further broken down into 22 groups, each containing 10 to 15 participants. Members of Section II were assigned to one or another of 60 groups, each containing about 10 participants.

The first of the 22 groups of Section I began to meet in March 1978, and the last group began in February 1979. The first of the 60 groups of Section II began to meet in February 1978, and the last group began in April 1979. Thus, 21 months elapsed from the time we received our funds to the time at which the last group of 10 participants began their treatment. Most of this time lag was due to the 12 months required to recruit the participants, some to the limited number of volunteers we were able to process each day.

SECTION I COUNSELING

The cardiological counselors of Section I groups conducted 90-minute meetings with their participants every two weeks for three months, monthly for three months, and then at two-month intervals for the remainder of the study. Besides their regular cardiological counseling, each group received visits every few months from a psychiatrist or psychologist. He offered them counseling about any anxieties they might have regarding their heart disease or other matters, but not on the subject of their Type A behavior. If, for example, a Section I participant complained about some stupidity on the part of his employer or one of his employees, his spouse, his children, or his friends, the psychiatrist or psychologist would simply change the subject. Likewise, if the visiting counselor noticed a Section I participant exhibiting impatience in his voice, gestures, or body movements, he would simply ignore it.

From the very beginning, Section I participants were told that, figuratively speaking, they were carrying and would continue to carry a "bomb" inside consisting of one or more old heart muscle scars left from their previous heart attack and severe obstruction of at least one of their three main coronary arteries. The bomb, they were informed, would probably never explode, but only if they avoided lighting one or more of several fuses. We described the fuses as follows:

1. THE INGESTION OF ONE MEAL RICH IN EITHER VEGETABLE OR ANIMAL FAT. Unfortunately, most persons exhibiting Type A behavior, whether they suffer overt coronary heart disease or not, cannot rapidly clear their blood of the fat they absorb from food. As we have explained, this results in the formation of globular masses of red blood cells in a process called sludging. Postinfarction patients are particularly susceptible to the dangers of sludging. They have hearts containing hundreds of vessels, often of very small caliber, which were newly formed after one of their coronary arteries became obstructed by a thrombus or clot. If these collateral vessels also become obstructed, even temporarily, by sludged blood masses, the patients may suffer angina, a new infarct, or even sudden death. *This danger exists for at least six hours after the ingestion of just one meal heavy in either*

animal or vegetable fat. Thus a meal containing more than two ounces of fat may, because of its propensity to cause sludging, prove fatal to anyone who has suffered and survived a heart attack.

An additional problem stems from the fact that the ingestion of considerable amounts of fat or protein leads to an *immediate* dilatation of the intestinal blood vessels. This forces the heart of the postinfarction patient to work harder and at the same time diverts blood from the heart's severely obstructed coronary arteries to the intestinal vessels.

While we understand the reluctance of many cardiologists to attempt to change Type A behavior, we cannot understand why so few of them are willing to emphasize the potential deadliness of a single fat meal. Thousands of patients, struggling to survive in coronary care units during the first few days after their acute heart attack, are being fed heavy meals that could by themselves snuff out their lives. Even the documented success of Nathan Pritikin, an intelligent engineer but not a physician, in relieving hundreds of coronary patients of their angina in a few days by the simple expedient of giving them no more than *one-thirtieth* of an ounce of fat in each of eight meals per day, does not appear to have made a serious impact on most cardiologists. And the danger of one fat meal was not discovered by Pritikin in Santa Monica, but was already known to the great eighteenth-century English physicians William Heberden and John Hunter, and reemphasized at the beginning of the present century by Sir William Osler.

2. PARTICIPATION IN ANY FORM OF SEVERE PHYSICAL EXERCISE. While millions of Americans are jogging, running marathons, playing hard competitive tennis, racquetball, and handball, lifting heavy weights, and playing other forms of sport, our Section I postinfarction participants were strongly advised not to. Such exertion, even if indulged in only briefly, can well lead to ventricular fibrillation (and instantaneous death) or a new infarction. Of

this we are absolutely certain. In fact, merely lifting or carrying an object weighing more than 25 pounds may prove dangerous to someone who has suffered a previous heart attack.

If these restrictions seem severe to the reader, let him remember that hundreds of *apparently healthy* persons die each year while engaged in some of the above pastimes. Yes, certain physical exercises do slow the resting heart rate; yes, some do allow the heart muscle to perform more efficiently; yes, some do provide an afterglow of exhilaration (or at least the pleasure of stopping, as when one stops hitting his finger with a hammer); yes, various sports do allow one to wear attractive costumes. None of them, however, has yet been shown to slow the process of coronary artery disease or prevent a heart attack in human subjects. We believe it is entirely possible that future research will indicate that such severe exertion as jogging and running *accelerates* the course of coronary artery disease.

Meanwhile, it might be wise to remember that the very experienced and superbly trained Greek courier Pheidippides dropped dead in 490 B.C. immediately after running from Marathon to Athens (a distance of approximately 25 miles, somewhat less than the 26 miles and 385 yards now standardized as the official distance for modern marathon races). We also might keep in mind that the nine Olympic Gold Medals Paavo Nurmi received for marathon running did not prevent him from having a series of heart attacks beginning in his late fifties.*

---

*While we are convinced that severe physical exercise of the type described here poses a serious danger, especially to Type A's, it should be noted that certain occupations require standards of physical fitness that can be maintained only through long-term regular exercise. The military services are an example of such an occupation; firefighters and police are others. It is important to recognize, however, that strenuous exercise programs undertaken for occupational reasons must be carefully monitored for consistency, with frequent fitness tests and regular screening for hidden coronary heart disease. The United States Army, Navy, and Air Force have been notable in this regard.

3. INGESTION OF CAFFEINE OR ALCOHOL. Because caffeine is a nerve stimulant which might set off a heart arrhythmia in veterans of a heart attack, we recommended that such persons drink coffee only in a decaffeinated form. If a participant already suffered from *any* type of arrhythmia, we *strongly* advised him to drink only decaffeinated coffee. If a participant without arrhythmia insisted on drinking ordinary coffee, we suggested it be kept to no more than three cups a day.*

Participants were asked not to drink more than two ounces of whiskey, gin, or vodka a day, and no more than two glasses of wine at a sitting. The ingestion of beer was not restricted because few of our participants appeared to drink more than two or three bottles or cans a day.

4. HIGH ALTITUDES. Persons living in the San Francisco Bay Area easily can, and frequently do, go from sea level to an altitude of 6,000 feet in the Sierras in the space of a few hours. This change in the amount of available oxygen can have a drastic effect on coronary patients.

Rather than set any rigid altitude limits for participants, we advised them to avoid any altitude at which (1) their resting pulse rate (before eating) was 15 beats greater than at sea level, (2) their breath was noticeably shorter, and (3) they experienced angina under conditions that did not cause it at sea level.

Because skiing in California is usually done at altitudes in excess of 5,000 feet, we urged our participants to eliminate this form of exercise. Not all of them did so, and three of the new heart attacks (two of them fatal) that occurred among our participants were associated with skiing.

5. PROLONGED EXPOSURE TO COLD. Exposure of the body or limbs to temperatures below 50 or 55° F. fre-

---

*One of our participants disregarded this advice, drinking seven cups of coffee between 5:00 and 7:00 A.M. one morning. At about 8:00 A.M., suffering severe angina, he was taken to the hospital.

quently causes the smaller blood vessels to narrow. If newly formed coronary collateral vessels of coronary patients contract in this way, the already reduced blood flow to the heart muscle may be further diminished. This in turn may bring on angina and, if prolonged enough, a second heart attack. This sort of vasoconstriction, together with the exertion involved, probably accounts for many of the heart attacks suffered by snow shovelers. We therefore required our participants to dress warmly at all times and to avoid prolonged chilling of their faces, hands, and feet.

These were the fuses we asked our Section I participants to avoid lighting. There was no need to list cigarette smoking; all our participants had quit smoking at least six months prior to their enrollment. Cigarette smoking by a post-infarction patient in our view is simply suicide, the only unknown factor being precisely when death will occur.

Although we were already aware that Type A's in general find it difficult to retain information about any matter not directly related to their work, we were surprised to discover this same failing in Type A's who had already suffered at least one heart attack. We thus realized that we would have to repeat our warnings about the bomb and the fuses over and over again. Even when the study was in its third year, group counselors still found it necessary to repeat them, especially during the period from Thanksgiving to the New Year—a famous time of excess.

Besides these warnings, Section I counselors gave slide-illustrated lectures describing the normal anatomy and functions of the heart and the manner in which coronary arteries become obstructed. They also answered any questions posed by their participants concerning the symptoms and signs of their CHD. In addition, the Section I counselors continually kept their group members informed of new diagnostic and therapeutic advances being made in the field of cardiology, such as the introduction of a new drug or a new surgical procedure to deal with an obstructed coronary artery, an arrhythmia, a leaking

valve, or a thinned-out bulging of a heart muscle scar.
And at all times, participants were urged to call for aid
immediately whenever a drug taken for any possible cardiac symptom or sign failed to work within seconds or
minutes at the most.

SECTION II COUNSELING

The eleven Section II counselors included psychiatrists,
clinical psychologists, and two cardiologists (Dr. Stephen
Elek, now deceased, and the senior author of this book)
who were capable of giving Type A behavioral counseling.
They met for 90 minutes with their participants each week
for the first two months, every other week for the next
two months, and then monthly for the remainder of the
study. In addition, we found it necessary to have the Section II groups visited every several months by one of our
Section I cardiologists, who would give them exactly the
same information and guidance they were giving their own
Section I participants. When we began the study, we
assumed that because the Section II participants were also
still seeing their own private cardiologists, they would not
need the extra cardiological advice Section I was getting.
We were dead wrong! As quickly became obvious, the
Type A inability to hear and retain medical information,
conjoined with the infrequency and brevity of participants' visits to their own time-obsessed cardiologists,
meant that most of our Section II participants had no
sense at all of the simple physical precautions they, like
any other heart attack survivors, needed to take. They
required the same *repetitive* presentation of cardiological
information to which Section I participants were being
subjected. It would, after all, have been a pyrrhic victory
if we succeeded in modifying the Type A behavior of
Section II participants only to lose them to the fuses and
the bomb through failure to drill them enough in the basic
precautions.

As it turned out in practice, therefore, the one major
difference between counseling given to Section II participants and that given to Section I participants was the

Type A behavior counseling. The details of this counseling—what it consisted of, how it worked, and a breakdown of its aims—are fully described in chapters 9, 10, 11, and 12.

COMPLIANCE FAILURES

Any Section I or II participant who missed three successive meetings without providing an acceptable reason for his absences, or who consistently indulged in dangerous activities (for instance, jogging or playing competitive tennis or consuming fat-heavy meals) was designated a dropout or compliance failure. Also, any person in Section II who did not follow the instructions or perform the drills prescribed for him to modify his Type A behavior was similarly designated. The National Heart, Lung and Blood Institute, whose funding was so important to our study, was almost as eager to find out how many of our postinfarction participants would comply with our instructions as they were to learn whether compliance would in fact afford protection against a new heart attack. After all, no matter what its potential, no program is much good if everyone drops out of it.

Quite a sizable fraction of both Section I and II participants did indeed drop out of our study. When we first designed it in 1976 and 1977, we were reasonably certain that more than a third of the postinfarction subjects we recruited would not stick with it for the entire five-year period. At the end of the third year, the figure was in fact about 40 percent of the total 1012 participants. There are a number of reasons why coronary patients drop out of any program designed to help them, whether the program concerns itself with exercise (at least 40 percent of coronary patients enrolling in exercise programs quit during the first six months), with diet (the officials of the National Heart, Lung and Blood Institute initially declined to subsidize the Pritikin dietary study because they thought it unlikely that enough enrollees would continue to observe the severe diet restrictions to get significant results), with ingestion of various drugs (over a third of all coronary patients "forget" to take regularly the drugs given to them; some even prefer to endure the pain and terror of an angina attack rather than to take a nitroglycerine tablet that would alleviate their distress in a few seconds).

Perhaps the chief reason for the dropouts is the fact that most coronary patients usually suffer comparatively little discomfort, apart from the brief and usually severe pain of the heart attack itself. It is unfortunately easy for them to convince themselves that they are perfectly well again. Of course they are not. The basic atherosclerotic process continues, "creeping on," as Osler put it almost a century ago, "slowly but surely, with no pace perceived" as the patients continue to be "all unconscious that the fell sergeant has already issued the warrant." Given this lack of overt symptoms, it is easy to see why the typical coronary patient, who is often much more easily swayed by his Type A sense of time urgency than by the perilous state of his heart, is likely to regard time spent with a cardiologist or in a life-saving program as time wasted. Time, in short, obviously means too much to him for his own good!

Finally, quite a few postinfarction patients refuse to believe that their coronary arteries are severely diseased, and have been so for a number of years. It is moreover difficult for them to accept emotionally and intellectually the fact that in suffering a heart attack a significant portion of the pumping muscle of their heart has been destroyed and is lost forever. This reluctance to accept the reality of their serious CHD is a variety of what we call "cardiac denial," the same syndrome responsible for their tendency to delay seeking medical care when precursor symptoms of a heart attack occur. (The national average of a ten- to twenty-hour delay in new cases, between the onset of heart attack symptoms and the seeking of medical assistance, may be laid to cardiac denial; that delay is the main cause of nearly half of all heart attack victims in the United States' dying before they reach a hospital.) Cardiac denial probably arises from the basic insecurity of the Type A individual and his habit of thinking that at least his body will never let him down. And when his body proves to be vulnerable, his only recourse is to deny reality, to deny or at least belittle the seriousness of the event.

So it was not surprising that a certain number of the postinfarction persons we enrolled in the 1977–1978 period dropped out of a program that not only demanded a good deal of their time but also repeatedly drove home these unpleasant truths: that their bodies indeed had let them down, and that heart attacks are never minor and ephemeral. We wish that all our participants had found the patience and nerve to stay the course; some, we are quite certain, would be alive today if they had.

CHAPTER 8

Results

In the July 1982 issue of *Circulation*, the official journal of the American Heart Association, an article appeared bearing the title "Feasibility of Altering Type A Behavior Pattern in Post-Myocardial Infarction Patients" and the bylines of no fewer than 15 authors. This was the first official publication to emerge from the Recurrent Coronary Prevention Project study. It reported what had happened to our participants after all of them had been in the study for at least one year.

This first paper carried no startling announcement of a breakthrough. On the contrary, it set forth in meticulous medical jargon findings that may well have struck some of our more statistically minded colleagues as tentative at best, unconvincing at worst, and in any case quantitatively insignificant. Together with our 13 coauthors, we knew better—that these results, while still premature, pointed firmly toward our goal: indisputable documentation of significant modification of Type A behavior accompanied by a dramatic reduction in the number of new coronary catastrophes.

All of us had waited eagerly, in that spring of 1981, for biostatistician Lynda Powell to complete her computations of the one-year questionnaires filled out by our participants (and, in the case of Section II, their spouses and monitors). What we needed to learn was whether the comparison of these questionnaires with the ones completed at intake would show any improvement in the Type A behavior of Section II participants.

We remember very well that morning in early April when Lynda entered our office. Her face, unable to conceal the pleasure her computer readouts had given her, signaled to us that we had succeeded. Then, speaking in the restrained precise voice of a psychologist-turned-biostatistician, Lynda said: "The data indicate that a moderate but very statistically significant improvement has occurred in the Type A behavior of Section II participants." In her written report, she went on: "The p value is far less than 0.001.* It is of interest that the average 14 percent improvement we observed by comparing the participants' responses to the questionnaires at the end of one year with those obtained in their intake questionnaires, we also observed when we compared the first-year questionnaire responses of their spouses and monitors with those obtained at intake. I might add that no significant difference in Type A behavior, as judged by these same first-year questionnaires, was observed in Section I participants or the comparison Section III participants. I am pleased with these results and I hope you are too." We were pleased indeed! No one could accuse us of relying on anecdotal evidence any longer; we had secured statistically valid proof that postinfarction persons could modify their Type A behavior.

What is more, at the end of this first year we were also

---

*This means that if we repeated the same study a thousand times, in 999 of the 1000 repetitions we would have observed a significant degree of improvement.

able to see that there were significantly fewer new heart attacks in the Section II participants than among our 124 remaining comparison (Section III) participants. For every heart attack that occurred in the behavior-counseled Section II participants during that year, *three* had taken place among the members of Section III.

Yet while there was no question about the protection against a new heart attack afforded Section II participants when compared with the comparison Section III subjects, it still was not yet statistically obvious that Section II participants did better than participants in Section I, who of course received nothing but cardiological counseling, thus making them the true control group. Although there were almost half again as many recurrences in Section I as in Section II, the number of recurrences in neither section was large enough at the end of one year to be statistically significant. Furthermore, the actual cases of instantaneous cardiac death were so few in both Section I and Section II that no statistically significant difference could be demonstrated. The instantaneous cardiac deaths in these two sections were, however, significantly fewer than among Section III comparison participants.

What these data were telling us was this: Participants enrolled in either of the counseling sections appeared to be receiving statistically significant protection against instantaneous cardiac death. Participants enrolled in Section II (and thus receiving behavioral as well as cardiological counseling) also suffered significantly fewer new nonfatal heart attacks than Section III comparison subjects. There obviously were processes at work even during the first year protecting both Section I and II participants from instant cardiac death, and Section II participants from recurrent infarctions of all kinds.

Analyses of the circumstances under which new heart attacks occurred (both infarctions and instantaneous cardiac deaths) revealed several interesting and possibly valuable leads. First, recurrences (including fatal recurrences) were three times more likely to happen on Saturday than on a weekday. We believe this is because Saturday is the day when the fuses are most likely to be touched off. It is the early hours of Saturday when the emotional exhaustion of the work week may still be intense; it is Saturday evening when a meal rich in animal or vegetable fat is most likely to be eaten; it is Saturday when indulgence in severe physical exertion may occur; it is Saturday when viewing televised sports (and, incidentally, listening to the hyped-up chatter of the commentators) may evoke a fatal arrhythmia; and it is Saturday when conflict with family members leading to anger and irritation is most likely to take place.

Our analyses revealed that recurrences occurred far more frequently in postinfarction persons who had undergone two or more heart attacks in the past or whose last attack had run a very turbulent course. Those who suffered from angina, easily induced shortness of breath, or high blood pressure, or who exhibited an irregular heartbeat, were also found to be at increased risk of a new attack.

By the end of this first year of our study, 57 participants had dropped out of Section I (21 percent); 100 participants out of Section II (16 percent); and 27 participants out of Section III (18 percent). It may be of interest to note that when we ran a survey of 124 of these dropout participants one year after they had left the study, we found that they had suffered twice as many recurrences as had the Section II participants who stayed with us.

We had planned to continue the RCPP study until all subjects had been counseled or kept under scrutiny for five full years. This would have meant that the study as initially designed would end in April 1984. However, by April 11, 1982, when all Section I and II participants had finished their third year of involvement in group counseling and the data obtained during these three years had been retrieved from the computer tape and subjected to statistical analyses, we realized that the original design would have to be changed. The results already obtained no longer simply *suggested* that our thesis was correct, they demonstrated it with statistical certainty. Section II participants not only showed a marked reduction in the intensity of their initially observed Type A behavior, they also showed a spectacular reduction in their cardiac recurrence rate. No drug, food, or exercise program ever devised, not even a coronary bypass surgical program, could match the protection against recurrent heart attacks that the Type A behavioral counseling program had been shown to bring about in a period of three years. Here is what we had achieved:

TYPE A BEHAVIOR HAD BEEN MODIFIED

By the end of our third year of counseling Section II participants, it was obvious that a significant decrease in the intensity of their Type A behavior had occurred. We could see this immediately in the responses to the third-year questionnaires filled out by Section II participants and confirmed by questionnaires from their spouses and monitors; these scores indicated a reduction in Type A behavior of approximately 30 percent. In strong contrast, responses to the third-year questionnaires given to Section I and Section III control participants indicated that very little improvement in Type A behavior had occurred in either section over the three-year period.

Questionnaires are admittedly not always free of bias even when respondents are relatively objective, as were the spouses and monitors of our Section II participants. Nevertheless the congruence between the questionnaire scores of the participants, their spouses, and their monitors suggests to us that a minimum of bias was at work. This suggestion was strongly supported by the results obtained from repeat videotaped interviews of all participants at the end of the third year. Conducted by Nancy Fleischmann, the same interviewer who had classified participants during the original intake phase three years previously, the appraisal was about as objective and accurate as one can hope for when evaluating Type A behavior. Not only was the interviewer herself completely independent of the study, but the method used—chiefly observation of the *psychomotor* manifestations of Type A behavior—the least subject to variability. Nancy's judgments were based, that is, not so much on the substance of participants' answers to her questions as on their ways of speaking, their facial grimaces, tics, and expressions, and certain body movements. To avoid the possibility of unconscious bias on her part (she might have been hoping, for example, that our study would succeed), we deliberately concealed from her the interviewee's status—whether the participant was in Section I, II, or III, or a compliance failure.

The results of the videotaped interviews also indicated approximately 30 percent diminution in the intensity of Type A behavior in Section II participants since the beginning of the study. Section I or III participants also showed some degree of improvement, though of a much less significant sort.

We believe that some of the improvement shown in these latter participants reflects the attempt that some of them made to alter their Type A behavior on their own, even though they received no counseling directed toward that goal. Although we tried very hard during these three years to isolate Section I and III participants from the behavioral counseling being given to Section II participants, we knew that a good deal of intercommunication occurred. This was particularly the case in large corporations like the Lockheed Missile and Space Company, more than 50 of whose employees were enrolled in the study (at least two-thirds of them in Section II, the rest in Section I). Repeatedly we discovered that Section II participants (or their wives) at the coffee breaks and at lunch time were being asked by Section I participants to tell them about the Type A behavior counseling they were getting. We heard about wives of Section I participants calling wives of Section II participants and asking, "What did your husband learn at his last heart meeting about changing his Type A behavior?" We, of course, tried to hold these "leaks" to a minimum, urging Section II participants not to talk about the Type A counseling, but we have to admit that we did so with mixed feelings. Knowing what we did about the probable lethality of unchanged Type A behavior, we probably failed to lay down the law about secrecy to Section II participants with sufficient conviction to stop the interchange of information completely. We comforted ourselves with the argument that it takes more than an occasional bit of information to alter Type A behavior, it takes many months of trying to change one's belief systems, reengineering events and drilling to effect significant behavioral alteration. To some degree, this rationalization usually mollified our scientific consciences.

MODIFICATION OF TYPE A BEHAVIOR PREVENTED
RECURRENT HEART ATTACKS

The three-year data, collated and statistically analyzed, left no doubt at all that the Section II participants, who had been receiving Type A behavior counseling, experienced significantly fewer new heart attacks than Section I participants, Section III participants, or dropouts. As the graph on page 152 clearly indicates, the average cumulative annual recurrence rate of Section II participants was lower than that of Section I and III participants from the very beginning of the study and continued to be so. Approximately two and a half years from the start of the study, this difference became statistically significant, meaning that the difference could not possibly be attributed to chance. By the end of three years, the difference was beyond any statistical challenge.

When we analyzed the data on a yearly basis, we found that the difference in recurrence rates between Sections I and II the first year was 48 percent, in the second year 62 percent, and in the third year *372 percent*! Indeed, when we observed during the third year alone that 14 of the remaining 162 Section I participants (8.6 percent) had suffered recurrences while only 7 of the remaining 384 Section II participants (1.82 percent) had done so, we knew that it was about time to discontinue the program as originally designed, and to make plans and find the funds to offer Section I the same type of behavioral counseling we had given Section II. Enough was enough, no matter how stubbornly reluctant some of our medical colleagues still might be to accept our conclusions. If they weren't convinced now they probably never would be, and meanwhile there were lives to be saved!

We found that the average annual recurrence rate of our Section II participants for the three-year period was 3.0 percent—about half that observed in Section I (6.6 percent) and in Section III (5.7 percent). It was no surprise to us that those Section I and II participants who were listed as compliance failures suffered significantly more recurrences than Section II participants. They are, we

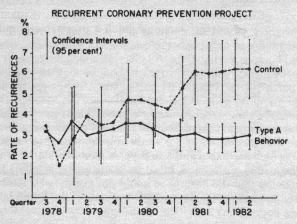

Graph illustrating the rate of new heart attacks in two test groups: the control group, whose members received only cardiological counseling, and the Type A behavior group, whose members also received counseling aimed at modifying their Type A behavior. By June 1981, the difference between the two groups was already statistically significant—that is, it was already too great to be accounted for by coincidence.

feel, not really to blame for failing to attend their group sessions or following the directions given to them by their group counselors. We would rather assume that we could have done a better job in getting them to persist. Our methods of intervention can hardly be considered flawless when we are unable to persuade a large proportion of our participants to give up habits and behaviors that so greatly increase their chances of suffering another cardiac catastrophe.

All in all, we observed 112 new heart attacks, of which 39 were fatal, during the first three years of our study. We often have been asked how many of these recurrences might have been forestalled. After closely studying each fatal recurrence and the events preceding it, we believe that 34 of the 39 could have been prevented if our counseling concerning the bomb, the fuses, and Type A behavior had been given to *all* participants and if *all* participants had followed our instructions. Such a prophylactic millennium is not likely to occur soon, unfortunately.

A committee of scientists selected by the National Heart, Lung and Blood Institute visited us at the Harold Brunn Institute to review our results. They concluded, after examining all our data, that the difference between the recurrence rate of the group receiving Type A behavioral counseling and that of the other two groups actually became statistically significant as early as the second year of our study, becoming overwhelmingly so at the end of three years. They accordingly recommended to the Institute that our study, having achieved its aims, should terminate at the end of four years rather than the planned five.

TWO UNANSWERED QUESTIONS

If Type A behavior plays a causal role in the development of clinical CHD, then abolishing or significantly altering this behavior *and only it* in an experimental study should lead to a reduction in the rate of recurrence of a myocardial infarct or cardiac death. Our study accomplished this. Type A behavior consequently becomes *the first of all the commonly accepted coronary risk factors to be directly demonstrated as bearing not just associational but casual relevance to clinical coronary heart disease*.

However, the study leaves two questions unanswered. The first is whether or not the participants in this study who changed their Type A behavior will be able to maintain the change once they cease attending monthly or bimonthly counseling sessions. Perhaps if we can continue our follow-up studies long enough, we shall be able to answer this question.

The second question is how many heart attack survivors, as well as *still healthy* Type A's, will be able to alter their behavior by themselves, following proper instructions but without participation in counseling sessions. Unfortunately, such an experiment cannot easily be done (who would subsidize such an inquiry?), and perhaps we shall never know the exact answer from a quantitative standpoint. But we are convinced in our own minds that many thousands of Type A's, given the correct guidance, can by themselves bring about a quite drastic reduction in the intensity of their Type A behavior.

We are reasonably certain about this point for several reasons. First, we have already received hundreds of letters from men and women (many of them still free of clinical coronary heart disease) who report that after reading and rereading the last few chapters of *Type A Behavior and Your Heart*, they have modified their own Type A behavior. A number of our medical colleagues would derisively label such letters as anecdotal or subjective. Well, let them do so. But if these readers feel that they have changed, the questionnaire results of this present study suggest that they should be believed, just as does our observation that quite a few of our Section I participants (again using *Type A Behavior and Your Heart* for guidance) were able to modify the intensity of their Type A behavior despite the fact that their cardiac counselor never uttered a word about it.

Many of the readers of this book may not yet suffer from coronary artery disease; they may never be afflicted in this way. Nevertheless, if they exhibit Type A behavior, a close study of the rest of this book, in which we describe all the methods used in helping Section II participants to control their Type A behavior, will not, we believe, turn out to be a waste of time.

A HIGHLY SATISFYING LETTER

We promised our Section II participants that just as soon as we were sure that their Type A behavior had been significantly changed and their *expected* recurrence rate had been diminished, we would notify them without delay. Although several more months were needed to complete data retrieval and analysis, on April 20, 1982, we were certain enough to write the following letter to the 384 remaining Section II participants. For us, the letter represented the climax of a long, long scientific struggle carried out over a quarter of a century in the laboratory, the consultation room, and the hospital room. That is why it can fairly be described as the most satisfying letter we have ever been in a position to write:

Dear Participant,

I should like to congratulate you for having passed through the third year of participation in our study without suffering a recurrence. And even more congratulations for those who have passed your *fourth* year.

I particularly want to congratulate you for your playing ball with us these past four years. The better part of many of you during these years must at times have almost given way to the backlash attempts of your old habits to reestablish their ascendancy in your personality. But most of you have held firm in

(1) remembering the bomb and fuses, (2) avoiding episodes of AIAI,* and (3) establishing your own monitor who will accompany you from now on, always alert to any backsliding on your part.

Perhaps never before in the history of medicine have so few accomplished so much. Because now that the results are being tallied, it is already quite clear that Type A behavior *can be changed*. And when it is changed, the recurrence rate in such patients is *phenomenally* lower than in those who remained as pure controls in this study. Thus when our three-year results are published sometime in 1984, the practice of cardiology will never be the same again—nor will the coronary death rate ever again be as high (approximately 700,000/year in the United States alone). Indeed, eventually it could well drop to 200,000/year. And this will be thanks to the 384 of you in Section II who stuck it out.

As some of you may remember when I first talked to you in 1977–1978 in the large Mount Zion Hospital classroom, although I never doubted that our study would be successful, I was in considerable doubt that I myself would be around to see it happen five years later. Well luckily, the outcome came sooner than expected so I have lived to see it.

On a more personal note, I am going to talk to you as if each and every one of the 384 of you were my private patients. Even though the critical statistics needed to save hundreds of thousands of future heart victims now have been obtained in this study (although we probably will collect additional data), there still remains your own individual life to think about. It is this life that I beg you to continue to save, year after year, so that you too can reach 72 years of age and still manage to "totter" about as I do. And you can best reach three score and ten by

---

*Our acronym for Aggravation, Irritability, Anger and Impatience—the four hallmarks of Type A behavior.

pretending every few months that you have just commenced this study and then carry on with as much hard energy as you possessed at the start, to keep yourself from reverting to a trigger-quick hostility, attempting to acquire too many junk things in too little time, or striving to be always right about the trivia of life. And of course reviewing the bomb and the fuses as often as a devout nun counts her rosary beads.

Very well done, my fellow Type A participants! I have come to like so many of you so very much these past five years—even when I nagged and nagged and nagged.

Your friend,
Meyer Friedman, M.D.
Director

PART THREE

TREATING TYPE A BEHAVIOR

CHAPTER 9

Who Needs Treatment?

A close reading of Chapter 2 plus some serious reflection about your own life and habits should establish for practical purposes whether or not you are a Type A. *Remember, it is not necessary to exhibit all the characteristics of the extreme Type A to fall into this category.*

Type A's in general have a regrettable tendency to avoid seeing themselves as they really are. They have no trouble spotting Type A behavior in others, but seem blind to their own failings. For example, a year ago we were interviewing the widow of a 48-year-old man who died unexpectedly and suddenly of a heart attack while playing tennis. "Did your husband ever read *Type A Behavior and Your Heart*?" we asked her. "Oh, he skimmed through it after I bought the book and insisted that he read about himself," she replied. "But it didn't slow him down or change him in any way, did it?" we asked. "Not one tiny bit. He just kept saying, 'I'm not like the men in that book. When do I ever jiggle my knees or finish other people's sentences?' 'You do it all the time, you dummy,'

161

I said. 'I do not, I do not,' he kept saying. So I just gave up," she said. She shrugged sorrowfully.

Perhaps half of all Type A men attempt to deny their affliction. We have dwelled upon this because unless they are more honest with themselves, little can be done to ward off the socioeconomic and cardiac catastrophes Type A behavior so often fosters. There are four groups of Type A's who we believe should take *immediate* steps to modify their behavior if they wish to reduce the frighteningly high odds of getting a heart attack. It would be wise for any reader who recognizes himself or herself as belonging to one of these groups to assume that he or she is at risk. Our studies have established that membership in any of these four groups is prima facie evidence of having been a severely affected Type A for quite a long while. This is true even if you have difficulty in recognizing a single Type A manifestation in yourself. Get an outside opinion from a spouse or friend, and accept this judgment without arguing about it.

Group I: Persons Already Suffering from Clinical Coronary Heart Disease

1. SURVIVORS OF ONE OR MORE HEART ATTACKS. The postinfarction patient, more than any other type of coronary patient, is most urgently in need of radical modification of Type A behavior, because he is a dozen times more likely to have a new heart attack than his still well contemporaries are to have a first one. Fortunately, such people are among the Type A's most amenable to treatment. Having already passed at least once through the valley of the shadow of death, they know better than most of us that they are mortal. And as we have been able to prove, modification of their Type A behavior can indeed forestall or prevent further attacks.

2. PERSONS WHO SUFFER FROM IRREGULARITIES IN THEIR HEARTBEAT. Millions of men, women, and children experience episodes in which their hearts appear to miss a beat, take extra beats, or temporarily beat so fast as to defy counting. Most of these arrhythmias, particularly in young people who show no evidence of any kind of disease or defect in the heart itself, are harmless, even though at times they can be frightening, and are almost invariably disconcerting. They can be brought on by tobacco, by the caffeine in coffee and strong tea, by alcohol (particularly an excess of wine), by various infections, by noncardiac diseases including a simple fever, and by various emotional states. But not all arrhythmias are so innocent.

We believe that any arrhythmia that *occurs for the first time in persons over 30 years of age and cannot be traced to any of the above causes should be regarded as potentially serious*. This is particularly the case if a Type A experiences any kind of arrhythmia that does not disappear during exertion, or that appears during the first five minutes after exertion. Such an episode in a Type A calls for a visit to a cardiologist for an intensive diagnostic session.

Persons who suffer from coronary heart disease (as indicated by an abnormal resting or treadmill electrocardiogram, by coronary arteriography, or by attacks of angina pectoris) and suffer from any type of arrhythmia should assume that the arrhythmia stems from their CHD. They should *religiously* take the drugs their cardiologists have prescribed for them. Anyone who finds himself or herself in this condition should regard modification of their Type A behavior a matter of first priority.

One point to remember: Even if coronary patients suffering from arrhythmias do succeed in altering their Type A behavior, they should never cease taking the antiarrhythmic drugs prescribed by their physicians—for the rest of their lifetimes.*

*New surgical techniques have been developed that call for the removal of the foci in heart muscle giving rise to dangerous arrhythmias.

3. PERSONS WHO SUFFER FROM ANGINA. If you suffer from angina pectoris, you almost certainly have severe coronary artery disease—that is, one or more of your three major coronary arteries are more than 75 percent blocked at one or more sites along their total length. Such persons are also almost always afflicted with Type A behavior and should make serious efforts to modify it. This holds true whether you obtain relief from angina by taking various drugs or by submitting to a coronary bypass operation. Neither the drugs nor the surgery, though they may ease the angina, do anything to prevent the further development of coronary atherosclerosis, which did, and continues to do, the damage in the first place. In fact, coronary bypass surgery—in making patients think that they have brand-new hearts and no longer need to be careful—may well lead later to the narrowing of coronary arteries that were in fair condition and needed no remedial measures at the time the surgery was performed.*

People suffering from angina should persist in trying to alter their Type A behavior even if the angina remains the same or worsens. In eight out of ten such cases, angina is caused by obstructing plaques composed of scar tissue, bone, and greasy puddles of fat and cholesterol. Such plaques will never shrink, no matter how much the Type A behavior is diminished. On the other hand, like smoking, continued Type A behavior is quite capable of making the plaques grow bigger. This can very well lead to *further* arterial obstruction, to an infarction, perhaps to sudden death. We are stressing this fact because we have known of dozens of cardiac patients who, disappointed to find that giving up cigarettes or changing their behavior pattern did not eliminate their angina, went back to smoking or to uncontrolled Type A behavior—and suffered a second, crippling heart attack or instantaneous cardiac death.

*We have observed individuals with a blockage of only 10 or 20 percent in one of the three coronary arteries at first examination develop an 85 percent obstruction within two years. These individuals showed absolutely no improvement in their Type A behavior during the same period.

It is now known that in about 20 percent of cases, angina is caused not by plaques but by the spasm of a coronary artery. It is at least conceivable that alteration of Type A behavior might reduce the frequency of anginal attacks in these cases too.

4. PERSONS WHO HAVE NO CORONARY SYMPTOMS BUT WHO HAVE CORONARY ARTERY DISEASE AS SUGGESTED BY TESTING PROCEDURES. Thousands of Western men and women who have no symptoms of CHD are receiving treadmill electrocardiographic tests as part of their annual checkups, and hundreds of such routine treadmill tests produce "positive" results. Of course in some few cases, the results may be wrong and the person's coronary arteries quite normal. In the great majority of cases, however, when a treadmill test is positive (that is, the patient shows characteristic electrocardiographic abnormalities or cannot continue the test because of angina or a marked drop in blood pressure), it is almost certainly a sign of serious coronary artery disease. The treadmill test should be followed by coronary arteriography. If serious obstruction is present in any of the three main coronary arteries, arteriography will reveal it, giving a very accurate description of the location and seriousness of the obstructing atherosclerotic plaques.

It is not for us to describe in this book what medical or surgical procedures should be followed if coronary arteriography discloses severe blockage. Such matters are to be decided by the individual's own cardiologist. Regardless of what medical or surgical action is taken after the discovery of serious coronary artery disease, however, or what medical or surgical regimen is prescribed, the patient should also immediately set about modifying his or her Type A behavior.

Incidentally, everyone should know that a *negative* treadmill electrocardiographic test in no way guarantees that you are free of coronary artery disease. At least half of all persons with one or more coronary arteries in very bad shape nevertheless pass an ordinary treadmill test with flying colors. So-called normal or negative treadmill tests have led scores of people to suffer instant death, often while exercising vigorously in the belief that they had nothing to worry about.

Only a coronary arteriogram whose results are negative can offer reasonable assurance that the coronary vasculature is relatively normal and that even severe exertion probably will not do any harm. Even so, reasonable assurance does not mean 100 percent. One out of every ten heart attacks occurs in persons whose coronary arteriograms appear normal.

Group II: Persons Suffering from Maturity-Onset Diabetes

We doubt if there is a cardiologist in America who is not aware of the fact that diabetes radically accelerates the course of coronary artery disease.

Juvenile diabetes almost always is due to the failure of the pancreas to supply adequate amounts of insulin to the rest of the body so that sugar may be taken in by the cells of the body and metabolized. Maturity-onset diabetes, the variety of the disease that begins in middle age or later, may have a more complicated explanation. In the last few decades some (but not all) investigators have argued that in maturity-onset diabetes a different form of insulin is secreted by the pancreas, or that something goes wrong with the body cells which prevents their absorbing sugar unless excess insulin is present in the blood.

Whether these investigators are correct or not remains to be seen. But we at the Harold Brunn Institute have observed that many healthy Type A individuals, when given a moderate amount of sugar to ingest, exhibit an abnormally high level of insulin in their blood. This phenomenon does not prove that Type A behavior plays a part in bringing on maturity-onset diabetes, but it does suggest that Type A behavior can affect the pancreatic discharge of insulin. It is also well known that norepinephrine, the "struggle" hormone that Type A persons secrete in excess, does interfere with insulin and sugar metabolism. Finally, most *lean* patients whom we have seen who suffer from maturity-onset diabetes also exhibit Type A behavior.

But whether or not Type A behavior is responsible for the occurrence of maturity-onset diabetes, the combination of diabetes and Type A behavior presents an extreme threat to the heart. Maturity-onset diabetics not only require drugs to help them metabolize sugar, they also urgently need relief from the Type A behavior most of them exhibit.

Group III: "Triple Risk" Persons

Persons who smoke cigarettes (10 or more per day), who suffer from hypertension, and who have a high blood cholesterol level* are commonly considered to be triple risks. Certainly any adult who smokes 20 cigarettes or more per day, whose systolic blood pressure is above 150 mm Hg and diastolic level over 90 mm Hg, and whose serum cholesterol level is 275 mg/100 ml of serum, is at least six to nine times more apt to suffer from clinical CHD in the next several decades than a person with none of these coronary risk factors. Indeed, even if only one of these factors is present, a person is statistically much more likely to succumb to a heart attack than if none is.

The National Heart, Lung and Blood Institute has subsidized a giant study, costing scores of millions of dollars,

*There is considerable difference of opinion today about what "normal" blood cholesterol level is. We believe that the highest blood cholesterol level generally observed in Type B's should be considered "normal." This *maximal* level is approximately 225 mg/100 ml of blood serum, while the *average* level of true Type B's eating the average American diet is approximately 210 mg/100 ml.

in an attempt to isolate, eliminate, or significantly modify these risk factors in thousands of persons. The hope was to achieve a dramatic decrease in the expected high incidence of new heart attacks in such high-risk individuals. Unfortunately, no thought seems to have been given, when planning this study, to the very real possibility that all three factors—excess smoking, hypertension, and hypercholesterolemia—are actually secondary effects of Type A behavior, and that such "triple risk" individuals are in fact invariably Type A's.*

If this turns out to be true (and we are reasonably certain it will), then the presence of two or more coronary risk factors suggests strongly that the increased incidence of heart attacks in these persons is in fact due to their Type A behavior, and that the only way to get at the crux of the problem is to deal with the behavior pattern. Thus triple risks should begin to make this effort not next month or next week but right away. Even those possessing only one of these coronary risk factors should do the same.

Group IV: Persons with Positive Family History of Clinical CHD or Hypertension

There is very little disagreement among practicing physicians and medical scientists that CHD tends to run in families. Fully half of all coronary patients were born into families where one or both parents at that time or later suffered from the same disorder.

Just as there are many specific conditions associated with the development of CHD, there is great variety in the way potential risk factors may be passed on from one generation to the next. For example, it is well known that

---

*This program, called the Mr. Fit Study, recently staggered to an end after five years of almost unbelievable epidemiological and clinical naïveté, a $115 million debacle.

there are certain defects in metabolizing cholesterol that are inherited. Children who inherit such defects may exhibit serum cholesterol levels as high as 1000 mg/100 ml, and almost always suffer heart attacks before reaching adulthood.

Again, one's inherited heart anatomy may encourage—or offer protection against—the early onset of CHD.* There may well be genetic influences at work determining the rate at which coronary atherosclerotic plaques develop, decay, and rupture, thus bringing on coronary thromboses and heart attacks. Inherited blood clotting characteristics may enhance or diminish the chances of an arterial thrombosis occurring in the first place.

It also is possible that the emotional constellation that leads to Type A behavior may also be, at least in part, genetically determined. This is hard to say for certain, because the various social factors involved in the genesis of the behavior pattern obscure the question. We are fairly sure, however, that Type A behavior in most cases does not develop solely from hereditary influences. One has only to recall how infrequently the *individual* hyperaggressiveness of Type A behavior is met with in Japan and how common it is among the nisei of California and British Columbia.

In view of the likelihood that a predisposition to CHD is heritable, and the possibility that children may follow their parents in a tendency to develop Type A behavior, we think it would be wise for anyone who exhibits Type A behavior and has a parent who suffered or is still suffering from clinical CHD, to take immediate steps to alter his Type A behavior.

---

*We know a pair of identical twins who suffered coronary infarctions of equal severity at about the same time and at precisely the same location in the heart.

A Special (Very Large) Group

The four groups of Type A's described above are most acutely in need of behavior modification. They are in real danger of losing their lives to a heart attack if they persist in their present practices and attitudes. But there is in addition another large group of individuals who, while they may be in less immediate physical peril, should very seriously consider taking steps to modify their behavior. In them, Type A behavior has created a wasteland of character and personality.

The aggravation, irritation, anger, and impatience which are the main exterior signs of Type A behavior are unlovely at best and truly hateful when present to a high degree. They usually evoke a negative reaction in others at both the conscious and the unconscious level. For example, the Type A's impatience, which habitually leads to the attempt to finish other people's sentences for them, to interrupt and make them speak faster, may very well come across as an attempt to dominate. It is in any case intensely annoying. Yet most people, more sensitive than the Type A to the feelings of others, are reluctant to speak directly of their distaste and repugnance for this behavior. It would be like complaining of someone's bad breath. Instead, they simply avoid the Type A altogether.

The Type A's habit of criticizing other people, often in violent, foul language, is equally repellent, even to other Type A's. It can be another serious obstacle to friendship. Yet it too is unlikely to be spoken of by those whom it offends. Once again, their choice will probably be to stay away.

If you find yourself unable to achieve lasting friendships, it therefore may make sense for you to consider objectively whether or not you are not in fact prey to Type A behavior. Ask a family member for a second opinion. Accept seriously what you hear, even if you don't like the sound of it. And if you do conclude that either hurry sickness or hostility or both are part of your makeup, take immediate steps to eliminate them or temper their unhappy effects. Type A behavior has many ways to hurt you but not a single way to help you.

CHAPTER 10

Getting Started

From now on, we are assuming that you exhibit Type A behavior to some degree, and we will be addressing you directly. (If we are wrong, and you are in fact Type B—as concluded from a careful reading of Chapters 1 and 2 and the fact that even extreme provocations don't trouble your equanimity—then the rest of this book may not be of much personal use to you. However, it will help you to understand better the three-quarters of your friends and family members who *are* Type A, and will also show you ways they can save their personalities and possibly their lives.)

As a Type A, you must first be honest with yourself. We are constantly being astonished by people whose Type A behavior is flagrant, yet who insist against all the evidence that they are only partial or part-of-the-time Type A's. How many times we have been asked "Can't you be an 'in-between'? Part Type A, part Type B?" Let us again emphasize that there are no "in-betweens"! There are only pure Type B's, who display no trace of Type A behavior, and Type A's, who can range from mild cases to severe. So if you are not Type B, you are Type A. If you are a Type A, your next step is to decide which components of the Type A behavior pattern you possess and how severe they are. Always keep in mind, incidentally, that the severity of your Type A behavior is directly proportional to the triviality of the stimuli that make it bloom openly. In other words, the smaller and sillier the cause of your anger, or the slighter the delay that touches off your hurry sickness, the more profound is your commitment to Type A behavior.

In the next three chapters, we shall describe how we helped our participants deal with their Type A behavior, component by component. The RCPP program involved many group sessions, discussions among participants, and a certain amount of individual counseling. While a reader working on his or her own obviously will not have the extra encouragement and support that such a program provides, we believe that it is possible to achieve a great deal independently by thinking about and practicing the advice given here. You will discover that we discuss at some length the background causes of Type A behavior, the hidden insecurity and damaged self-esteem that generally precede the more obvious free-floating hostility and sense of time urgency, and ultimately the drive toward self-destruction. We also talk about contending with Type A behavior on the overt level, and offer some very specific tactics for doing so.

It should be understood that there really are no shortcuts. Much of the time in our counseling sessions was devoted to repeated discussion of the whole Type A phenomenon, discussions that went on, some participants would say, to the point of acute boredom (which comes more quickly to a Type A anyway, remember). The immediate aim of the therapy was to bring about important changes in the Type A's belief system and daily activities, and to replace bad old habits with healthier new ones. To this end we employed drills, self-analysis, recommendations for corrective activities, and plenty of hard logic, the kind that even a dedicated Type A finds it difficult to argue with. All these will be found in the following chapters.

Before we start, let us once again remind you that what we are offering here is nothing less than a chance at liberation from a behavior pattern that is putting your very life at risk. It may help to think in terms of *freedoms*. We compiled the following list of ten freedoms to guide and encourage our RCPP participants; they represent the ultimate objectives in our joint effort to modify the Type A behavior pattern. Acquire them all, and we are virtually certain that you will be safe from a fatal heart attack at least until the age of 70, and possibly far beyond. Here they are; please mark them well:

1. The freedom to overcome your insecurity and regain your self-esteem.
2. The freedom to give and receive love.
3. The freedom to mature.
4. The freedom to restore and enrich your personality.
5. The freedom to overcome and replace old hurtful habits with new life-enhancing ones.
6. The freedom to take pleasure in the experiences of your friends and family members.
7. The freedom to recall your past life frequently and with satisfaction.
8. The freedom to listen.
9. The freedom to play.*
10. The freedom to enjoy tranquillity.

---

*"Blessed are they who play, For theirs is the Kingdom of Heaven"—Emily Dickinson.

CHAPTER 11

Alleviating Your Sense of Time Urgency

If you are burdened with a sense of time urgency and wish to reduce its noxious effects, you must be willing to take on some new ways of thinking and doing and to discard some old ones. These new processes may seem at first not only difficult but irrelevant, even nonsensical. Certainly many old habits will doggedly resist your attempts to replace them. You will have only sheer willpower to rely on and, we trust, a sense of the importance of the endeavor.

Recognize Its Presence

You obviously cannot eliminate your sense of time urgency if you are not aware that you suffer from it. We stress this truism because hundreds of thousands of Type A Americans have lived so long with their sense of time urgency that they come to regard it as a commonplace of life, as normal as thirst and hunger. It is not.

The psychological and psychomotor manifestations indicating the presence of a sense of time urgency, described in Chapter 2, should now be reviewed. If you note any of them in yourself, you can be quite certain that you are a prey to hurry sickness. This is true even if you exhibit only a few signs, and those only from time to time. (In the latter case, take comfort in the fact that your sense of time urgency, though present, may not be as severe as that of persons who suffer from *all* of them *all* of the time. But it should still be dealt with.)

When judging yourself, watch other people. If you notice that those talking with you appear to be rather tense, and talk rapidly as if they fear that you are about to interrupt them or volunteer an uninvited summary of what they are trying to say, you have reason to suspect they may be reacting (possibly unconsciously) to your own sense of time urgency. Certainly nothing quite ignites the sense of time urgency in a Type A so quickly and completely as his confrontation with another time-urgent Type A. "All my engineer friends talk fast, so I try to talk faster so that I can *win* the conversation," one participant in the RCPP study said. Silly, perhaps—but sad, too.

Find Its Causes

We observed that every one of the 592 Type A postinfarction participants in Section II of our study, that is, those who received Type A behavior counseling, harbored insecurities and in most cases insufficient self-esteem. While the insecurity was eventually noted in every one of these Type A participants, it was as a rule not *immediately* apparent either to the RCPP group leaders or to the participants themselves. Sometimes a year of involvement in group therapy passed before a given participant was able to pin down its nature and history. Yet it is certain that no one suffering from a sense of time urgency has much of a chance of controlling or tempering it without getting at the heart of the insecurities that bred it in the first place.

The prime insecurity of most Type A persons arises from the persistent fear that sooner or later they will be unable to cope with some task or situation, and as a result will lose status in the eyes of their peers and superiors. This insecurity is not as a rule concerned with one's sustenance or physical survival. We have never known any Type A generals who harbored any fear of their possible future death in battle. But what every single one of them did harbor was a haunting doubt that they possessed the necessary abilities to perform their present and future duties in such a way as to merit promotion.

It is very probable that your own insecurity (or complex of insecurities) also consists of a persistent, possibly unconscious fear that you lack innate intelligence, or education, or training, or flexibility, or downright courage (or a combination of these) to deal successfully with some contingency. Far too often, even a series of triumphs cannot allay this fear of failure.* Unlike the Type B, who uses his past successes to enhance his ongoing sense of security, the Type A subconsciously belittles the importance of his past victories and thus cannot use them to give him the confidence he needs to face new crises.

It is useful in determining the precise nature of your insecurity to think back to your earliest remembrances of it. It frequently begins in earliest childhood with parents (particularly the mother in the case of a male Type A, and the father in the case of a female Type A) who are overly inclined to find fault, who are all-knowing, or over-

---

*Doris Kearns relates how Lyndon Johnson reacted one day in the dry summer of 1969 to the delay in the dispatch of new parts for an irrigation pump at his ranch. "Once more I am going to fail. I know it. I simply know it. All my life I've wanted to enjoy this land.... *It's all I have left now.* And then this rotten spring comes along as dry as any we've had in fifty years. Then the Ford motor pump breaks down. And if we don't get our fields watered soon, everything will be spoiled. Everything."

protective, or incapable of providing verbal and tactile manifestations of love and affection.

If you are able to date the beginnings of your insecurity to your *very early* childhood, we believe you will recognize that one or both of your parents fit the above pattern. As we know from our intimate acquaintance with the 1012 coronary participants in the RCPP study, such parents are by no means rare. Of course, as we have pointed out in Chapter 2, there are other points in your life at which insecurity and flawed self-esteem may have begun to develop, ranging from childhood or adolescent emotional traumas to contemporary circumstances in the workplace or even from fears of technological or economic obsolescence. The common—and critical—factor is the damage done to one's self-confidence and pride, and the truly desperate measures the Type A turns to in a frantic attempt to retrieve the situation.

Whenever and whatever the point at which your feelings of insecurity and low self-esteem first emerged, you probably attempted to fight back. "Since my parents think I'm not very smart and not able to do as well as other boys, I'll show them how wrong they are by getting more things done than these other boys," the incipient Type A may think to himself, embarking upon his quest to achieve and to acquire as much as possible.

Unfortunately, the drive to achieve or acquire more as a compensation for insecurity gradually takes on a life and justification of its own. The phenomenon can be observed in any child who collects things—toy soldiers, stamps, marbles. At the beginning, he admires and fondles his first soldier, stamp, or marble. Later, however, as these objects are joined by others of their kind, the child no longer spends time admiring his latest acquisition but merely adds it to the rest. Now, it is no longer the individual treasure that fascinates, but the *number* making up the collection. What counts is what he can count.

In the adult Type A, this same process manages to debase many aspects of life. Numbers gradually in-fuse everything, taking the place of aesthetic and social pleasures. "How many?" "how much?" and "how fast?" —such bald questions as these, requiring simple numerical answers, increasingly displace the numinous "how lovely," "how warm," "how exquisite." An adjunct of this process, even more ruinous to the personality, is the progressive failure to use metaphors and imagery. Metaphors and imagery always wane as numeration waxes.

The Treatment

REPLACE OLD BELIEFS WITH NEW ONES

If our three years of observing our RCPP participants can serve as a guide, then we must emphasize that accepting new beliefs and discarding old and well-established ones is seldom easy. But it has been our experience that unless this procedure is successfully accomplished (it sometimes takes a year or more), no real relief can be obtained from the tribulations and dangers of a sense of time urgency. Moreover, if you do succeed, we can promise you—without a single reservation—that you will be acquiring not only considerable immunity to the premature occurrence of clinical CHD and hypertension, but also a more satisfying and pleasure-filled way of living. Let us now look at some false beliefs you must change.

MY SENSE OF TIME URGENCY HAS HELPED ME GAIN SOCIAL AND ECONOMIC SUCCESS. If someone told you that whatever socioeconomic successes you have enjoyed in the past were due to your propensity to become impatient and irritated, you would quickly recognize the absurdity of the statement. Yet impatience and irritation represent two of the four components typical of Type A behavior (along with the two "A's," aggravation and anger, they make up the AIAI acronym), and they above all other emotional states are associated with a sense of time urgency.

As a Type A, you have almost certainly made the common mistake of paying attention only to those leaders of our society who exhibit a behavior pattern similar to your own, assuming that it was their Type A behavior which was responsible for their successes. The fact is that in most cases these leaders were successful *despite* their possession of Type A behavior, because of entirely different traits and skills. For example, President John Kennedy exhibited severe Type A behavior. Why attribute his successes to his easily aroused impatience and irritation (that is, his sense of time urgency), when it is obvious that they should be laid to his ambition, luck, unfaltering energy, courage, intelligence, education, the financial help and advice of his father, and his remarkable charm? It remains a mystery to us why Type A's so obstinately refuse to recognize the presence of Type B behavior in many national leaders, both American (for example, presidents Lincoln, Truman, Ford, and Reagan, and generals James Longstreet, Winfield Scott, John J. Pershing, Omar Bradley) and British (Prime Minister Winston Churchill, field marshals William J. Slim and Bernard Montgomery).

The second reason you associate Type A behavior with success is your habit of trying to compensate for your insecurity by *struggling* for success, attempting to accomplish more and more in less and less time in hopes of winning a sort of victory. In the beginning, this may have eased your insecurity somewhat, but in the end it succeeded only in implanting a sense of time urgency, and making your insecurity worse. Hurry is open-ended; by definition, you can never hurry enough. The sorry practice is an old one. In the eighteenth century Lord Chesterfield wrote, "Whoever is in a hurry, shows that the thing he is about is too big for him."

Carefully review the failures that have occurred in your life and career. We suspect you will discover that many if not most of them were the result of errors that could have been avoided if you had been patient enough and taken time enough to arrive at a good judgment, or a creative and innovative approach to the problem.

Once you begin to realize that it was not your sense of time urgency that brought you your successes, you can easily move ahead to an honest appraisal of the true causes. Admittedly, some successes may have been due to pure chance. But in nearly every other case, you will probably find that one or more of the following factors played a major role:

1. Your creative ability
2. Your aptitude for making correct decisions at critical points
3. Your talent for systematizing, organizing, and simplifying various procedures
4. Your capacity for inspiring the confidence and cooperation of your subordinates, peers, and superiors
5. Your awareness of the consequences of your actions; your ability to keep in mind the future importance of whatever you accomplish on a given day, in a given week, month, or year
6. Your capacity for performing tedious, often dull and boring, activities to reach your goals

It should be immediately apparent to you that your sense of time urgency runs directly counter to each and all of these factors. They would not have been able to play a part in your successes, as they most certainly did, had you not curbed your easily aroused impatience and irritation. Ask yourself this: When has impatience led to new ideas and methods, to a good decision, to the fruitful organization of a business or professional activity, to the calm appraisal of the future value of something being done now, or to a willing involvement in slowly paced, tedious, but critically necessary work? This may be a long question, but the answer to it is very short: never. You must ask yourself various versions of this question not once but repeatedly until they and their single answer play a *permanent* role in your *conscious* thinking.

I CAN'T DO ANYTHING ABOUT IT. Repeatedly we observed in our RCPP study that many postinfarction participants, even after they recognized that their sense of time urgency had been hurtful, not helpful, to their careers, still found it difficult to believe that they might be able to diminish its intensity, much less abolish it altogether. This initial despair springs from the difficulty most of us have in separating behavior, which may be quite modifiable, from the intrinsic personality, which is generally very resistant to change. For example, when Freud read Goethe's essay fragment "On Nature" and abruptly gave up the idea of being a lawyer in favor of a career as a medical scientist, it is extremely doubtful that his personality had been significantly affected. Similarly, when an obscure South African Indian attorney named Mohandas Gandhi decided, after reading John Ruskin's essay "Unto This Last," to quit his law practice in South Africa and return to India, he did so because the essay changed some of his beliefs, and consequently his behavior. But no basic change in Gandhi's personality occurred.

You must recognize and differentiate habits and addictions from the far more permanent emotional, mental, and spiritual elements making up your personality. Luckily, even in late adulthood, new habits can still be learned just as old habits can be discarded. Older persons can become addicted to various drugs and noxious agents; in the same way they can rid themselves of old addictions, to nicotine and caffeine, for example, not to mention cocaine, amphetamines, or even heroin.

Some physicians, however, find it difficult to believe that the acquisition and abandonment of habits is a two-way street. They tend too often to believe that to acquire a habit is easy but to relinquish it almost impossible. Such physicians also find it difficult to accept the concept of free will, which is surprising in view of the fact that every patient they tend has come precisely because he, the patient, believes he can and should take a hand in guiding his destiny rather than allowing an unchecked sickness to determine his fate. These physicians also should bear in mind what William James, America's greatest psychologist, wrote a century ago: "The greatest discovery in our generation is that human beings, by changing the inner attitude of their minds, can change the outer aspects of their lives."

Your ability to change your behavior will, however, demand more than just good intentions. No bundle of habits, some of them decades old, will give way easily to new ones. As James warned, "nerve currents propagate themselves easiest through those tracts of conduction which already have been in use." Thus at first, it may well be an uphill battle. But it *is* being won. We witnessed hundreds of our RCPP participants succeed in greatly altering some of their habitual ways of thinking about and doing things. After all, what is lifelong learning but a process in which old thoughts and actions are constantly being modified or replaced by new ones?

MY COVERT INSECURITY IS TOO DEEP-SEATED TO CHANGE. Very few persons can travel through life without experiencing periods of insecurity. This appears to be the toll that man must pay for his ability to look forward. Unlike the flowers that flourish oblivious of the fact that they soon will fester and "smell far worse than weeds," man is aware that sickness, decay, and death wait to destroy him. More than most persons, the time-urgent Type A, because of his many decades of insecurity, is especially conscious of this universal fate.

Unfortunately, instead of developing a humane philosophy to deal with what they know is coming, most time-obsessed Type A's resort to another strategy, one which is completely self-defeating—to accumulate as rapidly as possible either currency or currency-convertible objects.

Physicians, attorney, broker, banker, engineer, politician, athlete, scientist, cab driver, even clergyman, he approaches the late autumn or early winter period of his life determined to build his future security less and less upon his talents and skills and more and more upon money.

This funneling of all one's talents and skills into a per-fervid search for tangibles is understandable in itself, but it almost never serves to appease one's basic sense of insecurity. As we have pointed out in Chapter 2, insecurity is quite independent of one's actual financial means (or lack of them); it almost certainly originated with child-hood or youthful traumas.

What you first must do to quell your sense of insecurity is to face up to the fact that you have it. Such an admission usually brings it into the open, making it at last possible for you to examine fully its nature and its origins. One thing is certain: Your insecurity cannot be alleviated if it continues to stay in hiding. Moreover, once you see it for what it really is, you will no longer need to blame it on economic fears. In other words, your insecurity is not in fact an honest concern about obtaining adequate food and shelter for yourself and your family. More than likely, it has instead to do with uneasiness about being adequate to the role you and society have chosen for you, with doubts about whether or not you are going to be able to maintain the *status* you have achieved.* Such status, of course, is totally out of your hands, and frequently in the hands of those who are not your true friends but actually your competitors or even enemies. It is their regard you are really striving for. What a hopeless pursuit! And how pointless, because even defeating your competitors or rivals will supply no solution to the basic problem—your ceaseless doubt that you possess various qualities and

---

*In this regard, here is Henry Kissinger trying to explain why he couldn't get along with William Rogers, Nixon's first Secretary of State: "But our attempts to meet regularly foundered. Rogers was too proud, I intellectually too arrogant, and we were both too insecure...." (*The White House Years*, p. 31; Boston: Little, Brown and Company, 1979).

capacities. Convinced of your inadequacies, you have been trying to fight back by battling to acquire material objects or to participate in more and more events. The result is a gradual erosion of exactly those parts of your personality that, properly guided and used, could go a long way toward ridding you of your insecurities.

REPAIR YOUR DAMAGED PERSONALITY

What exactly is happening to your personality? First, your sense of time urgency increasingly discourages you from recalling your past. It convinces you that you can't spare the time for it, and drives you to fill the void somehow by an increasing use of *numbers*. Your whole mental past becomes little more than a dry and unattractive agglomeration of numbers. Numbers are unfitted to nourish one's personality; a healthy personality needs roots in memory and a richly detailed sense of one's personal history.

Second, just as your sense of time urgency makes you feel you can't spare the time for memory, it makes you feel that you are too rushed to take part in the lives of your friends or your family, even to be truly interested in them. Over and over again you are unconsciously telling yourself: "I'm too busy acquiring or losing numbers to get involved with those people." The bleak consequences are obvious.

Third, your sense of time urgency is progressively expunging all color and complexity from your thinking and your speech, as "how much" and "how many" take over. Figures of speech, similes, metaphors—all these wither and die. In a very real sense you more and more begin to resemble a binary computer.

Finally, the purely acquisitive drive stimulated by your sense of time urgency is impoverishing your personality by constantly encouraging you to reach for more and more of the things worth having at the expense of the things worth being.

Several centuries ago Jonathan Swift wrote, "Whoever

is out of patience is out of possession of his soul." He might have been speaking of you. You can regain the possession of your soul only if you possess the resolution and courage to initiate certain remedial measures. Let us now examine these measures.

RECOVER THE USE OF YOUR MEMORY. The first step is to recognize that you have been using your memory almost solely for one purpose: to store essentially quantitative data that may serve to enhance your ability to acquire more and more things in less and less time. Your sense of time urgency has prevented you from using your memory to recall the past, thus depriving you of the pleasure and the spiritual growth that reading one's life backward can provide. If you persist in using your memory solely to appease your anxieties about the future, you will never be able to understand what Emily Dickinson meant when she wrote, "Such good things can so often happen to people who learn to remember." "Such good things" will simply not happen to you.

The second step is to make a conscious and systematic effort to recall, on a daily basis, not just data which may be useful to you in the future but also the important events of your past, whether they are happy or sad. This daily drill should be accompanied whenever possible by the repeated perusal of old photographs of friends and family members whose company you have enjoyed, or places and scenery that evoke feelings from earlier days. It may be a few months before this conscious recall of your past becomes less a self-imposed drudgery and more of a nostalgic pleasure.

The third step involves looking back across the events of each day in a deliberate search for things worth remembering. Too often in the past, your sense of time urgency never allowed you to do this; you were too preoccupied with the anxieties consequent on trying to accomplish too much. The best way to make sure of remembering an event or experience is *consciously* to label it memorable while it is actually happening. Say to yourself, "This is an experience I want to remember." Then do so, repeatedly, while it is still fresh in your mind. The more often you recall a particular experience, the better it will stick with you, and the richer your stock of memories will be.

The fourth step is to compare your past and your future critically with one another. It is not really possible, of course, to evaluate your present in this way; it slips too rapidly into the past. But a regular assessment of where you have been, in terms of where you think you are going, cannot help adding depth to your emotional state.

Finally, it may be helpful in restoring a real liveliness and vigor to your atrophying memory processes for you to recognize that humans alone, among all the creatures on this planet, appear capable of recollecting their past experiences with pleasure. A dog may recall where he can find food, water, and shelter. He is also capable of recognizing other animals, including people. But it is extremely unlikely that he is capable of *consciously* bringing to mind any aspect of his earlier life, even his parents! Why should you forfeit by default this almost divine gift?

RECOVER THE USE OF VERBAL IMAGERY IN YOUR DAILY THOUGHT. We have described how your sense of time urgency insidiously but surely substitutes numbers for similes, metaphors, and other verbal images in your speech and thought. The first step in reversing this process is to recognize just how extensive this loss has become. Observe for several days how frequently you use the words "how" and "what" in questions aimed at eliciting a numerical answer: "how much?" or "how many?" or "how fast?"; "what is the price?" or "what's the yield?" Your predilection for those interrogatives is a sign of your willingness to accept numbers in place of words and the complexity of imagery.

This impoverishment has not been entirely your fault, by the way. Our society is also doing its utmost not only to make you think exclusively in numbers but to transform you personally into a small series of digits. Indeed, you are no more than a number to the computers of your city, state, and federal governmental agencies, your insurance companies, your bank, and most of the shops you frequent. Once upon a time, however, only convicts were transmogrified into numbers!

The second step is to involve yourself in activities that cannot be represented or contained by numbers. This should include reading plenty of books—literature, drama, biographies, political books, or books dealing with phenomena of nature. (You would, however, probably do well to shy away from books on business or finance; such subjects may further encourage your already overstimulated enumerative processes.)

It may well be difficult at first for you to appreciate an intelligent (but not necessarily scholarly or difficult) book (for example, a historical work by Barbara Tuchman, a novel by Flaubert, Updike, or Bellow, a biography by Robert Massie or David McCullough). You may well feel like dismissing the whole enterprise by shortsightedly insisting that books like these bore you. You would do well in this instance to find the courage to suspect that perhaps these books, in a manner of speaking, find you boring, bemired as you are in a monotonous series of numbers.

There is more to this exercise than reading. You should also begin to take note of the way a given author (particularly a poet) builds phrases and sentences containing striking metaphors and images. Study the words used. Thus John Keats can compose a sentence such as "As though a rose should shut and be a bud again," while Emily Dickinson writes "She sped as petals of a rose/ Offended by the wind," and "The swamps are pink with June." When you come upon a striking figure of speech, lay your book down and try to construct new phrases and images dealing with the same objects. And as you do, take note of the manner in which the left side of your brain,* dominated by your still-intense sense of time

---

*It is now well known that the left hemisphere of the human brain concerns itself with the manipulation of numbers and other logical activity, while the

urgency, is shrilly insisting that this whole exercise is a sheer waste of time. Of course it isn't; the pleasure you will feel when you do devise a fresh and appropriate metaphor will prove that, and also, incidentally, prove that your right cerebral hemisphere, beleaguered as it has been, still exists.

Third, make a practice of visiting whatever museums and galleries may be available to you, on a frequent and regular basis. Carefully observe the images created by great painters and sculptors. Restrain yourself, or rather your overdeveloped left hemisphere, from dwelling upon the monetary value of the artifacts you are viewing. Your task is to appreciate, not to appraise. Again, as in reading a book, you may find it difficult at first to take pleasure in prolonged viewing of a particularly sophisticated form of art—for example, a painting by Jackson Pollock or Vassily Kandinsky. Once more be advised that before you declare such paintings boring, you should think again about who's boring whom.

Now go a step further. When you view a particularly striking painting or sculpture, imagine trying to write a letter describing it to someone you know well. Note how much trouble you have in dredging up from your mind the precise adjectives and nouns you need to make your correspondent visualize and enjoy what you are seeing. If the picture is a portrait, you will probably have to find ways of describing such details as the color of the hair, eyes, skin, and clothing, the position of hands and arms, and the facial expression, as well as the nature of the materials employed by the artist to paint his picture. This is not an easy exercise, but no matter how difficult and pointless it may at first seem to your time-urgent left cerebral hemisphere, persist in it. The practice is bound

right hemisphere is involved with the emotions and less clearly defined subject matter. It should be obvious that much of what we are recommending in this section is intended to give support and nourishment to your right-brain functions. Roger W. Sperry received a Nobel Prize in 1981 for his work demonstrating that the left hemisphere attempts to dominate the right; in Type A's this attempt is all too often successful.

to help bring back a feeling for descriptive words into your thinking.

Fourth, begin to write letters again, on a regular basis, to one or more relatives or friends. When writing these letters do not, like Type A Ernest Hemingway, stuff them with statistical descriptions of your achievements.* Tell what you have done and what you expect to do; what has happened and may happen to you; what you have seen and been thinking (apart from numbers). As you write these letters, resolutely try to employ new metaphors and images, turning often to your dictionary and your thesaurus for help. Incidentally, these two books should become as much a part of your life as your hand calculator or desk computer.

The fifth and final step to take to help free yourself from the tyranny of your numerative ways of thinking and expressing yourself is to attend, on a regular basis, a symphony hall, a ballet theater, an opera house or a playhouse or a movie theater. The programs given in these places may also appear to be a total waste of time to your numbers-benumbed mind. But if you persevere in listening to a symphony or watching a ballet, opera, play, or film, you will eventually discover that your speech has been enriched by this systematic nurturing of your right cerebral hemisphere and its unconscious activities.

TAKE INTEREST IN THE LIVES OF OTHERS. If you are like the majority of Type A persons who suffer from a sense of time urgency, you are increasingly stifling in egocentrism. To interest yourself in the activities not only of your friends but of your spouse and your children becomes more and more difficult. Even major events in your child's

*In describing a collection of Hemingway's letters, a *Time* reviewer wrote: "But much of the collection reads like the scoreboard of a ferocious competitor." The reviewer then describes how Hemingway, in various letters, related that he received 227 wounds, that he and his companions "... killed 3 big bull elk—2 bucks—2 bear—an eagle and a coyote," bagged 122 enemies in combat, and had intercourse three times on his fiftieth birthday.

life may well fail to tear your mind away from its absorption in a trivial or ephemeral business transaction.

We recently listened to a very rich Type A corporate president describe, at great length and with obvious self-satisfaction, how he had succeeded in getting a surgeon to halve his fee for removing a cancerous breast from the president's daughter. His account of this victory did not strike us as untoward until he mentioned to us in an almost offhand way that this same daughter had recently discovered a new growth in her right armpit. In this case, his obsession with numbers and the consequent destruction of his personality had ironically shielded him from the otherwise horrifying emotional impact of recognizing his daughter's true state—her imminent death, in fact. But at what a spiritual cost! There had been a time earlier in his life when even a slight fever suffered by this daughter took complete precedence over all his business matters, big and small.

You can regain an interest in other people. First, however, you must recognize that you have, in your struggle to achieve more and more in less and less time, allowed this interest to yield to an increasingly exclusive preoccupation with your own activities. "After all, he knows I'm his friend. If he needs my help (i.e., financial help), I'll give it to him," you have no doubt often said to yourself as an excuse for the fact that you feel no lasting concern for someone you may be willing to share a lunch or a game of golf with, promptly erasing from your mind anything which he may have told you of his interests, activities, triumphs, defeats, and continuing problems. To stop this evasive process, which is in fact deeply dehumanizing, you must make a conscious effort. After every meeting with a friend, recall what he or she discussed with you. Say the friend spoke of his son's trying to get a job, a deal he was working on, the possibility of his wife's undergoing a hysterectomy, his daughter's attempt to matriculate at Princeton—recall these matters and spend a few minutes wondering how each came out. Then, immediately before meeting your friend again, run over them in your mind so that you can ask him how they all came out. Reflect on how often a friend has told you of similar things which you instantly forgot once you left him and consequently failed to ask him about when you saw him next. Might not your failure to remember and express interest about such matters, some of them terribly important to the person involved, come across as cold and insulting?

You might respond, of course, that the same thing has frequently happened to you, and you are probably right. After all, three out of every four urban American males are, like you, afflicted with Type A behavior. (A Type B friend would probably not have waited until the next lunch to follow up on subjects of importance to you; he would have called.) Nevertheless, the failings of others are no excuse. The right thing to do is obvious, and there is always the possibility, even probability, that if you begin to take a real interest in what your friends think, hope, do, and experience, they in turn may evince the same interest in you. If this occurs, you will have rehumanized not only yourself but several of your friends.

PAY ATTENTION TO THE THINGS WORTH BEING. Your personality does not remain static; it grows, or it slowly shrivels by allowing itself to be taken over more and more by the sole purpose of acquisition.

There is, on the face of it, nothing particularly heinous about striving for the things *worth having*. When, for example, you were first making your way in the world, you were perfectly right to strive for such things worth having as a good position and career, a life-enhancing spouse, children, a fine home. But a time comes when the things *worth being* must take pride of place. For the great economist John Maynard Keynes, this time came when he was still a young Cambridge undergraduate. He wrote to his father that he could think of nothing having "so great a value as personal affection and appreciation of what is beautiful in art or Nature." The conviction grew as he became older. "When the accumulation of wealth is no longer of high social acceptance . . . [t]hen, the love of money as a *possession*—as distinguished from the love of money as a means to the enjoyments and realities of life—will be recognized for what it is, a somewhat disgusting morbidity, one of those semi-criminal, semi-pathological propensities which one hands over with a shudder to the specialists in mental disease." These are strong words, but Keynes had many opportunities to see at first hand just how spiritually devastating the unbridled acquisition of currency or its equivalent in expensive objects can be.

It is never easy, whether one is 5 or 55, to achieve the things *worth being*. They are solely the result of working on one's self and one's character, and frequently involve challenging established ways of thought and action. If a wealthy friend were to purchase an object well *worth having*, a fine painting, a rare private press book, or a splendid assemblage of audio equipment, you would probably not be surprised. But you would be justifiably surprised if this acquaintance launched on a study of art history and painting, or undertook to learn how to do fine printing, or began violin lessons; that is, attempted to achieve some of the things worth being.

A goodly portion of the things worth being grow naturally out of the aims we have already suggested in this chapter: to develop a memory accustomed to recalling events and happenings of one's own past; to restore one's ability to communicate in rich verbal imagery; and to take a keen and vivid interest in other persons. But there are more things worth being, and here are a few of the most important of them:

IT IS WORTH BEING CULTURED. It cannot possibly harm you, and it may do you a considerable amount of good, to learn to appreciate painting, sculpture, ballet, opera, and music. Quite possibly you once enjoyed such things, then let your interest wane in the face of professional obsessions (as Charles Darwin confessed he did). If so, you may at first find it difficult to believe that your personality has suffered any serious damage from your dereliction; after all, as Anne Morrow Lindbergh once pointed out in *A Gift from the Sea*, "the acquisitive habit is incompatible with true appreciation of beauty." Actually it is not only the acquisitive mind but also the enumerative mind that is estranged from beauty. The general manager of a Midwestern symphony orchestra recently admitted to us that he had become so absorbed in financial concerns that he actually found himself begrudging time spent listening to his own orchestra play. "Why should I be here listening to them play *Le Sacre du Printemps*, which I've heard at least a dozen times before, when I could be working out some financial problems?" he admitted asking himself not long before. Fortunately, he is aware of the sad irony in this. He had earlier resigned from a career in law to enter the musical world because he loved music so much.

So, even if you find that visits to museums, opera houses, and symphony halls are irksome at first, do persist. You also should make an effort to read widely—the classics and modern literature, history, biography, general science, and politics. It will not harm you to commune with the truly great men and women of the past and present. Who knows? They may be able not only to entertain you, but to contribute to your store of knowledge and common sense. And the best of them will be in their books. There is a famous ancedote of Max Beerbohm's refusing to stroll with Henry James in order to rush to the London Library to read the latest short story by—who else?—Henry James. And just before his death the painter Thomas Hart Benton described to us hearing Harry S Truman talk about the books in his home library in Independence, Missouri, saying that when he read them he felt he was meeting the only truly great people he had met in his entire life. (Considering the men Truman had met, from F.D.R. to Churchill to Stalin, that's quite a comment.)

While great men had perhaps best be met in their books, your personality can be enhanced by making a definite attempt to meet and talk with people who are knowledgeable or expert in various fields that lie outside your own. To get a feeling for art, a good "Sunday painter" will do; to understand something about genetics, you need not approach Francis Crick. Your family physician can serve as an instructor. The important thing is an occasional conversation with an artist, a musician, an engineer, a professor (or a businessman if you are a professor), a veterinarian, or even a choreographer. Be inquisitive. Ask them questions about their vocations. If they see that you are truly interested in the answers, they will be happy to find a jargon-free way to inform you of their activities. Remember that the specialist is not cut off from you because of his jargon; it is because he has reason to suspect that you really don't care about what he does or thinks. Unfortunately, only too often his doubts are well founded. The fact is that Type A's are not exemplary listeners. Your job will be to change that.

A note of caution is in order. You probably will not succeed in interesting yourself in any cultural or educational activity that you found dull, boring, or irritating in your high school or college days. Build on interests you once had, actually or potentially, before your drive to acquire more and more things worth having erased them from your conscious mind. If you once enjoyed plays, or good music, or reading good books, these earlier pleasures are still waiting in your right cerebral hemisphere to be reactivated. Just don't wait too long.

IT IS WORTH BEING AWARE OF THE TRANSCENDENTAL. Despite the evangelistic religious revivals that periodically sweep across the country, secularism steadily corrodes the spiritual fabric of modern society. In the West, even Catholicism, probably the most perdurable of

all Christian sects, has sustained disastrous losses this
last half-century, not only in its lay membership but also
in religious personnel. Approximately 100,000 nuns and
25,000 priests have left the Church in the last few decades
and many of those who remain are becoming increasingly
restive. It may be that never before in the experience of
man are so many people attempting to live in so absolute
a spiritual void!

There are undoubtedly many reasons for this disastrous loss in faith, among them the rise of science. Science
has played a significant part in making most religions
appear increasingly irrelevant to the human situation. Science of course does not attack religion directly; it attacks
by conditioning our minds to have faith only in phenomena stemming from measurable and dependable, no-
nonsense observations. Indeed, if you introduce miracles
into science, you destroy science, and conversely, if you
remove miracles from religion, you destroy religion, at
least conventional religion.

However, as we emphasized earlier in *Type A Behavior
and Your Heart*, man cannot flourish if his entire world
consists only of objects that he can see, hear, touch, taste,
or smell. Instinctively, whether he be a New Guinea
tribesman or a Wall Street tycoon, a human being tends
to feel that life on this earth must be subject to some sort
of higher purpose. Even those scientists who insist that
there is neither Design nor Designer but only chance at
work in our universe seem strangely dour and miserable
when their rationalism forces them to this conclusion. Is
this because they who have been brought up to trust
implicitly in the principle of cause and effect find it awkward to accept the idea that our universe is an effect
arising from no cause whatsoever?

Many people quite sincerely need, if they are to lead
an emotionally satisfying life, a belief in the survivability
of the soul. This need is certainly not universal, but it is
interesting to note how the absence of such a faith is
associated in many cases with the pressured unhappiness

of Type A behavior. Visiting the United States in 1831, Alexis de Tocqueville observed how despite their frenetic drive to achieve more and more things in less and less time, Americans seemed to him "as if a cloud habitually hung upon their brow." He attributed this inquietude to the fact that they had lost sight of their religion and the promise of everlasting life that is offered. "He who has set his heart exclusively upon the pursuit of worldly welfare is always in a hurry, for he has but a limited time at his disposal to reach it, to grasp it and to enjoy it," he wrote. "Besides the good things which he possesses, he every instant fancies a thousand others which death will prevent him from trying if he does not try them soon. . . . Death is often less dreaded than perseverance in continuous efforts to one end." Now, a century and a half later, most Type A's do not believe in any existence except their present one, and "a cloud" indeed hangs "upon their brow."

If you have *never* had any belief, even in your childhood, in God or in the spiritual immortality that most varieties of religion promise, it is unlikely that you will be able to develop one now by any act of will. If, however, you once felt some form of religious faith, you may be able to recover it. That this can occur in millions of persons is attested to by the large numbers of "born again" Christians among us.

From our own experience in counseling postinfarction participants in the RCPP study, we know that 50- to 60-year-old men and women can and do recover their religious beliefs (particularly if they had been believing Catholics) and in doing so, lose some of their most troublesome Type A traits. Our participants did not find the process at all easy. Their sense of urgency frequently made them feel that meditating about the numinous was a sheer waste of time. Nor was it easy at first for them to read the Bible, because the Bible did not speak to them in numbers and equations but in stories, metaphors, and images. But with great resolve, drilling, and in some cases a sort of personal revelation, quite a few of our participants found their way back to the religious beliefs they had held earlier in their lives. (We should note that there were several RCPP participants who took up Christianity with a flourish, using it as a well-rationalized outlet for their free-floating hostility. When they attempted to proselytize some of their friends and failed, they expressed annoyance at the willful "stupidity" of those who refused to see the light.)

If you find it impossible to recover or acquire a belief in the existence of God or a life after death, there are alternative possibilities—for instance, the myths and legends basic to Western culture, which Carl Jung probably would have described as fragments stemming from and nourished by our collective unconscious. While no one can explain, for instance, exactly why Greek and Roman myths still have the power to move us, there is no doubt that they do. We almost regret that we cannot believe in their reality, if only because they are composed as much of poetry as of religion. In a welcoming spirit, try reviewing these myths and their heroes and heroines; read the plays and poems written about them by Homer, Sophocles, Virgil, and other classical writers. You may well discover a springtime pleasure in their company. And there is the stuff of dozens of other legends and myths, from King Arthur to Joan of Arc to Chaucer's storytellers on the Canterbury road, waiting for you to be stirred by them and to be granted a sense that the world is full of glories and mysteries.

Besides religion, myths and legends, traditions and rituals can also enhance the spirit. They serve to align and join your past with your present thoughts and activities, thus giving fresh dimensions to your personality. There is in addition something soothing and stabilizing about them. Reestablish traditions which once played a part in your life before Type A behavior gained a grip. Enrich your future by creating new traditions for yourself and your family. The process is imbued with a charm quite outside the limits of time, a charm that will serve to ease and comfort those areas of personality rubbed raw by your unbridled sense of time urgency.

These traditions and rituals need not have anything grand or splendid about them. To be helpful to your personality, they need only be pleasant and gain a certain extra meaning from being repeated. Thus you might make a practice of drinking a bottle of especially good wine to celebrate important events in your life—the graduation of a child from college, an engagement, a marriage, an anniversary, or a major career triumph. Or you might choose to mark such occurrences by always going to dinner at the same restaurant, perhaps even wearing the same clothes. Or you might initiate a tradition of visiting the same hotel at the beginning of each spring, or at Christmas, or on your birthday or your spouse's. In short, search for events that fuse beauty with memorability and lend themselves to periodic repetition. Would you not glow with happiness at the thought of taking part in ritual annual reunion with a friend who lives in another city or town, in which you toast each other with a drink of very old bottled-in-bond bourbon? A silly business, you might be tempted to say. But in all seriousness we ask you to remember that it is the delectable and exquisite trifles of experience such as these that make our hearts merry—and healthy too.

REVISE YOUR DAILY ACTIVITIES

If you want to get rid of your sense of time urgency, you have only one option available to you: Eliminate some of the activities with which you are overstuffing your available time. Time itself is inflexible. What you do with it is not. And the relationship is absolute. Albert Speer caught the truth of this when he wrote, after being imprisoned for twenty years, "When there are no events, there is no time." In interviewing more than a hundred convicts at a California state prison, we rarely encountered a prisoner afflicted with a sense of time urgency. On the contrary, almost all of them, like Speer, found the passage of time insufferably slow.

Your first step, then, is to determine what you can safely dispense with. As a general rule, you should very carefully question your participation in any event or activity that does not have a five-year history of importance to you; whose success cannot be prayed for; whose success is related solely to your drive to acquire more and more of the things worth having; whose success will serve only to satisfy your ego; or whose execution can be delegated to one of your subordinates. In assessing the true importance of an event or activity, you should bear in mind that your sense of time urgency will be constantly encouraging you to inflate even the most trivial of them to a status of great moment. Churchill was speaking of this typical Type A myopia when he wrote, "When a man cannot distinguish a great from a small event, he is of no use."

After you have eliminated the "trash" events and activities cluttering your life, you should next adopt the following practices:

- Allow yourself idling time before and after your toilette and breakfast. Regard your breakfast as an event to take pleasure in, not a hurried prelude to a hurried day. If this means getting up earlier in the morning, do so.
- Begin taking several "mini-holidays" during the workday, in which you can daydream, meditate, or just plain nap. Such holidays need not be longer than 10 to 15 minutes.
- Make no attempt to get everything finished by 5 P.M. if you must pressure yourself to do so. It is far better to work later if absolutely necessary, or to take work home with you. It is not the number of hours that you work, but the pressure under which you spend those hours that can accelerate the onset of coronary heart disease in you. It is

far better to work 10 hours a day without time urgency than eight (or even four) hours a day with it. A good index of whether you are working under too much pressure is the ease with which you can stop working for a few minutes to indulge in pleasant conversation with your associates, to gaze at pictures on your walls, or the foliage outside your windows, or to lean back and meditate.

- Take great pains not to indulge in any polyphasic activities. If you catch yourself brushing your teeth while taking a shower or urinating, watching television and trying to read a newspaper, dictating or eating or making notes while driving your car, reading memos or signing checks while carrying on a telephone conversation, or trying to think about one subject while seeming to listen to a friend discuss another subject, do not attempt to rationalize the activity. Just stop it.

CREATE AN INTERNAL MONITOR

We believe our success in overcoming the sense of time urgency that afflicted all our Type A RCPP participants may be attributed in large part to our success in encouraging the creation in each of them of what we call an internal monitor. At first we advised participants to talk over with themselves any violation of the precepts set forth in this chapter, on the assumption that they would be reinforced in their understanding of the error of their ways. If a participant found himself watching television and trying to read a newspaper at the same time, for example, he began immediately to discuss with himself what he was doing. The same thing was to be done if he slipped into his old habit of thinking and communicating primarily in terms of numbers or began ignoring the activities of friends and family members in favor of some self-centered interest.

The problem with this approach was soon apparent.

An internal discussion was vulnerable to rationalizations, and Type A's are superior rationalizers. Something firmer was needed. This was the concept of the internal monitor—a sort of embodiment or incarnation of all principles aimed at reducing a sense of time urgency. To this monitor there was no appeal. It not only pointed out the transgression, it also responded flatly to any rationalization by saying, in effect, "Just do as I say. You know you are in error."

This internal monitor thus served as a constant form of self-discipline, and one which we have observed to be highly effective. Our participants reduced their sense of time urgency to a measurable degree, and also reduced their susceptibility to new heart attacks. Silly as such a mental trick may seem, it clearly works. You would do well to try it for yourself.

ANALYZE YOUR DREAMS

Freud placed great emphasis upon the interpretation of dreams as a means of exploring the troubled psyches of his patients. Jung also paid particular attention to dream interpretation in his attempts to probe what he called the collective unconscious. We had a more mundane purpose in mind when we urged RCPP participants receiving Type A behavioral counseling to record their dreams. We wanted to show them how dream analysis could tip them off to the fact that they were taking on too many activities or participating in too many events. Too often they succeeded in rationalizing such excess in their conscious minds, but the unconscious cannot be so easily fooled. The increased tension frequently turns up in the form of dreams, usually nightmares, in which *past* periods of tension, anxiety, fear, or frustration are reexperienced. Here are some examples:

1. John Treadway, 40, a very well trained engineer, suffered a heart attack in 1976. For a number of months prior to the attack, he had felt that his immediate superior was

asking him to do far too much in too little time, but he did not complain openly. In the weeks prior to the attack, he repeatedly dreamed that he was slogging through marshes trying to recover some duck decoys. The tramping alone was difficult enough, but he was also being beaten with a whip by someone whom he could not see or recognize.

While recovering in a coronary unit after he had his heart attack, Treadway decided that when he was well enough to return to work he would ask to be transferred to another project. This change was accomplished. About four years later, when he had already been a participant in the RCPP study for two years, he was told that when the project to which he had transferred was finished he would have to return to work in a project headed by his former boss. He did not like the idea of returning to work under this man but thought that after the two years of counseling in the RCPP study he might be able to deal with it. However, just before he was to return to work under this former superior, he began to have the same dream that he experienced four years earlier, prior to his infarction. This truly frightened him and he resigned from the company in 1980. Two years have passed since his resignation and he has not had another heart attack, nor does he show any symptoms of increased risk. He has never experienced the nightmare again, either.

Undoubtedly Freud could have mined this dream for the meaning and childhood origins of the duck decoys, the marsh, the sexual message of the whip. Heaven knows what Jung might have made of it. Our conclusion is simpler. It was easy to see that whatever else it meant, the dream reflected Treadway's deep emotional distress, and strongly suggested both to him and to us that he should go to great lengths to avoid working again under this particular superior.

2. Dr. Chung Fong, 63, a distinguished Sino-American biologist, suffered a heart attack in 1975. Dr. Fong was born and educated in the United States, receiving his

undergraduate and graduate degrees at Yale University. Believing he might be able to make a real contribution to China's health problems, he and his wife then emigrated to China, where he quickly became one of the country's leading academic scientists. He also became a friend of Premier Chou En-lai, who assured him that if he ever wished to take his family back to the United States to live, the arrangements could be made.

In time, Dr. Fong and his wife were accepted into the most privileged bureaucratic ranks. The prospects for their two children, however, were dreadful. Dr. Fong's parents had belonged to the pre-Revolutionary governing class and the children had been born in the United States. Nothing Dr. Fong could possibly do seemed likely to prevent his children from being permanently stigmatized by these two factors. Dr. Fong finally decided to try to leave China, even if it meant going alone and arranging for the rest of his family to join him later. The whole process took years, in spite of Premier Chou's promise, but he finally succeeded after a number of harrowing episodes.

Today, although almost fifteen years have passed since Dr. Fong left China, whenever he attempts to achieve too many things in too little time he suffers from nightmares. Invariably, these nightmares involve not his present-day tensions but some of his terrible experiences in escaping from China.

3. Richard Harris, an able sixty-year-old attorney, suffered a heart attack twelve years before entering the RCPP study. In his youth, he had attended a public high school with low academic standards before being admitted to Harvard. He found it very difficult to survive his first year or two at the university. He remembered this period as the most emotionally traumatic of his life.

Naturally enough, this period is still the stuff of Harris's nightmares, even though it was many years ago. When he began to analyze his dreams as a participant in the RCPP study, he found that any attempt to cram his life too full of activity sent him back in his sleep into such ancient collegiate agonies as having far too little time to finish an examination; hopelessly chasing a train while hampered by a suitcase with a broken clasp; struggling to find a classroom that had mysteriously vanished. Knowing the significance of these dreams, Harris was able to monitor his behavior.

Why do such stress dreams almost always recall earlier episodes? This question has been asked by thousands of soldiers suffering combat fatigue whose nightmares frequently mix frightening childhood experiences with more recent combat traumas. We are not psychiatrists, so we can only speculate that the unconscious mind is a much stranger place than our waking logic would suggest, and that stress in the present appears to reactivate previous stresses which, though submerged, were never really resolved. In any case, it is clear that nightmares reenacting episodes of stress earlier in life are a definite sign of Type A stress in the present.

If you wish to know whether or not you are suffering from a sense of time urgency, a way to find out may be to place a notebook and pencil by your bedside. When you awaken from a dream, write it down. When you get up the next morning, read what you have written and try to analyze it, keeping in mind that the message is usually an indirect one and often anachronistic in content. If you find that in your dream you are struggling to get somewhere on time or perhaps already late, in real life you are probably trying to do too much in too little time.

TIME URGENCY DRILLS

A fair number of the 1012 Type A heart attack survivors in the RCPP study were quite well aware in advance that they suffered from a sense of time urgency. They also recognized that it had probably played a significant role in bringing on their heart attacks. Most of them realized,

too, that their hurry sickness had not advanced their vocational careers. Yet they had not been able to free themselves from it.

Part of the difficulty was their failure to recognize their
covert insecurities and to deal directly with them. Another
reason was their failure to substitute new for old and
essentially harmful belief systems. But even if they had
succeeded in taking these steps, they would have been
faced with a still more difficult problem: to establish new
habits in the place of old ones. To do this, good intentions
are not enough; it is necessary to engage seriously in a
program of repetitive drills in which new patterns of
thought and action come to exist on both the conscious
and unconscious level.

You already know that any old habit, whether it is
physical, mental, emotional, or addictive, is not easily
uprooted. During out first three years' experience of
attempting to help our RCPP coronary participants modify their Type A behavior, we observed that the most
arduous part of the process was the drilling. This is easy
to understand when you recall how many years you spent
drilling as a child to become proficient in reading, writing,
and speaking; to become truly accomplished in baseball,
football, or basketball; or merely to increase the length
of your attention span. Our brain does not find it easy
either to accept new habits or to discard old ones.

Yet hundreds of our RCPP participants did succeed in
getting rid of old and harmful habits, replacing them with
new and helpful ones, and thus ameliorated their sense
of time urgency. They were able to accomplish this by
doggedly executing the drills described below. Admittedly, many of them began by paying only lip service to
the process, but even this eventually turned into deeper
involvement as time went on and they persisted. (Shake-
speare noted this phenomenon when he had Hamlet say,
"Assume [the] virtue even if you have it not. . . . For use
almost can change the stamp of nature. . . .")

We have made a distinction in the list below between

the *general* drills which we expected all members of the Section II (counseling) division of the RCPP study to observe from the beginning, and the *special* drills which were meant to be done on a scheduled basis. Section II participants received a booklet containing 12 pages, one for each month of the year. Every page listed seven of the special drills, to be performed on the basis of one a day and then repeated week by week through the month.* Each time a drill was performed, the participant was to check it off. In this way, group leaders at the monthly meetings could easily see whether participants were doing their job.

In addition, each page of the booklet contained four aphorisms that participants were asked to read and think about for a week at a time. A list of these aphorisms will be found in the Appendix.

General drills

a. Review at least once a week the probable causes of your sense of time urgency. Mull over the causes of your insecurities and consider the damage they have done to your personality and your behavior.

b. Remind yourself every morning of the fact that life is by its very nature unfinished and that you should not expect, or even wish, for *all* your projects to come to an end completely at a given hour, week, month, or even year. Just as your heart and liver have no set date at which their chores will be over, neither has your brain. The electrocardiogram and electroencephalogram prove electrically that the heart and brain are always actively at work. When you no longer have problems or challenges to overcome, your electrocardiogram and your electroencephalogram will register as low, straight, waveless, and lifeless lines! While

---

*Some of the drills aimed at controlling free-floating hostility will be described in the next chapter.

you are alive, your life consists not of separate end-
ings and beginnings but of continuously occurring
problems and potential solutions.

c. Listen to the conversation of others, always bearing
in mind that the more you listen, the more you will
gain from their experiences. You will also gain their
respect. A good conversationalist is invariably a good
listener.

d. Stop trying to think of or do more than one thing at
a time. The more you indulge in polyphasic activity,
the more trouble you will have in concentrating your
whole attention on a single subject.

e. If you see someone doing a job more slowly than you
know you would do it yourself, do not interfere. You
will then be able to congratulate yourself not only
upon your superior skills but also upon your wisdom.

f. Before you tackle a task, ask yourself: (1) Will the
execution of this task matter five years from now? (2)
Must it be done right away? (3) Can it be delegated
to someone else? The answers should temper your
habitual haste to rush in and try to do too much in
too little time.

g. Before you speak, ask yourself: (1) Do I really have
something to say? (2) Does anyone wish to hear it?
(3) Is this the right time to say it? If the answer to
even one of these questions is no, keep silent. Merely
asking these questions more often than not will keep
you silent. The point of this exercise is to combat the
Type A's self-centered habit of inflicting stories or
opinions on people who often aren't all that interested
in hearing them, and then unconsciously speeding up
the discourse in an attempt to finish in the face of
their growing boredom. "But people are usually interested in what I have to say," you might argue. We can
only suggest that the next time you find yourself relat-
ing some incident that seems to you interesting or
important, you excuse yourself to go to the bathroom
before coming to the point. Then when you return,

keep silent and see whether anyone asks you to pick up where you had left off. (Don't be angry if no one does.)

h. Tell yourself at least once a week that few enterprises ever fail because they are executed too slowly or too well. Then ask yourself if conditions of haste ever aided the formulation of good judgments and correct decisions.

i. Whenever you can, buy time with your money. Oddly enough, as things are now it is usually much easier to get even a top corporation executive's time than it is to get his money. The converse ought to be true. An executive has a very good chance of replacing any money he gives away, but he has no chance of regaining the time he has lost.

j. Refrain from projecting your own sense of time urgency upon those with whom you come in contact. Many Type A's speak rapidly not only because of their impatience with the pace of their own speech but because they think their listeners are impatient. When you catch yourself saying, "I know you're in a hurry but I'll make it short" or "This won't take long," you can be fairly certain that you are projecting your own sense of time urgency.

k. Try to wean yourself from employing numbers in your everyday speech. When you see a new and attractive automobile, a painting, an exquisite house, or a beautiful gem, try to express its impact upon you in adjectives, not digits. Eliminate "how much" and "how many" from your nonprofessional vocabulary.

l. Begin to read books that have nothing to do with your vocational concerns. First supply yourself (if you have not already done so) with some reference books—for example, a good unabridged dictionary, an encyclopedia, a biographical dictionary, an atlas, a thesaurus, a dictionary of quotations. Then begin to read some novels by, say, George Eliot, Tolstoy, Turgenev, Saul Bellow, or John Updike. At first, you may find these books boring partly because you have lost your ability to concentrate (concentration being the opposite of polyphasic thinking). But after several months, by which time you should find it considerably easier to keep your attention focused, you will probably be ready to take on books that require still greater concentration. These might include the writings of the Greek historians (Herodotus, Thucydides, and Plutarch) and dramatists (Aeschylus, Euripides, and Sophocles), or any book of Will and Ariel Durant's series, *The Story of Civilization*. As you read such books and come upon a word whose meaning you do not know or have forgotten, look it up.

Incidentally, in *Type A Behavior and Your Heart*, we recommended reading Proust's seven-volume novel, *Remembrance of Things Past*, as a therapeutic measure. Judging from our experience in the RCPP study, this recommendation was a mistake. As far as we could determine, only one of the six hundred RCPP participants who received behavioral counseling finished all seven volumes. This person, a distinguished major general, made it very clear to us that his reading of these seven volumes, like some of his Korean war experiences, was a trial of endurance that he never wished to essay again. We have concluded that you will have to lose a large part of your sense of time urgency before you can hope to finish even the first volume of Proust's colossal masterpiece.

Still, with six months or so of this drill behind you, you may well find that reading has become a pleasure again, one which you regret having neglected for so many years.

m. Learn to interrupt long sessions of working with periods of relaxation. It is far better that you work twelve hours a day without tension than a shorter period under pressure. But it is difficult to work continuously without building up tension inside you. Take a five- or ten-minute break every hour during work sessions. Stretch out, or daydream, or talk with an associate. If your pet is nearby, play with it—after all, that is why it lives with you! When Emerson felt himself getting tense, he would walk to his garden and pull up a few carrots.

n. Begin to use similes and metaphors in your everyday speech. Do not be discouraged if at first this seems awkward and difficult, or to your ear sounds strange. For too long you have been squeezing every bit of color and life out of your verbal style. Recognize the fact that speech stripped of adjectives and images is not only dull but eventually makes you colorless and dull.

o. Seek beauty wherever and in whatever form you may find it. Enjoy exquisite things, even if you cannot buy them or keep them for yourself, in museums, books, the collections of others; in scenes recalled from your travels or deliberately sought out all around you. You can provide a stimulus to your spirit by thinking over beauty you have seen or experienced in the past. If you find that your memory is empty of such things, this should prove to you that you have already wasted too much of your life on trash events and numbers.

p. Begin to drive in the slow lane of three- or four-lane highways, either on the far right or in the second lane if entering vehicles make the righthand lane dangerous. The idea is to reduce your urge to drive as fast or faster than anyone on the road. Practiced for several months, this drill usually results in a willingness to drive at a steady, moderate pace controlled by the car ahead of you.

q. Following lunch or dinner or a visit with friends, make notes of their concerns as they were told to you. Just prior to your next meeting, review these notes. Then make a point of following up with inquiries about how things have turned out. Sure it will seem artificial at first, but by forcing yourself to become involved like this you will eventually find yourself doing it instinctively and with genuine interest.

r. Whenever you can, try to establish rituals in your

daily life. For instance, on a regular basis repeat as closely as possible the circumstances attending a pleasant or notable event. The spirit-enhancing effect of a ritual does not arise from the importance of the event it celebrates but rather from the act of re-creating the pleasure of the event in retrospect. Lovers are particularly aware of the joy of rituals.

Specific drills

a. Visit an art museum, a park, a zoo, or an aquarium.
b. Note carefully the various components making up a tree, a flower, a bird, a sunset, or a dawn.
c. Alter one of your usual habits or ways of doing things.
d. Record on tape an hour of your dinner-table conversation with your spouse. Then play the tape back. Note whether your speech is pleasant to listen to, or too rapid and showing a frequent tendency to interrupt. You may be surprised to hear yourself as others hear you.
e. Walk, talk, and eat more slowly.
f. Recall past times and events for 15 minutes.
g. Leave your watch off.
h. Do absolutely nothing but listen to music for 15 minutes.
i. Ask a member of your family, at dinner, what he or she did that day, and listen to the answer.
j. Find a long line in a supermarket and get at the end of it. As you wait and find yourself becoming restless, ask yourself why you find it so boring to be alone with yourself. Look at the other persons in the line and in the store and think about them. What sort of persons are they? What sort of life have they led? What problems have they had? Are they rich or poor? Are they intelligent, stupid, or in-between? Are they sad or happy? Decide whether they seem to you handsome or pretty. And when you feel this waiting is a waste of time, ask yourself this question: "Why do I

find it so boring to commune only with myself?"

k. Ask yourself: "What did I do right today and what happened that is worth remembering?"

l. Invite someone to lunch and make certain your guest is encouraged to talk about his or her interests and problems, not yours. In other words, leave the table richer in the knowledge of someone else's life.

m. Try to hear out at least two persons on separate occasions without interrupting even once.

n. Devote 15 minutes to planning a new avocation.

o. Telephone or write to an old friend who has a job or profession different from yours. Note how difficult it is for you to find subject matter that you know will interest this friend.

p. During an entire workday, practice moving your entire arm, not just your fingers, when writing. This maneuver tends to lead to muscular relaxation.

We strongly recommend that you set up a drill schedule. Assign yourself one specific drill for each day of the first week of a month, repeating the sequence week by week for the remainder of the month. Make up similar schedules for the other eleven months of the year, introducing new drills and repeating some of those already done, until all of them have been covered. At the end of a year, repeat the entire schedule. The best way to keep track of all this is to make yourself a 12-page drill book (one page per month). At the bottom of each page, write down four of the aphorisms listed in the Appendix; they are to be read and pondered carefully for at least a week at a time each.

Our RCPP participants had one advantage over you in that they enjoyed the support of the other participants of their particular groups and the guidance of their group leaders. But the group leaders gave no advice that is not included in this book (in fact, we doubt that any group leader gave as much specific advice as you'll find here), and you may be able to get some help from your family, which probably has good reason to want to see an end to your Type A behavior. The following procedures will help you get the most out of the drills:

1. Tell your spouse, children, and friends that you are going to adopt some new habits and discard some old ones. You might even make some wagers to that effect. We often have advised any patient who wished to quit smoking to tell a friend he would pay a thousand dollars if he failed. Very few patients followed our suggestion, but those who did never smoked cigarettes again.

2. Resist the constant temptation to skip a drill or to revert to an old habit "just this one time." As William James once wrote, "Never suffer an exception to occur till the new habit is securely rooted in your life. Each lapse is like the letting fall of a ball of string which one is carefully winding up; a single slip undoes more than a great many turns will wind again. . . ."

3. When you practice a drill designed to establish a new habit, deliberately remind yourself that you are establishing new pathways in your brain where the nervous currents responsible for the habit can propagate.

4. Do not taper off an old habit. Break it off sharply and exert your *conscious* will to contend with the excuses it offers in favor of its continuing to exist.

5. Keep always in mind that a new habit is not really established until you follow it *unconsciously* and any failure to do so leaves you feeling uncomfortable.

6. Work on establishing just a few new habits at any given time. Nothing is more helpful in establishing a new habit than having already established a related new habit.

CHAPTER 12

Alleviating Your Free-Floating Hostility

Free-floating hostility is, with a sense of time urgency, one of the two overt aspects of Type A behavior. It is of interest that it was present in Dr. John Hunter, the great English surgeon of the eighteenth century and a victim of coronary heart disease, whose case was the first in history to be described in both its pre- and postmortem phases. Hunter's biographer was his brother-in-law. He played down the doctor's easily aroused hostility, describing his "temper" as "very warm and impatient, readily provoked, and when irritated not easily soothed. . . . He hated deceit, and he was above every kind of artifice, he detested it in others and too openly vowed his sentiments. . . . In conversation, he spoke too freely, and sometimes harshly of his contemporaries."* It is unfortunate that although anger

---

*The *English Dictionary of National Biography* described Dr. Hunter a bit more bluntly: "In manner, Hunter was impatient, blunt, and unceremonious, often rude and overbearing, but he was candid and unreserved to a fault." Hunter himself also was aware of his easily aroused hostility, saying that his life was "in the hands of any rascal who chooses to annoy and tease me."

and angina were observed together in this first fully documented case of CHD, the connection between these two symptoms remained unexplored until recent times.

While free-floating hostility is overt in that its presence eventually becomes apparent to families, friends, and associates of most Type A's, it may not be readily recognized by the Type A himself. This is because, as we pointed out in Chapter 2, Type A's are skilled at finding excuses for their unattractive behavior.

We already have described, in Chapter 2, the kind of things that arouse aggravation and anger in hostile Type A's. Here we shall simply give a few specific examples of typical free-floating hostility manifested by our RCPP participants. The first is part of the written response from a participant to a question asking if he believed his hostility had diminished after a year in our study.

> I do not believe that I have excess hostility; this is due in part to the fact that my intellectual, physical, cultural, and hereditary attributes surpass those of 98 percent of the bastards I have to deal with. Furthermore those dome-head, fitness freak, goody-goody types that make up the alleged 2 percent are no doubt faggots anyway, whom I could beat out in a second if I weren't so damn busy fighting every minute to keep that 98 percent from trying to walk over me. To answer your question however, if I

The "rascal" turned out to be a colleague at St. George's Hospital who, on Oct. 10, 1773, chose to contradict Hunter during a discussion. Very upset, Hunter immediately withdrew to an adjoining room, where he groaned and expired instantly.

Hunter possesed the acquisitive proclivity of the Type A. In his case, the things he regarded as worth having were 13,000 anatomical, pathological, and biological specimens, ranging from the tiny muscle fibers of insects to the skeleton of the 7'7" Irish giant O'Brien. During the latter's lifetime, aware that Hunter might attempt to skeletonize his corpse for his collection, he directed in his will that his coffin be securely sunk in the sea. By bribing the undertaker, Hunter nevertheless intercepted the coffin, carried it in his own carriage to his London home, and, sure enough, reduced the dead Mr. O'Brien to a skeleton.

could curb my inate [sic] modisty [sic], humility and empathy for my fellow man perhaps . . .

Our second example is the verbal blast of one of our participants (as he reported it to us, in some embarrassment) at his slightly overweight wife when he heard her cracking some English walnuts in their kitchen as he sat reading a newspaper in the living room. "I went to the kitchen and I let her have it: 'If you knew how you look in the bedroom with those huge rolls of flabby fat quivering on your big belly and thighs, you then would know why hearing you crack those Goddamned nuts cuts me to the quick.'"

From such examples as these, it should be clear to you that the answer to free-floating hostility is not simply the removal from the Type A's presence of every person, thing, and event that touches it off. Almost all living things except trees, bushes, plants, and certain tame species of animals would have to be exterminated. In fact, we have known hostile Type A's to be aggravated even by roses (because "they have so many Goddamn thorns") and camellias (because "they don't have any smell"). In order to bring your free-floating hostility under control, you must cease trying to change other persons and other things and instead concentrate on altering *your reactions* to them. This will be neither easy nor quick, but it can be done; we know it can because we have witnessed hundreds of RCPP participants do it.

Recognize Your Own Free-Floating Hostility

As usual, the first step in contending with your free-floating hostility is to accept the fact that you have it. The telltale signs are as follows: (1) if you become irritated or angry at relatively minor mistakes of your family members, friends, acquaintances, or complete strangers or find such mistakes hard to overlook; (2) if you frequently find yourself critically examining a situation in order to find something that is wrong or might go wrong; (3) if you find yourself scowling and unwilling or unable to laugh at things your friends laugh at; (4) if you are overly proud of your ideals and enjoy telling others about them; (5) if you frequently find yourself thinking or saying that most people cannot be trusted, or that everyone has a selfish angle or motive; (6) if you find yourself regarding even one person with contempt; (7) if you have a regular tendency to shift the subject of a conversation to the errors of large corporations, of various departments and officers of the federal government, or of the younger generation; (8) if you frequently use obscenities in your speech; (9) if you find it difficult to compliment or congratulate other people with honest enthusiasm. If *any* of these descriptions applies to you, then—unless both your spouse and a close friend *spontaneously and with obvious sincerity* object, you should conclude that you possess at least some free-floating hostility. Always keep in mind the fact that the greatest obstacle to recognizing the nature of your own hostility is your Type A eagerness to find excuses for it.

Detect the Cause of Your Free-Floating Hostility

We already have emphasized that insecurity or inadequate self-esteem, or both, underlie a sense of time urgency and free-floating hostility. It has been our experience studying hostile Type A persons before and after their heart attacks that in most cases both insecurity and low self-esteem must be present to account for free-floating hostility. In other words, those few Type A's who harbor insecurity despite the fact that they have always enjoyed adequate love and affection from their parents, siblings, and friends, do not as a rule exhibit free-floating hostility. Freud spoke of the psychic comfort derived from being one's mother's "undisputed darling"; if there is a single fact about a hostile Type A we are prepared to say is *always* true, it is this: He was never his mother's "undisputed darling." This goes equally for the hostile Type A chief executive officer of a multibillion dollar corporate conglomerate or a hostile Type A janitor working in the basement of a ghetto apartment complex.

Those RCPP participants (approximately 45 percent of the whole group) who reported on questionnaires that they had not received sufficient love and affection from their mothers, also unanimously noted that their free-floating hostility had begun before they had reached eleven years of age. We were startled when some of our middle-aged participants openly, almost belligerently derided either or both of their parents, who in most cases had been dead for many years. Exactly like Type A Ernest Hemingway ("I hate her guts and she hates mine. She forced my father to suicide") or Maria Callas (who wrote to a friend, after refusing to pay her father's hospital bill, "I hope the newspapers don't catch on. Then I'll really curse the moment I had any parent at all"), scores of our RCPP participants preserved their anger for many years. Here are some of their comments:

When my father was dying of cancer, my wife thought I should visit him, but I refused to see him.

When I told him on the phone that I made the All-American football team, he said, "Well, pretty good, but I always thought your brother was a better player than you." That did it! I knew that I never would be able to please or satisfy him in the future, never, never, never! You know, we never had an honest-to-God conversation in my entire life. No sir.

My trouble began when I was three years old and a kerosene lamp fell on my head. My mother screamed *at* me and verbally abused me. Sure, forty years later, I realized that she had yelled at me only because the accident had frightened her, but nevertheless from that time on I found fault with everybody, particularly my teachers in elementary school.

I don't ever remember my mother ever kissing or hugging me. Not once! The best I ever could expect from her was a grudging grunt indicating that she couldn't find anything at that moment to complain about.

I don't know why even after forty years, my mother and I can't talk to each other without her getting my hackles up. I tell myself to "cool it," that she's an old woman, but it doesn't do any good, she just sticks it in and turns it.

It is noteworthy that as our RCPP participants were saying such things, their voices became harsh and unpleasant, and they exhibited many of the hostile psychomotor manifestations of Type A behavior described in Chapter 2.

There can be no question that many parents of Type A's were deeply unloving. Hemingway's mother did disapprove of and try to dominate him. Indeed, she supposedly sent him (along with a package of cookies) the gun that his father had used to kill himself with. According to Adrianna Stassinopoulos's biography of Maria Callas, her mother also was so upset that she hadn't turned out to be a boy that she refused to nurse her for several days. But one question remains unanswered: How lovable were the Type A's, even as infants? How many of them accepted kisses and other caresses but did not return them? There is no way to know now how often they stubbornly opposed reasonable requests, exploded in violent temper tantrums or sibling jealousies, habitually scowled and whined their way through childhood. Logic tells us that the curse must begin somewhere, however; more than likely, at this infant stage, it is with the parents, or at least in the family. Sibling rivalries can be destructive too.

Of course, a loss of self-esteem does not always take place in one's very early childhood. It can come in high school or college, touched off by a conviction that you are not well liked by your fellow students. Some of the RCPP participants suffered from free-floating hostility that either developed or was reactivated in their early, middle, and even late adulthood. The most frequent causes of it were (1) unsatisfactory marital relations, (2) strife with offspring, and (3) quarrels with superiors, peers, or subordinates on the job. The problem with analyzing this sort of hostility lies in the fact that there is no way to tell what came first—whether a basic pre-existing hostility was not itself responsible for the poor relations between the parties. Nothing is more contagious than hostility, and a hostile Type A is like a plague carrier. Apart from these possible exceptions, however, the free-floating hostility of most Type A's should be traced to causes much earlier than middle or late adulthood.

Treating Hostility

REPLACE OLD BELIEFS WITH NEW ONES

We have already explained how any hope of getting rid of a sense of time urgency depends on getting rid of some old beliefs and adopting new ones. The same goes for getting rid of free-floating hostility. However, it has been our experience that the process is much more difficult in the latter case. This is probably because the changes in beliefs we have recommended for dealing with time urgency make "cash register" sense, whereas those intended to reduce free-floating hostility may strike you as much less obvious and direct. The difference probably lies in the fact that the presence of free-floating hostility in you may itself be harder for you to accept than the presence of a sense of time urgency.

Subtle or not, it is imperative that you do something about any hostility you may have. We found in our RCPP study that of all known coronary risk factors, including even a sense of time urgency, free-floating hostility appeared to be the one whose continued presence was most closely associated with a second heart attack or sudden death. The presence of this factor also decided whether a participant's life would continue to be mean-spirited, just as its absence betokened a new spirit-enhancing existence.

Let us now consider some of the false old beliefs that must be changed, and the new ones that should take their place. Remember as we proceed that beliefs are in fact no more or less than filters through which we perceive and deal with the world outside ourselves.

I NEED A CERTAIN AMOUNT OF HOSTILITY TO GET AHEAD IN THE WORLD. While you could find some justification, of a superficial kind at least, for believing that your sense of time urgency was in part responsible for your vocational successes, it is a good bit harder to argue that a tendency to become easily irritated, aggravated, or angry about the trivial errors of other persons has contributed to whatever successes you may have enjoyed. Still, some Type A's will try.

It is absolutely clear to us that your free-floating hostility is responsible for flawing your relations with your wife and family members, your friends, your associates, and acquaintances. In the cases of hundreds of RCPP participants (and of thousands of other Type A's we have known or treated), the frequent family problems with wives and children can almost always be traced to the Type A's free-floating hostility. The same goes for the difficulties they so often encounter in their relations with business and professional associates, that is, their incorrigible penchant for reacting to events with anger rather than understanding.

I CAN'T DO ANYTHING ABOUT MY HOSTILITY. This belief is hard to shake. Over and over again, we have heard some version of this statement from our RCPP participants: "I know I'm being hostile when I shouldn't be, but I just can't help it." In an odd way, they may be right, or at least partly right, because our studies and those of others have made possible a hypothesis that their bodies have actually become addicted to anger, that is, to an excess of the "struggle hormone" norepinephrine, making them unconsciously seek out situations where anger will be elicited and the hormone secreted. The late novelist Cameron Hawley, after interviewing more than 50 post-infarction subjects (including presidents Lyndon Johnson and Dwight Eisenhower), expressed to us his belief that most of these men were "hooked on adrenaline"* prior to their heart attacks, purposely entering into or creating events which "would excite or anger them."

Nevertheless, even an addiction to some hormone released in excess every time you become aggravated or angry does not mean that you are helpless. We now know from the RCPP study that the intensity of the free-floating hostility of most Type A's can be significantly controlled and reduced with the help of drills, deliberate revision of certain activities, and a clearer understanding of the mechanism by which hostility does its harm. We need not be slaves to our hormones.

OTHER PEOPLE TEND TO BE IGNORANT AND INEPT. If our world were a perfect world inhabited by persons equally perfect, hostile Type A's would very probably still find plenty to complain about. We say this even after observing the decline of hostility in hundreds of our RCPP participants. It now seems apparent that the chronic predisposition of hostile Type A's to criticize and become irritated over the mistakes of others arises not out of any real desire to improve the world or to help those in need of help, but simply out of an urge to assuage their own low self-esteem. When the free-floating hostility is truly serious, the Type A appears to feel an almost physical

---

*More accurately, Hawley should have spoken of norepinephrine, because it is this hormone and not adrenaline that is associated with anger or struggle.

revulsion whenever he encounters what appears to him to be a case of inexcusable error, regardless of its seriousness or importance. For example, one of our RCPP participants was out driving with his wife through a shopping center when he noticed that an American flag hanging over a camera store was tattered. He stopped his car, entered the shop, and said to the proprietor, "Your flag outside is torn and I think you should replace it." The proprietor unfortunately happened to be a hostile Type A too and responded accordingly, demanding to know why our participant thought it was any of his business that the flag was torn. "I'm a patriotic American, that's who I am," rejoined our man, and proceeded to engage in a heated and increasingly violent argument about the flag. Finally, actually quivering with rage, he abruptly walked out, slamming the glass door so hard that it cracked. "I was embarrassed to tell my wife just what I did. I did tell her never to buy film from that store. After all I had been a Marine and I am a patriot. There should be more Americans like me."

This is typical of the thousands of accounts of rage we had to listen to during the first few months of the RCPP study, outbursts touched off by delays in the arrival or departure of planes, trains, and buses, by a busy telephone signal, a motorist's error, a fork with unaligned tines at a restaurant, a few drops of coffee sloshed into a saucer, or soup not piping hot. Gradually our participants began to recognize their rages for what they really were—infantile temper tantrums—and started bringing them under control.

Since you cannot possibly hope to avoid all irritants in your environment (including those that are irritating to anyone, not just angry Type A's), your only hope of diminishing your free-floating hostility is to change your attitude toward them. After all, the intensity of an irritant in a very real sense depends upon the irritability of the recipient. Certainly the world contains people who are both inept and annoyingly ignorant. Very little you can do will alter that state of affairs, but patience and a sense of proportion can make you feel better about it. The fact is that we have never encountered a single Type A hostile person whose own irritability did not far exceed the gravity of most of the irritants he encountered. So although your own free-floating hostility originally arose from and is sustained by your low self-esteem, it is also chronically exacerbated by your failure to recognize that many errors and mistakes are just not worth getting upset about.

You probably are not aware of the serious spiritual damage you may be inflicting both upon others and yourself by your obsessive fault-finding. When you constantly attempt to mold other persons to fit an image that you have constructed, you are guilty of what Thomas Merton once described as loving only the reflection of yourself you find in them. We hope that once you recognize the essential evil inherent in this practice, you will not find it difficult to desist; most of our RCPP participants managed to do so. You then may find yourself asking, in some wonderment, the question one participant did: "Why in hell did I ever concern myself with all the crappy little mistakes that other people made?"

I DON'T BELIEVE I CAN EVER FEEL AT EASE WITH DOUBT AND UNCERTAINTY. For far too long, your free-floating hostility has been fueled in part by frustration arising from your losing struggle to wrest unchangeable truths and certainties from the continuous unpredictability that is life. It is time now for you to face up to the fact that there has been and will be only two absolute certainties in your life: your birth and your death. You had no control over the former and you will have very little over the latter—in the long run, none at all. Stretching for three score and ten years (give or take a few) between these two poles is the line of your life, shaped a good deal less than you might think by deliberate choice on your part, and prey to circumstances of every description. It is your life—but it is not really yours.

Hostile Type A's not only expect their environment to present them with absolute truths and certitudes, they also strive to erase doubt and uncertainty from their own thought and actions. They behave as if they expected to remedy deep-seated insecurities and low self-esteem by simple fiat: by regarding everything they do, and every opinion they have, as invariably correct. This sort of attitude understandably often irritates and antagonizes family, friends, and working associates. Indeed, they often find it obnoxious. As Laurens Van der Post once remarked, "Human beings are perhaps never more frightening than when they are convinced *beyond all doubt* that they are right." With that in mind, carefully consider some of your more opinionated and self-righteous acquaintances. Are these the sort of people you enjoy counting as close friends? Is it not possible to detect in them some of the telltale signs of insecurity and low self-esteem? Do they appear to be really happy either with others or themselves? We suspect that the answers to these questions will impress you with the truth of Van der Post's observation. You might then ask yourself whether you would like to associate intimately and indefinitely with a person exactly like yourself. If the answer is negative (as we suspect it may be), be courageous enough to think through the reasons for your judgment.

In his early youth, John Keats made himself miserable searching for immutable principles. Then he formulated a theory of conduct embodying several life-enhancing ways of viewing one's world. For our purposes here, it will be enough to quote just one small section: "...at once it struck me [that a] man of achievement...is capable of [living] in uncertainties, Mysteries, doubts, without any *irritable reaching after fact & reason*." [Our italics.] Over a century later, the brilliant physicist Werner Heisenberg also made peace with himself by concluding that it is impossible to measure both the position and the velocity of a subatomic particle. His uncertainty principle is now a fundamental of nuclear physics. If Heisenberg had been a hostile Type A, it seems at least possible that his findings would have provoked a temper tantrum instead of the patience to explore them fully, a process which brought him a Nobel Prize and gave his fellow scientists a marvelously effective theoretical tool.

Recently we held an informal discussion with some of the senior faculty members of the U.S. Army War College at Carlisle Barracks on the subject of whether a military leader could function effectively if he entertained doubts about the correctness of his judgments. Our final conclusion was that a good military leader should carry and live with many doubts, actively encouraging and welcoming the dissent of his staff until the final battle plan evolves. Even then, the officers insisted, a good general should allow for contingency plans. Most military defeats, they argued, could actually be laid to firmly held bad assumptions on the part of leaders. A little doubt might have saved the day!

But you need not be a poet or a scientist or a general to live quite easily with doubts and uncertainties, or to learn the fruitful consequences of doing so. Good military strategists must incorporate them as part of their planning techniques. Celebrated attorneys know that no case can be expected to develop exactly as planned, and find ways of turning such unknown factors to their strategic advantage. Similarly there are very few good physicians who, after making a diagnosis, do not begin to entertain doubts about whether they are right. "What other defense does my patient have against a possible mistake on my part?" a respected medical colleague recently responded when we asked him about his self-doubts.

We know it is not easy for you to admit that you may have been dead wrong about a previous belief or opinion, especially if you delivered it with the arrogance so common among covertly insecure Type A's. Yet as Oliver Wendell Holmes, Jr., once said, "To have doubted one's own first principles is the mark of a civilized man." Strange as it may seem, an open admission of doubt, uncertainty, error, or even incapability will *not* increase your insecurity or decrease your self-esteem. It usually has precisely the opposite effect. It also will surprise and please a lot of your friends and acquaintances. It is far past time for you to come out from behind this mask of infallibility!

GIVING AND RECEIVING LOVE IS A SIGN OF WEAKNESS. This is one of the saddest false beliefs we know of. As you know, nature resolutely abhors a vacuum. This being so, you have little hope of getting rid of your freefloating hostility unless you have something to put in its place. This something is of course love and affection— precisely these emotional elements whose earlier absence in your life may have been responsible for introducing hostility into your personality.

We have referred to the importance of a surrogate mother in our attempts to modify the Type A behavior of our RCPP participants. We wish it were possible for you to make friends with someone who could give you the sort of unsullied affection and support that our men received, but finding someone of this caliber and gracious intent is not easy.

Many men, particularly those who are in their late forties and fifties, have turned to younger women in their unconscious search for such a person, turning back the clock of their lives by dressing in a more youthful style, taking up various strenuous sports, dancing, socializing with younger people, and all the while indulging in the hectic sexual rhythms of a "born again" lover. What all of this leads to in the majority of cases is spiritual catastrophe. Certainly in our experience we never have known a single hostile individual taking this pathway to have lost one whit of his hostility.

Sometimes the wife of a hostile Type A man can serve as a surrogate mother, but this is unusual. Wives who have been spiritually bullied by the demands of their Type A husbands for perfection in everything are too emotionally drained even to attempt the role. Such women, whether or not they are aware of it, are generally waiting passively for either their husbands' demise* or a divorce. Unfortunately most wives of Type A men are themselves Type A and often subject to the same emotional disorders. Many of these Type A wives, who also suffer from low self-esteem, married their Type A husbands in the hope of finding a surrogate father. It is not easy for them to mother a person they had hoped would father them.

The wives who do serve as surrogate mothers to their Type A husbands usually are over 55 years of age, exhibit far less Type A behavior than their husbands, possess a very good sense of humor, and appear able to put up with the typical Type A behavioral oddities with as much forbearance as a young mother usually shows to the temper tantrums of her toddler. As one tolerant wife (who unconsciously already seems to be trying to serve as a surrogate mother) told us: "I know George gets all hot and bothered about little things but shucks, he's been doing that even before we got married and that was thirty-four years ago. Deep down, Doctor, he has a heart of gold, so I just try to remember that. But he sure can be a devil when he doesn't get his way."

If you are a Type A man and believe your wife cannot fill the role of a surrogate mother, it will not be easy to find another woman who will be sufficiently mature, wise, tolerant, and understanding to provide you now with the affection, understanding, and comforting counsel you should have received a number of decades earlier from your parents. The converse is true for a Type A woman. This being the case, you will have to seek different varieties of love and affection from other sources.

---

*We have interviewed a number of widows of recently deceased middle-aged coronary patients. With few exceptions, these widows stated that they felt relieved after their husband's death. Their relief consisted essentially of no longer (1) having to think and act precisely as their husbands demanded, (2) being always fearful of frequent and unpredictable outbreaks of anger and vituperation, and (3) having to serve as "umpires" when husbands and children engage in "yelling contests." These memories of course reflect the husbands' free-floating hostility.

HIGH EXPECTATIONS ARE VERY NECESSARY TO ME. Until you raise your self-esteem, it is almost impossible for you to diminish your free-floating hostility. These two complexes are at opposite ends of your emotional seesaw. For example, if you have just received a huge bonus and praise from your superior, it is not very likely that you will go home, pick a quarrel with your wife, or give a long disciplinary lecture to one of your children. At least not *that* night, because for the moment your self-esteem is in pretty good shape.

But as a rule it is not, and one reason is the nature of your expectations. It is clear to us that in most cases the insecurity and dissatisfaction afflicting hostile Type A's is due not to any failure to achieve but to the unbridled and unrealistic nature of their expectations. In their habitual way, creating a struggle where one need not exist, Type A's are constantly setting goals and ambitions that are by definition unreachable, often rationalizing the process by claiming that they need the spur to get ahead.

You must face up to the necessary job of determining whether or not your expectations exceed your capabilities. If they do, you are old enough to accept the fact and calmly and courageously bring them down to size. They probably have been outrageously blown up for decades. It is time now to retrench and in so doing find a measure of tranquillity and perhaps an ease-up in your free-floating hostility. Some battles are simply not real, and it's high time you make up your mind which are actually worth fighting.

CHANGE SOME OF YOUR PRACTICES

FIND NEW WAYS TO GIVE AND RECEIVE LOVE. We hope that you now see how love is not a weakness but the source of spiritual strength that you have been seeking unconsciously since childhood. But believing in the efficacy of love is not the same as bringing it into your life. You must search for it and then work to install it as an active part of your conscious existence.

You may find it difficult to accept easily the tenderness that a wife, daughter, or son offers you. This is because in the past you have been less interested in their love than in their respect or, at worst, their total subservience to the code of ideals you constructed for their guidance. In demanding their adherence, moreover, it is quite possible that you unconsciously enjoyed playing the role of a bully. If that seems extreme, remember that a bully usually regards himself as having perfectly good reasons for acting as he does.

Begin to recognize that sweetness in your family relations is not a weakness. Heretofore you may have avoided acting toward members of your family with gentleness and compassion because you believed such a posture might encourage them in various errors. Or you may have been reluctant to admit that you have a very pressing need of their affection and concern, stupidly priding yourself on your self-sufficiency. Yet if you love your family in part because of their dependence on you, you also must allow them to see that you too require love from them in return, and that you don't mind being dependent on them for it. The cement of love binding persons together is their *felt* dependence upon each other. Make certain of the integrity and strength of that cement by welcoming openly and frankly a mutuality of affection between you and the members of your family.

We already have spoken of the spiritual strength to be gained from actively maintained friendships. Their number need not be great. In fact, a single true friend outweighs a hundred mere acquaintances in terms of spiritual value. Just as with members of your family, let your friends recognize that you have a very real need for their affection and care. There is no need to hide this; they will respect you for it. Frequently Type A's are loath to accept the fact that they are dependent upon others, not recognizing that the power to remain free is directly related to the number of persons upon whom one is dependent.

In addition to finding new sources of affection and love in old friendships, you may also seek new friends. We would suggest, however, that when encountering a new acquaintance, you ask yourself seriously why you would like to have him as a friend. Who is he? What does he believe in? Does he have a capacity for love, and is he able to give something important of himself? The answers to such questions as these will tell you whether you should take steps to befriend him. There is one precaution, however, that as a Type A person you should always keep in mind: Whenever you encounter someone whose general qualities exceed your own but whose friendship you desire, do not attempt to create a big impression by talking about your achievements. Just allow him to recognize that you wish to be a friend.

Old friends or new, you have an obligation to listen intently and with interest to the events of their lives, feeling real pleasure when they are pleased and sorrow when they are distressed. You must let your friends know that you stand ready to help them whenever and in whatever way they may need you. At all costs avoid giving them unasked-for advice and desist from trying to control any element of their deportment. Remember that you are trying to recover the honest joy of true friendship and the subtle pleasure of emotional dependence on others.

You also would do well to seek love and affection in the world of animals. Recent studies make it very clear that the possession of a pet may play a very important role in preventing death; in fact, one study indicates that during the first year after a heart attack, patients not owning pets died at five times the rate of pet-owning patients. The kind of pet did not appear to matter much—some patients had cats and dogs, of course, but others had parakeets, gerbils, and even an iguana. In view of this variety, it seems obvious to us that the protection conferred by this relationship doesn't have a lot to do with the affection given by the pet to his master (what sort of affection can an iguana give?) but rather stems from the patient's act of showing affection to the pet. In either case, one would be hard put to deny that affection and love regardless of their source do play a powerful role here.

We are certain that this same type of affection and love also can help prevent even a first heart attack.*

Nor does the target of love have to be animal. It is not ridiculous to talk about a gardener's affection for his plants. Perhaps such affection is not reciprocated; we will not venture to speculate about that. Nevertheless, even if it is one-sided, the relationship still contributes to the spiritual sustenance of its caretaker, and probably in turn to his physical well-being as well.

EMPLOY UNDERSTANDING, COMPASSION, AND FORGIVENESS WHEN DEALING WITH OTHERS. You will encounter very few persons with whom you will wish to become intimate. Meanwhile you will continue to meet, as you have in the past, scores of people who do not interest you, and dozens whom you intensely dislike and who immediately induce irritation and aggravation in you. Only too often they are also Type A's, to whose free-floating hostility you respond in kind. The easiest solution to the problem they present is to avoid them whenever possible. Certainly you have nothing to gain from such confrontations except possibly a mirror view of yourself at your worst.

A second measure you should always take when you cannot avoid communicating with other hostile Type A's is to avoid any subject about which both of you entertain even moderately set opinions. Since neither of you is likely to give way, the best you can hope for is that your already aroused irritation will not flare into sheer fury. F. Scott Fitzgerald was aware of the pitfalls in such confrontations when he wrote: "Very strong personalities must confine themselves in mutual conversations to very gentle subjects."

The very best way for you to cope with a variety of

*It has been known for over half a century that feeding a rabbit just a few grams of cholesterol daily will produce coronary artery disease in a few months. It was not discovered until 1982, however, that if a cholesterol-fed rabbit was gently fondled several times a day, its coronary artery disease was strikingly inhibited.

unpleasant persons involves the use of what we may term the lenses of understanding, pity, and forgiveness. When you encounter someone whose manners or actions may at first glance threaten to annoy or anger you, begin by asking yourself the following questions:

1. What is this person's background and what possible circumstances may have led to this sort of behavior?
2. How would I feel or act if I were in this person's position, given the pressures he is under, his capacities, and his expectations?
3. How long has it been, if ever, that anyone caressed this person and said, "Well done. I am proud of you"?
4. Has my own initial response to this person been gracious?
5. If I do become irritated or angry at this person, whom do I benefit? What do I accomplish?

Think about the answers to these questions. Consider them rationally, without letting your antagonism interfere. It is probable that you will find it possible to *understand*, at least to a significant degree, why this person is the way he is. And you will be in turn much readier to pity and forgive him his faults than to become annoyed or angered at them. In other words, by spending a moment getting perspective, then using the lenses of understanding, pity, and forgiveness through which to view him, you may well prevent his actions from touching off your anger. Why not? After all, if you were visiting a zoo and watching the monkeys, you would not react angrily if one of them squealed in rage and threw a banana peel at you. After automatically assessing the situation you would know better than to take it personally; after all, he is a monkey only doing what a monkey might be expected to do, especially a caged monkey. (This analogy is incidentally not far-fetched; truly severe hostile Type A's also are "caged" by their unresolved hates and angers.)

Here's an example of how the process can work. One of our male RCPP subjects was standing in line at a supermarket. When a middle-aged woman just in front of him reached the checkout counter, she began to chat with the checker and then handed her a baby she was carrying. The checker held the baby and cooed at it. Our subject, having been drilled to go through the measures described above, restrained his annoyance. "After I asked myself 'the questions,'" he reported, "I found myself admiring the checker because she still remained human enough not only to talk with a customer but even play with the baby. As a matter of fact, I was tickled with the baby too. After she returned the baby and the woman left, I stepped forward and said, 'That was sure a cute baby, wasn't it?' The checker smiled at me and said, 'Well, thank you, sir. That's my baby. My mother brings her here so I can see her sometimes during the day.'" Our participant paused a few seconds and then asked his group counselor: "Can you imagine what a horse's ass I would have felt like if I had blown my stack at the delay they were causing me?"

We do not believe that to understand all is to forgive all. But we do believe that if you try to understand the reasons why other people act meanly (or *seem* to act meanly) or selfishly, you not only will find many of them more bearable, you will find yourself more lovable. And you will prevent a surge of anger-induced norepinephrine from battering at your vulnerable coronary arteries and their fragile plaques.

SEARCH FOR BEAUTY AND JOY. John Keats claimed "a thing of beauty is a joy forever" and was disposed to find beauty in many things, from a Greek vase to the song of a nightingale. Perhaps it is harder for you, but try. Many things are beautiful, and many things can bring you joy. Nor need your search be confined to beauty in a fleshly form. Sculptures, paintings, jewels, books, songs, flowers, animals—a myriad things and creatures and even situations carry and convey beauty.

Yet there is more. Many people, by their acts of altruism, affection, loyalty, sacrifice, and compassion, have the power to bring you spiritual beauty and joy if you would only allow it. One of the tolls exacted by your unchallenged free-floating hostility is an inability to see how some men and women are capable of acting in magnificently nobel ways. What other species can boast the glory of a Jesus, or of a poverty-stricken monk who liked to talk to birds and bless them?

The point is really simple. Even if you free yourself for no more than a day from slavery to your hostility, there is a chance that your experience of the beautiful and the joyful could so illumine your life that you would be liberated for good. It is not easy for us, hard-bitten veterans of scientific medicine, as our practice of cardiology has forced us to be, to admit that such unquantifiable things as beauty and joy may be more important in protecting against premature CHD than any drug or surgical measure. But now, after our experiences in the RCPP study, we are left with no alternative.

INSTRUCT YOUR ADOLESCENT CHILDREN BY EXAMPLE, NOT BY WORDS. Most of our child-rearing Type A RCPP participants, intent on developing offspring who are not merely handsome, well-behaved, creative, and brilliant, but also successful, regularly lavished admonitions, criticisms, and monotonous homilies upon them. The adolescents, to their parents' dismay, generally responded by becoming sullen and rebellious. In a very real sense, those coronary patients were treating their own children exactly as they had been treated in their own childhood: with a minimum of unconditional love and affection and a maximum of harsh words. The insecurity and low self-esteem of the father were begetting the same emotional defects in his children.

When we discovered how widespread this practice was in our RCPP participants, our first question was how to stop it. The answer itself was obvious: Those guilty of the practice had only to cease giving verbal advice of any kind to their adolescent children, and instead act out the sort of person they wished their sons and daughters to become. A good straightforward solution. But hardly an easy one to put into effect, since carping at one's children, futile as it may be, gets to be a habit. Giving it up will probably not be easy for you, but it offers a real hope of transforming what may now sometimes seem to you to be the nearest thing to a reform school into a home where both you and your children may find repose after a buffeting day.

Two hundred years ago Horace Walpole remarked that after children have reached puberty they are not susceptible to unasked-for advice. We believe that he was right in this, and that indeed you would be well advised to refuse to give advice to any adolescent or postadolescent child—even if he asks you for it—until you answer the following questions in the affirmative:

1. Am I qualified to counsel my child on this matter?
2. Can I be absolutely certain, knowing as I do his intellectual and emotional capacities, that my advice can be followed?
3. Can I be certain that I will not be upset if my child refuses to heed what I say?

If the answer to any one of these questions is no, go no further. In any case, think twice before delivering your lecture. Mull over what Goethe once wrote: "We can't form our children on our own concepts; we must take them and love them as God gives them to us."

There is one exception to this no-advice rule. If you are aware that your child is going to commit or indulge in an act that is evil, you should act promptly and decisively, albeit with a minimum of bombast. (We define an evil act as one that may do or lead to serious damage or injury to others or to your child.) But if it is a question of preventing minor errors and mistakes—even though your advice might have avoided them—desist. Children who are allowed to make mistakes and then to recover from them gain self-confidence that cannot be obtained in any other way. Moreover, by ceasing to insist on correct behavior by your children at all times under all circumstances, you may well bring a new era of peace to your evening dinner table—to say nothing of relief to your spouse, who has had many reasons to fear a final explosion bringing an end to whatever fragments of family amity still exist.

STOP USING OBSCENITY. Soldiers are famous for sprinkling their conversation with obscenities and have been for centuries; the same can be said for other classes of individuals. It at first surprised us to discover that most hostile Type A men are prone to use the same words to vent their free-floating anger, whatever their occupation or social class. It finally became apparent to us when we observed how very rarely Type B's did this, and how Type A women are more and more likely to indulge themselves in the same way.

We asked a number of our RCPP participants why they so often felt impelled to express themselves in frankly obscene or scatological terms. From their responses we concluded that their use of four-letter words does not reflect a dearth of alternative expressions; on the contrary, they use these words simply because *they are* ugly, and seem to carry an extra weight of anger and violence and disgust. Watching their faces, we noted how often looks of fury flitted across as they recalled their last obscene outburst.

If it were true, as our participants seemed to feel, that anger could be vented effectively by recourse to obscenity, of course we would strongly urge you to let streams of noisome expletives flow freely. But from our observations we strongly suspect that obscenity, far from venting hostility, often intensifies it.

If in fact speech is, as has been said, the mirror of the soul, is there anyone who would like to see his soul expressed in terms of filth? Actually, it is quite easy to desist from obscenity. Moreover, in eliminating it from your conversation, you may well discover that some of your hostility has been eliminated too. Don't be surprised if your friends tell you how much more pleasant you are to be with since you cleaned up your language. Remember that not even a thief or a prostitute ever actually enjoys listening to profanity.

MONITOR YOUR HOSTILITY. In the preceding chapter, we recommend that you construct an internal monitor that can embody the principles needed to alleviate your sense of time urgency and react immediately to any transgression on your part. This internal monitor can be further developed to incorporate all the principles designed to alleviate your free-floating hostility. It should instantaneously order you to employ your new lenses of understanding, compassion, and forgiveness whenever you are confronted with any person or situation that threatens to touch off your irritation, aggravation, or anger. Code it to respond to any excuses you may come up with about why the irritation is called for with the words: "I will not accept your rationalizations. You have been made too sick too long by your hostility to be able to think sensibly." Assume that you are reacting with your usual hostility and your addiction to its hormonal products. Take out your "lenses" and use them.

IF YOU DO BECOME ANGRY, AVOID FOOD. We earlier referred to the deadly peril presented to any Type A already suffering from clinical coronary heart disease from any meal containing more than an ounce of either vegetable or animal fat. Indeed, it is probable that at least half of the 38 cardiac deaths that occurred during the first three years of the RCPP study were chiefly due to this cause. Once absorbed in the blood, such fat disappears very, very slowly, even in healthy Type A's, particularly if the person is either struggling against time or allowing his free-floating hostility to express itself. The excess norepinephrine generated by either of these two core emotional components of Type A behavior is probably responsible for slowing the clearance of the fat from the blood, which in turn leads to the blood's sludging (described in Chapter 2) that can choke off hundreds of small blood vessels for as long as 12 hours. If these small vessels are in the heart, a heart attack—and death—may and frequently does occur.

It is thus chance-taking of the most lethal kind for a person with *known* CHD to attempt to eat a meal if he is aggravated, angry, or even just stewing over an earlier unpleasant incident. On the other hand, many Type A's who do not suffer any symptoms of CHD usually can survive ingesting a meal heavy in fat, even if they are excited or angry while eating. The trouble is that quite a significant fraction of these persons over 35 years of age harbor serious coronary artery disease *and don't know it*. Their symptoms are still hidden. We suspect that for them to eat a fatty meal in a hurry or while hostile is as dangerous as it would be if their CHD were overt. In short, if you are adult and if you cannot keep from becoming irritated, aggravated, impatient, or angry, at least have enough common sense to avoid food of any kind during or immediately after your emotional perturbation. However, if you are accustomed to drinking alcoholic beverages, you might drink up to two ounces of whiskey under such conditions with relative impunity.

GENERAL DRILLS

This category of drills, like those designed to combat hurry sickness (see Chapter 11), should be practiced at all times.

a. Announce openly, to your spouse or to a close friend, your intention to eliminate your free-floating hostility. One of the most effective ways of dealing with a stubborn habit is to let others know you intend to rid yourself of it. This is because you are staking your pride on the battle. If you fail to effect the change, you will suffer a loss of face, and you know it. Your sense of pride comes to the support of your will. If you find yourself reluctant to take this course, it may mean that your self-respect has been abased to the point of impotence by your bone-deep belligerence. That's *really* something to worry about!

Dozens of our RCPP participants deliberately forewarned their spouses of their determination to bring their insensate irritability under control, requesting them to give a prearranged signal whenever they observed the signs of an eruption coming on. Furthermore, our participants promised (and this is an important point) that when they got the signal, they would make no attempt to justify their anger but would simply stop immediately. We had one bit of advice for the spouse who volunteered to give the signal, however: She (or he) should smile tenderly and lovingly when doing so. Remember that after all the Type A is trying to change, and recovering one's freedom from an addiction is always a difficult business. A warm word of congratulation at the right moment is appropriate.

b. Regularly express your appreciation for the encouragement and help of your spouse and others. If American husbands and wives continued in the years following their marriage to express their affection and admiration for each other as freely and frequently as they did in the months before, we seriously doubt that the present melancholy divorce rate would be as high as it is. Conjugal love cannot thrive exclusively on efficiency in a kitchen, or an office or, for that matter, a king-size bed. Skill in these things may be desirable, but they at best represent only the sinews and not the soul of a successful marriage.

What is urgently needed to make a marriage joyful and life-enhancing is the verbal and tactile expression of tenderness and gratitude. We do not know just why it is so difficult and embarrassing for a husband or wife of ten years or more to utter such phrases as "How deeply I love you," "You make coming home such a joy," "You are as attractive as when I met you," or simply, "Thank you." Such expressions were easy enough to utter during courtship. But now, even though your relationship may be close enough, they have probably dropped out of your vocabulary. Quite probably if you are a man your wife may still seem to you adorable, loyal, unselfish, and pretty, even though you don't tell her you think so. But you should realize that your silence may be interpreted as indifference or worse. Anyone taken for granted is automatically diminished, and sometimes even mortally sapped of his/her meaning. Therefore, do overcome your shyness and reluctance. Make a point of praising this human treasure with whom you are so fortunately associated. Add caresses to your words, caresses devoid of lust but rich in affection. A gentle grasp of a hand, a touch on the neck or shoulder or knee (or even on the derrière) can transmit messages of tenderness beyond words.

You also should drill yourself to express your affection and love for your children. It is hard to say why so many parents find this difficult, especially when adolescents are involved, but they do. Perhaps—at least so far as mothers are concerned—so much of their earlier communication with their children involved discipline, and discipline simply doesn't sort well with expressions of tenderness and affection. Here again it is necessary to confront and overcome well-established habits. Don't shirk it; even a partial victory will bring you remarkable gains. Try it yourself. Show love openly in the next few days or weeks. You may be surprised not only at their reaction but at the feeling of warmth you experience yourself.

Most men and women do not find it easy to tell even their closest friends how much they like them. But here again, it will hardly hurt you to try. Tell a friend how much you value him or her, how this friendship has made your life richer and more interesting. If a friend admires a scarf, a tie, a blouse or shirt of yours, send one as a gift; you can afford it.

Similarly, don't merely tell your best friends about books they should read, go out and buy copies for them. *Few events move a human being more than the receipt of an unexpected gift from a good friend.* One reason that it is so moving, incidentally, is that it happens so seldom, even among the very rich.

c. Practice living with uncertainties and doubts by deliberately attempting to adopt unfamiliar and unexpected opinions. You have no doubt experienced how unpleasant it is to be in the company of anyone whose mind is so firmly made up as to be impenetrable to new information. F. Scott Fitzgerald, suffering as badly as he did from alcoholism and Type A behavior, nevertheless saw the importance of flexibility when he remarked that the test of a good mind was the ability to harbor two opposing thoughts and still live at peace with itself and function.

The drill is this: After making up your mind upon any subject, immediately and *enthusiastically* begin to unmake it. For example, if you are convinced that Ronald Reagan has been a superb president, deliberately begin searching for reasons why he has been a poor president. You can detect and gauge the rusty fixity of your own mind by observing how irritating this process is (and how soothing it is to find evidence supporting your original beliefs).

d. Play to lose, at least some of the time. Most of your life you have been playing to win, no matter what the eventual cost. Recall how difficult it was for you to let even your pre-adolescent child beat you in a game of checkers, Ping-Pong, or dominoes. "They have to learn that this is a tough world and if they are going to win, they've got to earn it. No one gives nobody nothing," a Type A truck driver told us during one counseling session, failing to recognize that what he considered wisdom was in fact a dead giveaway as to the shakiness of his own sense of security. We mention this because more than 95 percent of our RCPP Type A coronary participants responded in the same fashion when asked if they ever deliberately let their young children win a contest. Type B's, on the other hand, almost always answered that they let them win occasionally: "Otherwise they might get discouraged and refuse to play." The contrast has much less to do with a clash of philosophies than it does with the radically different amounts of self-confidence and self-esteem in Type A's and Type B's.

In games of fun, then, allow your spouse and your children to feel the pleasure of victory occasionally, instead of forcing them to endure the endless defeats necessary to protect *your* security and self-esteem. A willingness to welcome defeat by your teen-ager in such games as Ping-Pong, tennis, and golf is likely to make him admire and love you more. He will remember how you taught him, not simply how you insisted on proving your superiority. Your insecurity may encourage you to rationalize along the lines of "it isn't honest to lose on purpose." We can only respond that if it means building up the egos of members of your family, bestowing pleasure, and promoting family cohesion, then by all means be dishonest. Nobody ever got arrested for this sort of midemeanor!

There is another reason to lose which may sound odd to you. By ceasing to concentrate on winning, you can sometimes improve your skills. Many Type A golfers and tennis players could be far better players if they worked at improving their game instead of always trying to come out on top

e. Start smiling at other people and laughing at yourself. This may at first glance appear to you to be a foolishly ineffective way to reduce the intensity of your free-floating hostility, especially at moments when you feel like throwing a chair at somebody. To our surprise, however, we found that it works. In fact, it turned out to be one of the best tools at our disposal in the RCPP study.

This fact would probably not have come as a surprise to Charles Darwin, who was fairly certain that emotion could not exist independent of an appropriate physical manifestation. Thus if our facial muscles could only form a smile and if we lacked the ability to weep tears, he believed, we probably would not be able to *feel* sorrow. Whether or not Darwin was correct, and he has his supporters on this point even today, his notion is very much of a piece with a comment made by William James in 1890: "Cerebral processes are almost feelingless, so far as we can judge, until they summon help from parts below. . . . If we wish to conquer undesirable emotional tendencies in ourselves, we must assiduously, and in the first instance, cold-bloodedly go through the outward movements of those contrary dispositions which we prefer to cultivate. . . . Smooth the brow, brighten the eye . . . speak in a major key, pass the genial compliment, and your heart must be frigid indeed if it does not gradually thaw. This is recognized by all psychologists, only they fail to see its full import." No other simple statement has helped us more in erasing free-floating hostility from the personality of our RCPP Type A participants.

You might be inclined to believe that any person simply twisting his mouth into a smile is behaving like a hypocrite. To avoid this charge we advised our participants to think deliberately of some beautiful or happy event as they smiled. After a few weeks of consciously combining the memories with their manufactured smiles, they found that the association became automatic—that every time they smiled their minds spontaneously called forth a pleasant thought. Beyond that, if a participant *first* brought to mind a pleasing memory, he immediately found himself smiling. In neither case did there any longer seem to be room for hostility.

We know that such a drill as this may strike the sophisticated reader as naïve and simplistic. We can only reply that our one purpose here was to supplant anger and irritation with pleasure and joy in the lives of our participants, and these maneuvers did the trick. So feel free to doubt the efficacy of this drill all you want, but try it and see how within a week or so the general aspect of your life is happier both in your eyes and the eyes of your family and friends. Besides, that artery-damaging excess norepinephrine is automatically reduced.

Many of our subjects in beginning the drill of smiling asked us whom they should smile at. The answer is that you should first practice smiling at yourself in a mirror, always carefully noting the eyelids and the corners of your mouth to make sure that the smile is loose, flexible, and authentic. Following this solitary exercise, begin to smile more frequently at your spouse, children, and close friends. As you become more comfortable and adept, smile at couples or well-dressed old ladies you encounter on the street, then at fellow employees, store clerks, barbers or hairdressers, waiters and waitresses, indeed even at those motorists and bus drivers who formerly attracted only your scorn and anger.

Finally, as you are learning to smile at a variety of other people, stop taking *yourself* so seriously.* Discover things about yourself to smile at, even laugh at. (Don't worry, there are plenty.) When you are at last able to view your own actions with a degree of skepticism and humor, especially those actions which you heretofore considered deeply meritorious and noble, you will find that you have come a long way in strengthening your self-esteem. And as we have said, free-floating hostility wanes as self-esteem waxes.

f. Do away with ideals that are really excuses for anger. More often than not, Type A's who are fiercely

---

*One of Harvard University's most distinguished scientists recently told us how he had for many years noticed that it was only those among his colleagues "who couldn't laugh at themselves" who appeared to suffer heart attacks.

addicted to their free-floating hostility argue that they are really idealists with a responsibility for keeping people up to the mark. Needless to say, they are always being disappointed by the failure of others to meet their standards. The fact is that the so-called ideals of the average hostile Type A are actually nothing more than traps unconsciously constructed to ensnare other persons, thus making the Type A feel superior and justifying his contempt. The Type A's distorted psyche is apparently hoping in this way to appease the destructive demands made upon it by his own lack of adequate self-esteem. A casual inspection of any complete dictionary makes clear that an ideal is a standard of excellence *conceived and existing only in the mind*, not in reality. An ideal constructed in the mind of a Type A is almost certain to be skewed and bound to be misused.

During the past few years, listening to so many scores of RCPP participants describe their hate-flawed ideals, we have come to dislike even the sound of the word "ideal." Unattractive as we found our participants' sometime practice of soiling their speech with obscenities, it almost seemed preferable to tired lists of the ideals they were always seeking and failing to find in the thoughts and actions of their fellow men.

If you want to construct standards for your own conduct, do so, but stick to generally accepted models. Be wary of refining these principles further according to your own beliefs. It is difficult to be afflicted with Type A behavior and keep your belief systems entirely straight. If you live according to the principles most other people consider adequate and helpful to society, ceasing to apply your ideals to all and sundry, you, your family, and your friends will be much happier, and no less moral. This is a trustworthy sort of general drill.

Keep track of just what makes you angry, and set it down in writing. Whenever you do become deeply aggravated or upset, make a note *as soon as possible* of the cause and circumstances. Then, at the end of each week, look over the list. We hope it will be a short one. But even if it isn't, ask yourself, in the light of what you've learned about free-floating hostility, whether the cause in each case really merited your reaction to it and the excess discharge of norepinephrine, and possibly ACTH, that accompanied it. Once again let us emphasize the importance of noting each instance *in writing* and *at the time*. In our experience the hostile Type A erupts so frequently and at such trivial stimuli that even at the end of one day, much less a week, he has already forgotten a good proportion of the incidents and their causes.

It will also help to show this list of anger-provoking events to your spouse or good friend. It will probably require courage to do this, considering the embarrassing pettiness of most of them.

Until you are well on the way to losing your hostility, avoid other angry Type A's. You are undoubtedly aware of certain individuals who by their manner, words, or practices invariably succeed in setting your teeth on edge. Take for granted that they are like you, and that their free-floating hostility is inciting your own. Only when you have changed enough of your own belief systems, established enough new practices, engaged long and conscientiously in these recommended drills, and as a result observed a significant decline in your own hostility, should you venture to approach them again. Do so in a gingerly fashion. And even then, ask yourself if they are people really worth spending time with.

SPECIFIC DRILLS

The specific drills against free-floating hostility are meant to be practiced on a regular basis, like the drills against a sense of time urgency given in Chapter 11. They should be added to the drill book described on pp. 207 and 213,

interspersing them with the specific drills presented earlier.

a. Look at yourself in the mirror at midday and
again when you first arrive home in the evening
to see if your face exhibits irritation, aggravation, or anger.

b. Buy a small but thoughtfully chosen gift for your
spouse or some other family member.

c. Ask yourself in the evening: "What did I do
wrong today and what did I do that showed kind-
ness to someone?"

d. Surprise your spouse by taking her or him to
the theater, a concert, the ballet, the movies, or
a nice restaurant. As you go, keep in mind that
you once thought of this person as your sweet-
heart.

e. Say "Good morning" in a *pleasant*, *cheerful*
manner to each member of your family, and later
to those you meet at your place of work.

f. Call or write to an old friend, recognizing as you
do how difficult it is for you to speak or write
about things that you know will be of particular
interest.

g. Deliberately say to someone "Maybe I'm wrong"
at least twice today, even when you are not at
all certain that you are in error.

CHAPTER 13

Alleviating Your Self-Destruct Tendency

Although the instinct for self-destruction is a phenomenon that has been recognized by many psychiatrists, particularly those of the psychoanalytic school, for over a half century, very few cardiologists seem to be aware of it. Yet it is at work in over half of their middle-aged Type A coronary patients. The cardiologists' obtuseness is in part due to their own Type A behavior, which seems to blind them to this tendency in others. A terribly busy and successful Type A cardiologist apparently has a hard time believing that an equally busy and successful Type A businessman harbors an unconscious wish to destroy his career or himself; he has just as hard a time believing that *he* harbors such a wish. If people were colors, how would two greens meeting each other ever recognize the blue component they share?

Still, no cardiologist could be completely ignorant of the Type A's self-destruct tendency if he were willing to listen to the remarks made by his coronary patients as they convalesce from an infarction, remarks so frequently made to nurses and other hospital attendants: "I really didn't want to live when I came in here with this attack." ... "I knew this heart attack was coming but I didn't give a damn." ... "What a relief to be here and out of the rat race I was in." ... "I just wonder if I will be able to return and face up to the mess I left or whether it's worth returning to." How could anyone hear such comments as these (and believe us, they are typical) without suspecting that Type A behavior had driven the speakers to the brink of self-willed oblivion? A ruined heart is in these cases a way out, furnishing many of its victims what one of them aptly called "the purple badge of honorable retreat."

This covert drive toward self-destruction rarely surfaces in the form of an open suicide attempt. Instead, it usually takes such indirect forms as overeating, heavy drinking, failure to exercise, and a forced-draft working schedule involving as many as 20 hours a day, month after month. Type A's guilty of these practices are quite aware of the danger they pose, but seem unwilling to change.

Some severely afflicted Type A's may resort to measures that are career-destroying though not life-threatening. For example, we have already mentioned the two intensely harassed board chairmen of huge multinational corporations who deliberately ruined their careers by failing to file federal income tax returns for years. Their business associates (who were unaware of the self-destruct tendency inherent in certain Type A's) found the behavior of these men inexplicable, and still do. Besides these two obvious cases, we have encountered scores of other Type A's responsible for business or professional decisions that can be explained only in terms of a subsconscious wish to destroy their careers or themselves.

This tendency to self-destruct is by no means present in all Type A persons, and almost never prior to adulthood. Moreover, it is deeply hidden in the unconscious and thus rarely recognized. If despite vocational success you find that you are subject to increasingly frequent episodes of unexplained melancholy and joylessness, or if you are having dreams in which your life appears to be threatened, you might well consider this a hint that the tendency is present and may be growing stronger.

There are probably a number of causes for the introduction and growth of the self-destruct tendency in so many Type A's. We shall describe some of them:

SENSE OF TIME URGENCY

The Type A's incessant struggle to speed up all life processes frequently plays an important role in either initiating a drive to self-destruct or aggravating the intensity of one that already exists. Strange as it may seem, many Type A's become so obsessed with accelerating every aspect of their lives that they finally seem to reach the point of wishing to accelerate their own demise. When a Type A is anxiously eager to see days rush by, he wishes years to pass rapidly too, and after that what besides his own end will satisfy him? Some Type A's insist that all this hurry is simply a desire to bring some project to a successful completion. This rationalization fails to explain why the Type A lacks enough time, on a day-to-day basis, to get done all the things he wants to.

Indeed, it probably is the emotional exhaustion induced by his incessant attempts to cram more work, more events, more of everything into a fixed amount of time that eventually gives rise to a self-destruct tendency in the severely affected Type A. Battered by his unbridled drives, other emotional components seek relief almost at any cost, even extinction!

SELF-HATE

The intensity of self-hate in a Type A is related very closely to the amount of free-floating hostility he harbors, and can be measured by observing how often and how strongly the hostility is expressed. Self-hate is an obvious component of any self-destruct tendency, and its counterpart hostility serves as a most effective mechanism for making things much worse. In the face of unremitting anger, the healing powers of love and affection can have little chance, indeed can scarcely exist. Thus stripped of emotional supports, his personality rendered even less attractive than it was before, the Type A may have a hard time finding anything of himself worth preserving.

LOSS OF THE SPIRITUAL COMPONENT

The personality of the severely affected Type A is further impoverished by the erosion of its spiritual resources as numerical data gradually take over the memory. The joys and pleasures of the past, the satisfactions of the numinous—all these vanish as numbers take their place. A personality so starved, we believe, is predisposed to self-destruction; certainly it is far less able to contend with a self-destruct tendency encouraged by other factors.

LOSS OF SENSE OF HUMOR

Almost no one, even a Type A, can simultaneously nourish both a self-destruct tendency and the ability to laugh at himself and his foibles. If you are capable of finding yourself ridiculous at various times, that proves you still have a sense of proportion and perspective, and probably a fair quantity of common sense. Of course we do not mean to imply that all persons lacking a sense of humor necessarily carry an unconscious wish to destroy their careers or themselves, but if you as a Type A no longer find anything funny about yourself, you probably ought to be concerned. You may be developing an urge toward self-destruction.

DEATH AS A SOLUTION

A certain number of Type A's, particularly if they already suffer from clinical coronary heart disease and possess moderate to large personal estates, are prey to suspicions that their demise may be wished for by members of their families. Unfortunately, the free-floating hostility of some Type A's is so distasteful that in some cases their families *do* yearn (at least subconsciously) for the peace and tranquillity death might bring. This concern doubtlessly strengthens the Type A's covert tendency to self-destruct, as does his disappointment and irritation with the way his family, friends, and acquaintances refuse to give way to his attempts to dominate them.

Finally there is the seldom-spoken but commonly felt dread on the part of the Type A (particularly if he already suffers from clinical CHD) that he may some day be physically dependent upon his spouse or some other member of his family. This looms as a terrifying denial of his life-long boast, "I'm all right, Jack." Plagued by chronic insecurity, the Type A had nevertheless always assumed that at least his body would never let him down. When he begins to fear that he's wrong, his drive to self-destruct is exacerbated. "Better dead than fed and led" is a slogan most Type A's are all too ready to believe in.

Treating the Self–Destruct Tendency

RECOGNIZE ITS PRESENCE

It should be apparent from the above that there are various ways of judging the presence and intensity of a subconscious drive toward self-destruction. Your first duty is to learn whether such a drive exists in you. Here are some things to look for:

As we already have mentioned, *inexplicable* episodes of melancholy strongly suggest the presence of a relatively strong drive for self-destruction in your unconscious. So do dreams in which the dreamer, caught in life-threatening situations, makes no vigorous attempts to escape. Your easy acquiescence in life-threatening eating, smoking, and physical habits, despite your awareness of their possible lethality, is another indicator that the will to die is gaining ascendancy over the will to live. What other conclusion can one reach upon hearing a coronary patient say that he knows his pack-a-day cigarette habit may kill him, "but I'd rather die than give them up," or when another insists, "If I can't ski and jog, I don't *want* to live."

When you find that little happening in your life strikes you as joyous, amusing, funny, or piquant; that almost all of your activities seem merely dutiful and fringed with anxieties; that nothing apart from your work seems either relevant or worthwhile; that most people you meet are boring or irksome, and their conversation is almost insufferable—then you can be fairly sure that there is far more of winter than spring in your spirit. Certainly it is high time that you began to find ways to restore your will to live.

You must force yourself, unwilling or reluctant as you may be, to become a spectator and an admirer of those natural processes that make our brief existence on the planet a matter of wonderment and delight. The violet glows deep blue, the robin sings his short song, the dog's tail wags, the aspen shakes its leaves, the trout rises in the stream, and the flag snaps in the spring wind, offering pleasure not only to others but to you too. Reread and contemplate those parts of Chapter 12 that talk about recovering a sense of life's beauty.

You must learn to take as much interest in your friends and their hopes, activities, and fears as you now do in the accumulation of numbers. Whether they represent the sales of your merchandise, the patients you have taken care of, the clients for whom you have litigated, or the articles or books you have written, such numbers have no lasting meaning; they are just a collection of integers inscribed on paper. Their basic lifelessness now is threatening to engulf you, and the insidious nature of the process should not disguise its evil nature. A review of Chapter 11 will alert you to appropriate actions. And remember, the more reluctant you are to take these actions, the more threatening and powerful your self-destructive urge has become.

If you are suffering periods of inexplicable melancholy

frequently and for long periods, you should consider visiting a psychiatrist or clinical psychologist. If we appear overinsistent on this point, it is because the situation itself may be urgent.

Finally, recognize the fact that any bad dietary, smoking, or drinking habit in which you indulge is just as dangerous to you as it would be to anyone else. Don't try to fool yourself on this score. You should consider these habits as direct manifestations of your drive for self-extinction. Whether you are prepared to do something about them or not is an obvious and vivid test of your remaining will to live.

TAKE POSITIVE STEPS TO TURN THINGS AROUND

If you harbor an urge toward self-destruction, conscious awareness of the fact will not make it disappear. Neither will mere wishing reduce its dire threat. You must take deliberate steps to restore your will to live and to eliminate the underlying causes of your tendency to destroy your career or yourself.

These steps will involve a series of decisions, none of them easy for any Type A to make, aimed at abridging your overinvolvement in your work and reducing your free-floating hostility. We have no wish to disguise the fact that you may be forced to take these steps by a sheer act of will, since the natural joy in life that guides most people may have been virtually wiped out in you by the power of your drive toward self-extinction. Remember that this drive flourished exactly as your pleasure in the grace notes of life withered and died; now, overcome by its implacable energy, you have very few resources left to you in your sadly belated wish to be saved. It will take a special kind of courage not only to halt your passage into the dark but to move back into the light again.

You must cut back on activities connected with your work, and probably some of those ironically identified as leisure-time. There is no other way to allay the emotional exhaustion caused by your incessant battle against the normal capacity of time. Review Chapter 11 on the specific measures you should take, keeping in mind that with a tendency to self-destruct already present in your personality such measures are no longer merely desirable. They are urgent and mandatory.

CHAPTER 14

How to Avoid a Heart Attack

It should be apparent to you at this point that a heart attack is not an unpredictable tragedy, an unavoidable bit of very bad luck like an earthquake, a tornado, or a bolt of lightning. The preceding chapters should, we trust, have made clear that most people actually have had to work quite hard and long at getting a heart attack. Just consider how much energy a Type A puts into fighting time and other persons at such length and with such intensity!

However, while diminishing your sense of time urgency and free-floating hostility by the measures we have suggested in the preceding chapters is critically important, these actions alone cannot guarantee you, as a Type A, immunity to a heart attack (or to a second attack if you have already suffered a first one). If you are over 25 years of age, your coronary arteries almost certainly contain sizable and probably decaying plaques obstructing more than half of the arteries' internal diameter (or lumen), the result of decades of hormonal assault induced by constant aggravation, irritation, anger, and impatience (AIAI). You may suffer from such plaques and still be entirely free of symptoms; 20 percent of a cross-sectional group of 150 supposedly healthy U.S. Army colonels (average age about 42) recently tested with the treadmill procedure were found to have an obstruction amounting to at least 75 percent of one or more of their three major coronary arteries. Some of these officers were understandably bewildered after they learned about the dangerous state of their coronary vasculature. For over a decade, believing that jogging and running would protect them against heart disease, they had been totally faithful to these exercises which had proved useless, at least in their particular cases.

The damage already done to your coronary arteries by years of eating cholesterol-rich foods and Type A behavior cannot be undone by any change in your diet, drug, type of physical exercise, or behavior pattern. These arterial scars will no more disappear than a scar on your arm will. With reduction in your AIAI and certain other precautions, however, *further* damage may be slowed or avoided. You should keep in mind that even coronary bypass surgery does not clean out the garbage that's already in one's coronary arteries; it simply allows blood to bypass the areas of obstruction.

Let us look now at the other precautions you should take if you wish to forestall cardiac tragedy:

You Must Quit Smoking Cigarettes

There is no doubt whatsoever that persons who smoke more than five to ten cigarettes a day are doing as much as they can to damage not only the internal lining of their coronary arteries but that of other arteries as well (particularly those supplying their legs and feet).

It is admittedly difficult to distinguish damage done by excess smoking of cigarettes from that done by Type A behavior; the heavy smoker is almost always a Type A. Certain epidemiologists employing a technique called multivariate analysis claim they can do so; indeed, they convinced a special panel of experts appointed by the National Heart, Lung and Blood Institute to that effect. Whatever the truth of this matter may be, we ourselves believe that excess cigarette smoking, like Type A behavior, probably induces an excess discharge of norepinephrine. Smoking is known to cause an excess of carbon monoxide circulating in the blood and this gas injures the lining of arteries. No matter how you look at it, cigarette smoking really is bad business for *all* the arteries of the body. Persons already suffering from clinical CHD and subject to attacks of angina are often disappointed to find that giving up cigarette smoking does nothing to stop the angina. Many of them then take up smoking again, not realizing that the damage done to an artery by smoking cannot be undone. Here again, the best one can hope for is to avoid making the damage worse.

While it is statistically true that *habitual* pipe smokers suffer from clinical CHD no more frequently than do non-smokers, the reason is almost certainly not the "harm-lessness" of pipe tobacco, or the tendency of the pipe smoker not to inhale, but rather the fact that the pipe smoker is most likely a Type B. A note of caution is in order for the Type A cigarette smoker who thinks that taking up a pipe will protect him. Cigarette smokers are used to inhaling, and are likely to inhale pipe smoke too by force of habit. If you are a cigarette smoker who has made the switch, try deliberately inhaling some of your pipe smoke. If it doesn't make you cough violently, then you have probably been inhaling it all along.

As was pointed out in *Type A Behavior and Your Heart*, the addiction of a cigarette smoker to the cigarette is by no means solely or even mostly due to the nicotine content of the cigarette. If this were so, then an oral dose of nicotine would satisfy the longings of a former cigarette smoker. It does not. *What the cigarette smoker is addicted to is the peculiar emotional sensation he receives when tobacco smoke comes into contact with the surface tissues of his lungs.* Thus a former cigarette smoker encouraged to inhale smoke from a cigarette made up of corn tassels (which contains no nicotine) feels almost as satisfied as if he inhaled real tobacco smoke. We are convinced that it is this "smoke-lung" reaction which makes cigarette smoking so addictive.

It is never easy for an inhaling cigarette smoker to quit, particularly if he smokes more than a pack a day. One of the most immediate and annoying withdrawal symptoms is a feeling of tremulousness, accompanied by a feeling of confused thinking, and even slurred speech. This is in part due to the sudden reduction in the smoker's chronically excessive norepinephrine (and epinephrine) discharge rate, which evoked and maintained a certain level of sugar in the blood. Following the abrupt withdrawal of this stimulus, the blood sugar falls, and the result is a mental and physical state comparable to that of a diabetic whose blood sugar has been lowered excessively by too large an injection of insulin. Although the acute withdrawal symptoms may last only a few days, nevertheless the lowered level of blood sugar, combined with general restlessness and unhappiness (the smoker of course misses the smoke-lung palliative sensation), frequently leads to eating too much sugar-rich foods. This in turn leads to increased weight, which sometimes is in itself enough to break the fragile will of the ex-smoker and give him what looks like a good reason to resume.

Like the ex-alcoholic, the ex-smoker is prey for many months, even years, to an unconscious conflict between a deeply rooted habit and his own willpower. No matter what tactics are employed, the rate of failure is well over 25 percent—unless the former smoker already suffers from clinical CHD, lung cancer, leg artery obstructions, emphysema, chronic bronchitis, or peptic ulcer. In the latter case the success rate is much higher, simply because willpower gets an effective helping hand from stark fear and bodily distress. It is a pity that such fear cannot be brought to play a role *before* illness develops!

We often have been asked if a Type A who manages to diminish the intensity of his AIAI syndrome but continues to smoke will receive some protection against clinical CHD. Our answer is, "Probably, but we aren't at all sure." We must answer in this way because though our participants in the RCPP study did reduce their vulnerability to recurrent heart attacks radically by changing their Type A behavior, all of them also had stopped smoking months or years before entering the study.

Incidentally, we have said nothing here about the extreme danger of lung cancer connected with smoking and inhaling cigarettes. The omission has nothing to do with a lack of concern on our part with this aspect of smoking; it's just that we are focusing on the heart.

You Must Eat Wisely

We now believe that some of the dietary advice given in *Type A Behavior and Your Heart*, while conforming in general to the coronary dietary instructions advised at that time by various health agencies, was more liberal than it should have been. In that book, the general diet we suggested permitted even the person already ill with clinical CHD approximately 160 grams (five and a half ounces) of both unsaturated and saturated fat per day.

The Pritikin Diet, a regimen devised and promoted by Nathan Pritikin and his associates in a book and at an institute in Santa Monica, restricts cardiac patients to less than a tenth of this amount. Ideally, perhaps, this extremely low-fat diet (approximately a half ounce per day) is to be preferred over other diets recommended by various authorities. But it may be a little too strict to be practical. In our experience, most of the coronary patients we know who have visited the Pritikin establishment revert to their old dietary habits a few months after leaving Santa Monica. It is quite easy to change the dietary habits of some persons drastically for a short period but it is far more difficult to do so permanently. Mr. Pritikin of course may think differently, but his direct observations have been mainly limited not only to a small subset of quite sick persons but also to a short time (generally a few weeks). There is no question, however, that hundreds of coronary patients have been relieved of their angina *by the particular ambience* of the Pritikin institute, and the dietary regimen they followed there.

Since 1978 we have been impressed by the lethal threat posed to a coronary patient of a *single* meal rich in fat (that is, a single meal containing a total of more than one ounce of either vegetable or animal fat). The danger arises from several causes. First, after the ingestion of any kind of food the blood vessels of the digestive tissues dilate, demanding a greater supply of blood. The degree of such dilation depends largely upon the nature of the food consumed, and of all types of food, fats cause the intestinal blood vessels to dilate most. Since your circulatory system is closed, a greater flow of blood to one segment—in this case, the digestive tract—means less blood for the other segments, including of course those blood vessels serving the heart itself. Anyone suffering from coronary heart disease is already getting a severely reduced flow of blood through his damaged coronary arteries, and this further reduction may (and frequently does) result in angina (which is nothing more or less than chest pain due to inadequate blood flow to the heart muscle), a heart attack, or sudden cardiac death.

Unfortunately, during the last few decades cardiologists have been so intent upon reducing the chronic blood level of cholesterol of their patients by advising them to replace their intake of animal fat with vegetable fat, that they have failed to keep in mind the fact that the above sequence of blood vessel dilation in organs outside the heart takes place as promptly and as intensely after the ingestion of corn oil, let us say, as it does after the ingestion of a pork chop. This myopia on the part of the car-

I. A Daily Diet Plan for the Coronary Patient or the Adult Type A Person

Type of Food	Total Daily Amount (oz.)	Approx. Cholesterol (mg. per day)	Approx. Fat[1] (g. per day)	Approx. Protein (g. per day)	Approx. Carbohydrates (g. per day)	Approx. Calories (per day)
A. 2 servings lean meat, fish or fowl	8	192	56	56	0	728
B. 4 servings vegetables[2]	16	0	3	13	48	271
C. 2 servings salad (no dressing)	8	0	2	4	12	94
D. 2 glasses skim milk	16	0	0	16	16	128
E. 2 slices bread	2	20	2	4	32	164
F. Oleo-margarine[3]	1.5	0	40	0	0	320
F. Fruits	6	0	0	1	24	100
H. One serving cereal	2	0	0	1	52	212
Daily Total	59.5	212	103	95	184	2017

II. *Dietary Precautions*
   A. Avoid These Foods
      1. Egg yolks
      2. All animal organs, including roe
      3. All shellfish
      4. Butter, cream, ice cream, and foods containing these
      5. All cheeses except cheeses processed to be cholesterol-free and low in fat
      6. All hors d'oeuvres
      7. Ordinary hamburger meat
   B. *Cut Down Your Intake of These Foods*
      1. All foods containing sugar, honey, syrup, or molasses

---

(1) A person with CHD should never ingest more than 32 grams (1 oz.) of fat in any single meal.
(2) All vegetables except avocado and eggplant, that is.
(3) Includes oleomargarine in foods.

C. *Eat As Much As You Like Unless You Observe That You
   Are Gaining Excess Weight*
    1. All vegetables (except avocado and eggplant)
    2. Egg whites
    3. Skim milk, buttermilk, yogurt
    4. Gelatin products (e.g. Jello-O)

diological establishment probably accounts for a large
number of sudden deaths within minutes or hours of eating
a fat-rich meal.

The second cause for the occurrence of angina, a heart
attack, or sudden cardiac death under these circumstances is the phenomenon of sludging (described on p. 62)
that occurs in cardiac patients and in Type A's whenever
the blood concentration of fat reaches high levels and
stays there for three to six hours. A fatty meal can cause
this.

The plan shown opposite outlines a general daily diet
that we believe will be safe for most persons who already
suffer from clinical CHD. It is possible that its meat-fish-
fowl allowance of eight ounces per day may in some cases
permit the coronary patient too much fat. Certainly the
daily total should *never* be consumed in a single serving.
If you find yourself with angina, palpitation, or breath-
lessness while following this diet, its fat content may be
too large for you and you should probably turn to the
more restrictive Pritikin diet.

The dietary recommendations we give here should be
seriously considered not only by the person already sick
with clinical CHD but by most adults. Certainly Type A
adults would be well advised to adhere to it because at
least two-thirds of them may be certain that they already
have significant atherosclerotic plaques obstructing one
or more of their three coronary arteries. We believe that
this diet would also well serve young Americans, but we
are not so naïve as to think that many of them, or their
parents, are likely to accept it.* A fair number of parents

---

*While most epidemiologists are convinced that the usual American choles-
terol-rich diet lays the groundwork for coronary heart disease in adults, it is

already have struggles enough these days to keep
their children from becoming addicted to alcohol or mind-
eroding drugs.

You Must Avoid Dangerous Forms of Physical Activity

When *Type A Behavior and Your Heart* first appeared in
1974, quite a few people were jogging and running for
exercise. Now, in 1982, there has been an enormous
increase in their numbers. Millions of "born again" ath-
letes are pounding away on pavements, cinders, and dirt.
By now hundreds, perhaps thousands, of them have died
instantaneously of a heart seizure, broken their necks
falling over some unseen obstacle, been injured or killed
by automobiles or motorcycles.

It is far from easy to come up with statistical proof of
the dangers of jogging and running, but Dr. William Stur-
ner of the office of the Medical Examiner in Rhode Island,
together with several associates, recently published a
suggestive study in the *Journal of the American Medical
Association*. They studied cases of sudden death in con-
junction with jogging and running in Rhode Island over a
period of six years (1975–1981), analyzing them in terms
of the runner's age, experience, physical condition, and
cause of death. Their data gives us a chance for the first
time to make some informed guesses about running-asso-
ciated deaths in the entire United States.

extremely difficult to convince children and adolescents to cut down on their
consumption of such things as ice cream, pizza, tacos, chili, cheeseburgers,
milk shakes, cakes, cookies, and pies. In part the problem is the failure of
pediatricians to occupy themselves with a disease that will not strike their
patients until long after they themselves have retired from practice, in part
the inability of maternal pressure to oversome peer pressure, in part the
reluctance of the National Academy of Science to offer effective criticism of
the fat and cholesterol "lushness" of the typical American diet. It has already
been shown that this diet helps produce significant atherosclerotic wounds in
one or more of the three coronary arteries in 75 percent of American young
people before they reach the age of 25.

The article reports that during the time of the study at least 12 men died while running or immediately afterward in the state of Rhode Island (population about one million), apart from those killed in accidents. Extrapolating this number for the entire United States (population about 225 million), we come up with approximately 455 cases of sudden deaths *per year* among joggers and runners—almost all of them caused by heart disease. (According to statistics compiled by the Insurance Institute of Highway Safety, another 54 or more deaths are due to motor vehicles hitting runners on the road each year—more than half after dark. Thus the total of running-related deaths is in excess of 500 a year.)

At least 90 percent of those dying suddenly in Rhode Island were found to harbor seriously diseased coronary arteries, and some of them also exhibited large infarcts at autopsy. However no more than half the runners, whose average age was 47, had been *aware* of the desperate condition of their coronary arteries. These pathological findings in general agree with those observed in other studies dealing with persons dying while running or jogging. The Rhode Island study also reported that approximately 7 percent of all persons aged 30 through 64 jogged at least twice a week. Those who died had run, on the average, approximately 10 hours per week and had been running, again on the average, approximately three and a half years. Obviously, even experienced runners were vulnerable to sudden death; long practice gave no particular protection. In sum, the study concluded, *sudden cardiac death is seven times more likely to occur in individuals during jogging or running than while they are engaged in more sedentary activities.*

We regard this as extremely significant. Here we have at least 500 deaths taking place each year in individuals indulging in a physical activity that has never been shown to protect the coronary arteries in the slightest way, and which some of us suspect actually damages them. It is true that such exercise slows the resting heart rate and improves the muscle tone of the heart. But why should we cardiologists be interested in slowing down a normally beating heart, or in making heart muscle that is already doing a very good job of contracting "pump iron"? We should instead be interested in preventing the interior of coronary arteries from looking like clogged sewer pipes.

If there are no data proving that running provides immunity to clinical CHD, why has it become such a fad? Some of the reasons were discussed in *Type A Behavior and Your Heart*, and need not be repeated at length here. Suffice it to say that no one has encouraged this sort of violent exercise more enthusiastically than American physicians, particularly cardiologists. Moreover, they are so totally convinced that jogging and running afford protection against CHD that they have not only urged it on many of their coronary patients but they themselves do it. As a result, dozens of them have collapsed and died. Admittedly, *any* activity is at least potentially lethal. But why should a middle-aged person engage in an activity that turns him into a machine?

Recently a report appeared in one of our most prestigious medical journals describing the coronary vasculature of five young marathon runners who died while running. Two succumbed to heart attacks while the other three were hit by trucks. All exhibited severe CHD. Whether the marathon running done by these men actually damaged their coronary arteries remains to be decided, yet we have heard several cardiologists argue that if these five dead men had not run, their arterial disease probably would have been even worse. The only way we can respond to this sort of "heads I win, tails you lose" position is to remark that no physician would think very highly of a drug that did no more for his patient than to make him say that he might have felt worse without it. When penicillin was first given to patients suffering from various bacterial infections, the patients had not the slightest doubt that they were miraculously improved!

We also now know (as we did not when *Type A Behavior and Your Heart* was published) that a normal electrocardiographic treadmill test is no proof that a man is free of serious coronary heart disease. Actually the test seems unable to detect the presence of one or more dangerously obstructed coronary arteries in one out of three persons taking the test. The combination of an injection of radioactive material and a treadmill test allows somewhat better detection of diseased coronary arteries but it is by no means foolproof. The only essentially foolproof test is a coronary angiogram, which involves the visualization of the coronary vasculature by a cinematographic recording after the intracoronary injection of a radio-opaque dye. Unfortunately this is still too risky a procedure to use on apparently healthy individuals. Most cardiologists believe that before 1990 rolls around medicine will have discovered an effective and completely safe diagnostic instrument to scan the coronary arteries.

In the meantime, if you are a Type A male over 25 years of age, we would strongly advise you not to indulge in either jogging or running. Nor do we look kindly on handball or racquetball or singles tennis played too intensely. What we do advise enthusiastically is an hour of *pleasant* exercise *each day*. Walking, skating, swimming, bicycle riding (on level ground), gardening, fishing, golfing, horseback riding, downhill skiing (after proper acclimation), hunting, bird watching, ballroom dancing (but no folk dancing), or any sort of physical activity that will not raise your pulse rate above 120 or 125 beats per minute or your blood pressure above 150.

We believe that nature did not intend the hearts of human beings to go awry before the age of 70. But on the other hand, nature did not intend man to force his heart to perform at its utmost capacity for extended periods. Just as a racing car that is forced to run at 200 mph for hours at the Indianapolis Speedway may well break down no matter how well designed it is, so a heart, forced by jogging or running to beat 200 times a minute against a blood pressure more than double the normal level, will sometimes stumble, slip into a chaotic rhythm, and quite possibly cause the instantaneous death of its owner.

What we have written here may displease you strongly; we have ourselves not enjoyed writing it, and it is possible that we lack some objectivity in our opinion about the lethality of violent physical activity. If we do, however, it is not through any dislike of violent exercise per se, but because we have repeatedly had the distressing task of attempting to console women widowed by the inability of their husbands to give it up. What could we say to these women? Should we have offered them the sleazy rationalization that if their husbands had not jogged or run or played hard tennis or racquetball, they might have died even sooner?

We know that many of you, like some of our RCPP participants, will want to ask your own doctor's opinion of our views about the possible perils of vigorous exercises. By all means do so. If he disagrees with us and urges you to continue, well then perhaps you should. But before you do, may we suggest to you (as we suggested to our RCPP participants) that you take one further step: Ask your physician to give you a note, *in writing*, specifically confirming his advice to continue strenuous exercising even in the absence of a defibrillator. Only one of our RCPP participants was able to obtain such written permission. If you do obtain it, give it to your spouse for safekeeping. If you cannot obtain written permission from your physician to go on exercising violently, do not question his refusal, just reread this entire section and then discuss the situation with your spouse. We believe that you should abide by his or her decision.

We know through investigation that over 80 percent of the recurrent heart attacks among participants in the RCPP study could have been prevented by adherence to the advice and precautions described in this and preceding chapters. Yet gaining protection against a heart attack is in many ways simpler than getting one. Look at what you must have done to suffer a heart attack. You must have eaten a diet in your youth that was high in cholesterol and fat, struggled incessantly against time and other persons, poisoned yourself with tobacco smoke, and battered your coronary arteries by racing your heart wildly against high blood pressure in frenetic physical activities. From this it should be obvious that heart attacks do not just happen, they have to be *worked* for!

CHAPTER 15

Can You Modify *Your* Type A Behavior?

After more than three years of observing Type A post-infarction participants in the RCPP study, we now are certain that a majority of heart attack survivors can reduce the intensity of their Type A behavior. In fact, so many of our participants were successful in this that we now believe that even healthy Type A's can equally well forestall their first heart attack by modifying their behavior pattern. This should be good news particularly for those persons who are already afflicted with hypertension or hypercholesterolemia (an excessive amount of cholesterol in the blood), or who smoke cigarettes. The presence of one or more of these recognized risk factors, combined with Type A behavior, makes the prospect of coronary heart disease not a possibility for them, but a probability. Ameliorating their Type A behavior thus furnishes them with a measure of hope, the more so because this behavior pattern may well have been responsible for initiating and maintaining their high blood pressure and level of cholesterol, as well as encouraging their consumption of cigarettes, in the first place. (On the other hand, let not a single reader ever allow himself to believe that his high blood pressure, or his high blood cholesterol, or even his immoderate cigarette smoking had anything to do with originating his Type A behavior! Hundreds of animals have been exposed to tobacco smoke and have been observed to be hypertensive or hypercholesterolemic without developing anything even remotely resembling Type A behavior.)

With this note of encouragement, let us describe the kind of participant in our study who found it possible to scale down the magnitude of his Type A behavior significantly. Admittedly the profile is to a degree informal; there is no way to describe such a person in quantitative terms. But certain characteristics do appear to be associated with a capacity to change. Here are some of them:

Absence of Certain Type A Psychomotor Manifestations

Type A participants of the RCPP study who finally succeeded in modifying their behavior pattern significantly did not exhibit extreme physical restlessness—more or less continuous finger tapping, knee jiggling, or frequent changes in position or posture. Nor did they display, with any frequency, the tic-like movements (described in Chapter 2) that betray intense free-floating hostility—pulling back of the corners of the lips, opening the eyes widely so as to expose the whites above and below the iris, or contracting the various neck or shoulder muscles. They rarely indulged in tuneless humming or showed excessive facial perspiration.

Finally, few or none of them showed the *extremely* rapid speech patterns typical of the confirmed Type A. Those individuals whose speech was chronically so rapid as to require intense concentration on the part of listeners usually failed to alter their Type A behavior or, for that matter, to slow down their speech.

Ability to See Yourself As Others See You

Almost all of us find ways to play down or overlook completely many of our failings. Type A's are exceptionally good at this. The RCPP participants whom we observed to be capable, at an early stage, of tempering the intensity of their Type A behavior were those willing to scrutinize their feelings, thoughts, and actions with a minimum of self-delusion.

One of the first faults they were able to identify in themselves was their penchant for venting their hostility—harping upon various racist and sexist topics, on the presumed inefficiencies of governmental officers and employees, the stupidity of most car drivers, and so forth. "I began to realize," one man confessed, "that no matter whom I began to talk to, sooner or later I'd find myself bringing the conversation around to the decay downtown. I even felt irritated and unhappy when anyone so much as suggested that not all cities were decaying at their centers. When I thought about it, I realized that my hostility was at the bottom of it. I was just looking for subjects to feel upset about."

Another fault fairly readily noted by Type A's capable of modifying their behavior was their envy of those in the same vocational field whom they saw as relatively more successful. Type A's rarely envy persons who are successful in businesses or professions completely different from their own. For example, a Type A banker with a relatively modest salary rarely envies, in any active way, a very rich real estate agent or industrialist, but he is very much aware of and frequently quite jealous of the progress of another banker. Oddly enough, we rarely observed any

Type A in the study to envy any other individual on the grounds of physical, emotional, or even intellectual superiority in an avocational area. Type A envy is almost exclusively vocationally oriented.

In the same way, the Type A's most likely to change were those able and willing to admit certain character flaws in themselves, even though they had previously been unable to do so. These included, for example, admitting that their own petty larcenies (such as taking Scotch tape or stationery from the office) amounted to about the same thing as the failings they were in the habit of criticizing violently in others, and conceding that their vaunted morality often contained elements of hypocrisy and snobbishness. Our most hopeful cases, again, were able to recognize and admit their own occasional lack of loyalty to their spouses, their friends, and acquaintances and to confess that they lacked sufficient security and self-esteem.

On the positive side, these particular Type A's possessed some attributes of which they had good reason to be proud. They had the ability to work hard at their jobs; they retained at least some affection for and interest in other people, animals, and things; they were still curious about some phenomena not directly related to their work; a few of them maintained a fairly decent acquaintance with literature, music, drama, and the arts; and almost all of them were capable of generosity to others. Most were also able to assume, when necessary, burdensome responsibilities, a laudable attribute whose importance we do not mean to belittle by pointing out that though Type A's possess many faults, an unwillingness to assume responsibility is as a rule not one of them.

Potential for Cutting Back on Events and Numbers

A sense of time urgency of course is one of the chief manifestations of Type A behavior and it cannot be alleviated unless those afflicted are willing to eliminate some of their activities. We observed that RCPP subjects who were willing relatively early in the counseling period to do this, and to curb their drive to acquire more and more *things*, found it comparatively easy to reduce the fierceness of other aspects of their Type A behavior.

One of our participants, a lawyer we'll call Henry Schwartz, coolly and dispassionately reviewed the extent of his vocational activities while convalescing from a heart attack. He discovered for the first time that as an attorney he had 502 clients, but only eight of this number accounted for over 90 percent of his income. After his recovery and return to the practice of law, he accordingly informed these eight clients that he was going to devote all his time to them. He sent a letter to his remaining 494 clients informing them that he could no longer represent them and referred them to a choice of other competent colleagues. In addition, he closed one of his two law offices, sold a small investment business he ran in another city, and ceased serving as an evening instructor in a local law school. Had Schwartz not suffered a heart attack, he might never have found time for his stocktaking. It made clear to him that he had gone right on battling against the insecurity he first experienced several decades earlier when he began the practice of law, in spite of the fact that he had long since become financially and professionally secure. "Do you know what happened in the year after I made these changes?" Schwartz asked. "I made just as much money as I had the year before. The next year, I made twice as much. And yet I was seeing and enjoying my wife and kids, something I'd never found the time for before my heart attack."

Schwartz did not find it all difficult to modify his Type A behavior in accord with our counseling.

The same can be said for another participant brought to his senses first by a heart attack. "When I realized that I was just collecting a lot of numbers that I really didn't need, I felt ashamed. At 58, I wasn't any wiser than I was at 10 when I collected cigar bands. What the hell is the real difference, I asked myself, between collecting cigar bands and collecting commissions from life insurance sales? That's when I called up the main office at Hartford and said to the big boss, "Jack, you've always told me that I had to increase my quota because so many of your young folks wanted my job. Well, now you can give my job to one of your hustlers, because I've decided to retire.'"

The man who made this statement is now growing carnations near La Jolla, but he still returns to his monthly RCPP group meeting. Almost every vestige of Type A behavior has disappeared from his face, body, and voice. He now laughs easily, becoming reflective when he thinks of the district office he managed for so many years. "That Goddamned rat race. I can't even force myself to visit the fellows who used to work for me there. I did it once and from the first minute I entered the office I knew that they wanted me out so that they could get back to their numbers game." We are certain that this man is in no danger whatever of suffering another heart attack for quite a few years.

Note that both these men gained a new sense of self-esteem not by achieving more but by sharply abridging their activities and expectations. They also gave up the world of numbers to enter the far more joyous world of persons, pets, and plants.

Not everyone in the RCPP study managed this, of course. We recall a participant who from the outset made clear that he would or could not give up his ambition to acquire more and more rare stamps and fine paintings even though he detested his position as the president of a small lumber company. "I endure the Goddamned pressure because it gives me enough money to continue buying stamps and canvases," he said. Decades ago, he decided that his wife was almost unbearably monotonous and colorless, but that a divorce was not feasible. "If I tried to get one, we'd have to sell the collections." He admits that none of his paintings or even his rarest stamp can afford him more than the doubtful satisfaction of studying auction records to figure out what his prize possessions may be worth. He still lives by the immature acquisitive fervor he developed as a little boy when he first began to collect stamps. If a philatelist Mephistopheles were to appear and offer him an 1856 one-cent British Guiana magenta in exchange for his soul—or at the price of doubling his sense of time urgency—we suspect that he would gladly accept the offer. This despite his three years of enrollment in the RCPP study. Goethe and Balzac may have gloried in describing characters like this one, but we take no pleasure at all in it. From the standpoint of our study, he is a perfect failure.

Relative Ease in Seeing and Accepting Realities

Among the RCPP participants who proved most amenable to significant alterations in their Type A behavior were those who most readily grasped certain psychological and philosophical realities and related them to their beliefs. These realities included an understanding of the following:

- That their security had never been enhanced by application of any of the basic components of Type A behavior (anger, hurry sickness, and so forth), but on the contrary had hampered both their vocational and social progress. As long as any participant remained reluctant to discard his belief in the value of any of these components, he failed to make progress in altering his Type A behavior as a whole.
- That Type A behavior had seriously damaged their personality, and that its repair and enhancement (particularly in the area of cultural interests, disdained since high school or college) was a matter of urgent concern.

- That their life is in its deepest sense always unfinished, and they no longer made desperate efforts to try to get everything wrapped up by 5 P.M. each day.
- That one should pay far less attention to things worth having and much more to things worth being.
- That deep within many Type A's flows a self-destructive stream. Very few participants recognized the existence of this unconscious urge at the beginning, but within a few months some did. They were among those who made good progress toward behavior modification.
- That memory should be greatly valued and used with some frequency to recall and relive pleasant or joyous events of the past.

A Comparatively Low Level of Hostility

Those participants in the RCPP study who exhibited few or none of the psychomotor signs of severe hostility (frequent clenching of the fists, a hate-filled face, or a harsh, staccato, arrogant voice or laugh) usually proved amenable to behavior counseling. This was true even if they admitted to irritation or anger at some of the antics of other people, especially erratic or hyperaggressive motorists. On the other hand, participants who found almost all other people stupid or "only out for what they could get," whose faces were marked by a chronic scowl, and who from time to time glared with bulging eyes or frequently bared their teeth in a tic-like movement, proved totally unable to rid themselves of their Type A behavior. Indeed, some of this latter group remained convinced to the end that a thirst for fame, not a wish to help people protect themselves from a second heart attack, was really behind our research efforts. (We hope that there is not much truth in their suspicion; but if there is, allow us to point out that scientists are fallible human beings too.)

A Sense of Humor

The distinguished editor and writer Norman Cousins, almost hopelessly crippled a decade ago by a mysterious disorder that was relentlessly ravaging his joints and other important body tissues, decided in desperation to give up on his baffled doctors and take his cure into his own hands. Leaving the hospital, he began reading, almost continuously, a series of funny articles and stories. In a remarkably short time, as he later reported in *Anatomy of an Illness as Perceived by the Patient*, he recovered completely. Mr. Cousins was of course convinced that his diet of jokes and laughter had done the trick; in any case, they seem to have done more for him than his Boston doctors could.

We must make clear that our idea of a protective sense of humor, one that can help ward off a heart attack, is of a rather different sort. Indeed, many of our Type A post-infarction participants were superb tellers of jokes and quick to see the humor in the jokes told by others. But as Mr. Cousins himself should have discovered, having suffered a heart attack within a few years of successfully treating his arthritic disorder with comedy, what is wanted is an ability to laugh not just at jokes but at oneself. The person most effectively protecting himself against the continued progress of coronary artery disease is the person willing to see himself and his affairs as ludicrously unimportant in the planetary scheme of things. Anyone equipped with this kind of perspective rarely succumbs to an early myocardial infarction. In fact, we cannot recall, in our total clinical experience, a single person under the age of 65 years who, having kept constantly in mind the basic ephemerality and triviality of his daily problems and activities, later suffered a heart attack.

A Peaceful Environment

While most of the difficulties the Type A encounters in his environment can be traced to his own character and behavior, this is not always the case. Sometimes individuals find themselves thrown willy-nilly into vocational or social situations that simply cannot be reconciled with serenity and equanimity.

For example, the presence in the home of a mentally or emotionally deranged spouse or child provided strains that severely compromised the ability of certain RCPP participants to deal with the most crippling aspects of their Type A behavior. Similarly, participants whose financial resources were inadequate, or whose job forced them to work under an unreasonable, hostile, ruthless, or even alcoholic superior, were much less likely to benefit from behavior counseling than those spared such personal misfortune and tension.

An Effective Internal Monitor

We have described the important role played by the internal monitor in restraining the Type A's impulse to do too much in too little time or to explode wrathfully over the actions of other persons. This personification or incarnation of self-control plays a very powerful role in the reduction of Type A behavior.

Our most successful RCPP participants were in the main those who learned relatively quickly to construct their own monitors and to use them effectively in interfering with or interrupting any train of thought or feeling engendered by the greed to do more things or the hair-trigger tendency to blow up at someone. As one of these participants told us, "I had a conversation yesterday with a guy who usually has me climbing a wall after a few seconds, but my monitor kept saying, 'Hey, cool it, just keep feeling sorry for the son-of-a-bitch, if only because he's just as much a horse's ass as you used to be.' I ended up laughing at myself and my AIAI just blew away." Remember that it is not enough simply to fabricate an internal monitor; it must be powerful enough to come into play repeatedly if necessary during any confrontation. It also must be vigilant enough to deal with any affront before it can reach the Type A's emotional centers and set off a hostile explosion.

Willpower to Persist in Drills

Almost a century ago William James stressed the necessity of conscious and repetitive drills by means of which new beneficial habits can be formed and old injurious ones eliminated. This process is necessary because our brain is deeply conservative, with a predisposition to process our thoughts, opinions, and even our motor activities via already well-used neurogenic pathways, some of them established many decades ago. It tends to resist doggedly any attempt made to establish or impress one or more new pathway ruts, that is, habits, in its substance.

Those participants who had the willpower to drill regularly, almost always succeeded in modifying their Type A behavior; those who lacked willpower did not succeed. It is as simple and tragic as that!

These are the characteristics that seem to be associated with an ability to modify the intensity of one's Type A behavior. Their absence is an indication of an inability to change. Certainly in the RCPP study we encountered far too many people in the latter category. When we watched them continue in their fretful, unhappy downward spiral, mindlessly ignoring the loveliness that life could have afforded them, we shook our heads in sadness, trusting that our own internal monitors would shield us from frustration or anger over our failure to bring them round. We knew what they had lost; we nearly lost it too.

PART FOUR

THE BOTTOM LINE

CHAPTER 16

And Once More, Before We Leave

It has been a decade since the last chapter, "And Before We Leave," in *Type A Behavior and Your Heart* was written.

In that chapter, we predicted that there would be less coronary heart disease to treat in ten years' time. The reduction would be due, we hoped, to more attention on the part of pediatricians to the diet of children and adolescents, causing them to consume drastically less animal fat and cholesterol; that Americans would smoke fewer cigarettes or none at all; and finally, that many Type A's would have altered their destructive behavior pattern. We also hazarded the opinion that coronary bypass surgery would improve markedly and that by 1984 a dependable, economically feasible artificial heart would be available to replace a heart too badly damaged by disease of its coronary vasculature to be repaired surgically or medically, even in part. We also believed that potent new drugs would have been discovered, particularly drugs capable of halting ventricular fibrillation and preventing instant cardiac death.

Well, those ten years have passed. How valid did our hopeful prophecies turn out to be? We must admit that the results are mixed. First, cardiac surgery has improved markedly, to the point where only one out of a hundred patients undergoing bypass surgery in the best clinics fails to survive the operation. A bypass operation is now essentially as safe as a gall bladder or prostate operation, and usually less painful and distressing. Almost 110,000 of them are performed each year in the United States alone, at a cost of approximately two billion dollars. The coronary bypass is possibly the most frequently performed elective surgical procedure we have. And a workable artificial heart is in existence. Just as we were finishing this book, an air-driven artificial heart was implanted in the chest of a dentist named Barney B. Clark at the University of Utah Medical School in Salt Lake City. Though this brave man survived only 3½ months, it was not his artificial heart that failed him, and it is plain that a new era in the treatment of heart disease has begun.*

---

*A number of physicians and surgeons deserve credit for this achievement, but in our estimation one stands out above the others. Willem J. Kolff, M.D., Ph.D., a Dutchman who is now 72, in 1944 published his doctoral thesis *De Kunstmatige Nier* (issued three years later in English under the title *New Ways of Treating Uremia*). This work led directly to the renal dialyzers used so widely today to prevent uremia in persons with inadequately functioning kidneys. Kolff, after a decade spent perfecting his dialysis machine, turned to the fabrication of an artificial heart.

For over a quarter of a century, as founder and director of the Institute for Biomedical Engineering and Division of Artificial Organs at the University of Utah, he struggled against a myriad natural (and man-made) obstacles before at last achieving the first successful replacement of a human heart by a mechanical one. He received little or no financial aid from any large private or federal government source; at one point he was even forced to sell some of his own precious books to rare book collectors in order to defray laboratory expenses.

Still, because of what he has done he is much more to be envied than pitied by fellow physicians. His success in inventing two extraordinarily ingenious techniques for replacing failing organs, the kidney and the heart, will bring him enduring fame. No matter what the future holds in the way of improvements to his artificial heart (as his kidney machines have been vastly improved since 1944), Willem Kolff will be remembered as the man who began it all.

Our prophecy concerning the discovery of new drugs has proved to be correct. Today the cardiologist has available at least a half dozen new chemical tools able to ease the pain of angina, or to help the muscle of a heart gone flabby to pump more efficiently. And very soon a new drug will be available to the American physician that promises to be a most potent inhibitor of ventricular fibrillation or cardiac arrest. Since approximately one person dies every minute from this deadly phenomenon, we hope that federal bureaucratic red tape will do nothing to delay access to it for even one unnecessary minute.

What we failed to anticipate in *Type A Behavior and Your Heart* was the almost miraculous increase in the number of American men, women, and children capable of administering cardiopulmonary resuscitation. Perhaps as many as 150 million Americans now have received instruction in this lifesaving procedure. Thousands of them have already had occasion to put their knowledge to use on the floor of a department store, on a city sidewalk, in a restaurant or a stadium.

Nor did we guess that during this last decade almost every hospital in our country would establish a coronary care unit far better equipped than the pioneering installation devised by Dr. Hughes Day* in 1962 at the small and relatively unknown Bethany Hospital in Kansas City, Kansas. Another pleasant surprise was the distribution of thousands of mobile and portable defibrillators† not only to all hospitals in the United States but also to indus-

---

*Dr. Day's first article describing his invention of the coronary care unit and "code-blue" emergency system associated with it was declined publication in 1962 by the editor of a national medical journal with the comment, "There is nothing new to write about in the field of cardiac resuscitation." A decade later, the editor of the *American Journal of Cardiology* invited Dr. Day to write an article describing the "History of Coronary Care Units."

†Dr. Paul M. Zoll, the inventor of the defibrillator in 1952, told us that this discovery also failed at first to impress his colleagues. When he applied for a $5,000 grant from a prestigious national organization, he was turned down on the grounds that effective external electrical stimulation of the heart was not possible. Twenty-five years later, however, he received a Lasker Award for his invention.

trial clinics and, most important of all, to the paramedics manning ambulances throughout the country. It now is becoming somewhat more difficult to die instantaneously of ventricular fibrillation.

Given all these advances in ways of prolonging the lives of persons already stricken with severe coronary heart disease, it should not surprise the layman to learn that during the past 15 or 20 years a 20 percent decrease in coronary deaths has taken place. However, the cause (or causes) of this very significant decrease is still the subject of endless speculation among cardiologists, particularly those who have argued in favor of changing the diet of American adults or of exercising vigorously. These latter cardiologists (most of whom are epidemiologists) like to intimate that adult diet and exercise are the *probable* causes of the observed decline in mortality, but dare not be absolute about it; after all, to do so would be to say in effect that coronary care units, defibrillators, bypass surgery, and widespread use of cardiopulmonary resuscitation meant nothing at all—in which case why continue to spend billions of dollars on them? No one knows better than they that such a step would be the height of foolishness.

A second reason why this particular group of "diet-exercise" cardiologists do not claim flatly that the decline in mortality can be laid to their efforts is that there has been no decrease in the number of *new* cases of coronary heart disease occurring each year. In other words, in spite of all the exercise classes and road running and diet modifications for adults, just as many people are developing CHD as ever. This fact is well known to cardiologists, but not to the laity. Indeed there has been something approaching news blackout on the subject.

In the last chapter of *Type A Behavior and Your Heart*, we predicted hopefully that modification in Type A behavior might itself lead to a reduced incidence of CHD by 1983. Although it is probable that hundreds, perhaps thousands, of persons already ill with CHD have been able to modify their Type A behavior significantly, just how many still healthy Type A's have done so is a question we cannot answer. We suspect that not many have found the will and the courage. While hundreds of cardiologists during this past decade have advised their coronary patients to read *Type A Behavior and Your Heart*, we doubt that many of them insisted on a thorough reading and rereading. Most cardiologists are so severely afflicted with Type A behavior that they are unlikely to have read the book carefully and introspectively themselves; besides, as we have said, while most of them are willing to grant that Type A behavior may accelerate the onset of CHD, they do not think it can be modified.

This latter belief may soon change. Before this book is published, at least two articles reporting the results of the RCPP study will have appeared in prestigious medical journals. The statistics contained in these articles will make it overwhelmingly clear that Type A behavior *can* be changed in coronary patients, and when it is, *this change provides the most potent protection yet discovered against recurrent myocardial infarction or instantaneous cardiac death*. Our colleagues, tendentious as they (and we) well may be, are almost without exception well-intentioned men and women. We are confident that when they read these articles their opinions about the unalterability of Type A behavior may change. After all, it has taken a number of years and several dozen major confirmatory studies of our original work to convince the majority of American cardiologists that Type A behavior plays some part in the development of clinical CHD.* It may well take still more years before cardiologists accept the possiblity that this behavior pattern can be modified in a goodly portion of their patients, if not in all of them.

As for us, after observing scores of RCPP participants rather easily modify their Type A behavior and begin to experience a fuller, finer, often more productive life, we

---

*Most British and French (but not German, Finnish, or Russian) cardiologists still shy away from this position. Japanese physicians, however, are beginning to recognize the potential coronary danger of Type A behavior.

are completely convinced that there is no need for all Type A's to remain enslaved to their sense of time urgency and their free-floating hostility until they are freed by either a sudden cardiac death or by a severe (and often severely crippling) myocardial infarction. Certainly the time must come when millions of them will be as a matter of course informed by their physicians of the consequences of a failure to do something about their behavior.

"You making haste, haste on decay," Robinson Jeffers warned us over a half century ago in his poem "Shine, Perishing Republic." What would he say if he could see us now, even more frantically dashing, darting, and sprinting almost senselessly through life? Let us not fool ourselves, moreover, about this simple but truly terrible fact: If Type A individuals ever succeed in taking over our society completely, it will scarcely be worth living in! We have resisted this conclusion for a long time, but it now seems to us unavoidable. The lovelessness at the center of the Type A's spirit embitters all it touches. Yet if a therapeutic process can be set in motion to help Type A's find serenity and affection in their own lives, we may cease worrying about what they will do to ours. We need not hate; such passions can be subdued, provided serious steps are taken. We believe that such steps can be and should be taken *soon*!

There is much talk these days about the Japanese and their economic successes, many of them at our expense. It strikes us as important to remind our readers, as we finish this book, that the Japanese are not getting ahead—as so many Americans believe—by indulging in a still more intense version of Type A behavior. Quite the contrary! Type A behavior is not very common among the Japanese who live in Japan. According to the best evidence we have seen, the Japanese success is due largely to their ability to plan and act on behalf of the whole group instead of the first person singular, to work long, hard, and *together* rather than competitively and aggressively against each other as individuals, to think in the long term rather than the short. In many ways, they have avoided the American obsession with the bottom line and its string of numbers, commas, and decimal points.

Or perhaps one might say that the Japanese, unlike most Type A's, are able to see the *true* bottom line—not the one composed of numbers, but the one that summarizes what a person has done with his life, the joy he has brought to others, the care with which he has conserved and enlarged his spirit. That, in the long run, is the only bottom line that matters.

APPENDIX

A List of Aphorisms Useful for Revision of Beliefs

1. "For every minute you are angry, you lose 60 seconds of happiness."—Ralph Waldo Emerson

2. "When a fixed idea makes its appearance, a great ass also makes its appearance."—Nietzsche

3. "...And it occurred to me that there was no difference between men in intelligence or race so profound as the difference between the sick and well."—F. Scott Fitzgerald

4. "Unhappy is a society that has lost the words to understand the world."—Daniel Bell

5. "Nothing has happened [to me] but loneliness."—Emily Dickinson

6. "Love is nature's second sun causing a spring of virtues when he shines."—George Chapman

7. "Before I had my heart attack, I didn't have any friends. When I played poker, I played to win from the bastards."—Jesse Lair

8. "Think of persons as adventures."—Lawrence Durrell

9. "Good conversation should be a dialogue, not a duel of monologues."—Anon.

10. "There is no learning to live without learning to love."—John Powell, S.J.

11. "Perhaps the best test of man's intelligence is his capacity for making a summary."—Lytton Strachey

12. Ask yourself why you are so much more aware of the irritating qualities of other persons than their good qualities.

13. Coronary patients are not condemned to lead bandaged lives.

14. No family survives as a unit if it is bound together only by ties of loveless duty.

15. "Common sense is only wisdom applied to conduct."—William James

16. "Experiment to me/ Is everyone I meet/ If it contains a kernel."—Emily Dickinson

17. Wisdom embraces as one of its indispensable components the processes of pity and forgiveness.

18. "Culture is acquainting ourselves with the best that has ever been known and said in the World."—Matthew Arnold

19. "He who is hurried cannot walk gracefully."—old Chinese proverb

20. "No new truth is ever really learned until it is acted upon."—John Powell, S.J.

21. No nation has ever been warred against solely because its inhabitants excelled in creating great poetry, music, or painting.

22. And when all the clocks and calendars have stopped their counting for you, what then has your life added up to?

23. You must find time to bring order to your past, and to remember it.

24. There are two creatures in nature that exhibit impatience: men and puppies.

25. The moment numeration ceases to be your servant, it becomes your tyrant.

26. "There is, in my view, one thing you can depend on: People who are interested in power are not interested in people."—John Ward

27. "Nothing is so vulgar as to be in a hurry."—Oliver Wendell Holmes

28. "When men have killed joy, I do not believe they still live."—Sophocles

29. If our measurements and documentations manage to do away with all our religious beliefs, what have we gained?

30. "There is no second act in American lives."—F. Scott Fitzgerald

31. "There is something in the American character that regards nothing as desperate."—Thomas Jefferson

32. The only love that counts for anything is that which reveals itself not just in deeds but in words.

33. If we did not exist as human beings, what plant or animal would miss us?

34. Very few things worth measuring can be measured.

35. "Knowledge is folly except Grace guides it."—George Herbert

36. "If you make the organization your life, you are defenseless against the inevitable disappointments."—Peter Drucker

37. "The most difficult thing in life is to know yourself."—Thales

38. If you are ashamed to pray for something, it may not be worth obtaining.

39. The most important obligation of friendship is to listen and to remember that which you heard.

40. "No man who has once heartily and wholly laughed can be irredeemably bad."—Thomas Carlyle

41. "Memory is reading oneself backward."—Walter Benjamin

42. "Genius is nothing but a greater aptitude for patience."—Buffon

43. "To let friendship die away by negligence and silence is to voluntarily throw away one of the greatest comforts of this weary pilgrimage."—Samuel Johnson

44. "Only the brave know how to forgive. . . . A coward never forgives, it is not in his nature."—Lawrence Sterne

45. "Do not say things. What you are thunders so, that I cannot hear what you say to the contrary."—Emerson

46. "The heart of a man changeth his countenance whether it be good or evil."—Ecclesiasticus

47. "Mental health is the ability to work and to love."—Heinz Kohut

48. "Democracy is the recurrent suspicion that more than half of the people are right more than half the time."—E. B. White

49. "You shall have joy or you shall have power, said God, you shall not have both."—Emerson

50. "The next thing most like living one's life over again seems to be a recollection of that life."—Benjamin Franklin

51. "Talk *low*, talk *slow*, and don't say *too much*."—John Wayne's advice on acting.

52. "The creative act is the defeat of habit by originality."—Arthur Koestler

53. "Mark this well, you proud men of action: You are nothing but the *unwitting* agents of the men of thought, who often, in quiet self-effacement, mark out most exactly all your doings in advance."—Heinrich Heine

54. "Love is an attempt at penetrating another being, but it can only succeed if the surrender is mutual."—Octavio Paz

55. "The Indian Summer of life should be a little sunny and a little sad, like the season, and infinite in wealth and depth of tone—*but never hustled*."—Henry B. Adams

56. When has God judged us by counting the things we own?

57. On the average, a man having no avocations on retiring receives only 13 Social Security checks before he dies.

58. One's voice sounds lovely only when one possesses an inner repose.

59. A mind continually preoccupied with the future garners nothing for its memory.

60. "One ought, every day at least, to hear a little song, read a good poem, see a fine picture, and if it were possible, to speak a few reasonable words."—Goethe

61. "The metaphor is probably the most fertile power possessed by man."—Ortega y Gasset

62. "Success is a result; it must not be a goal."—Flaubert

63. "For those who seek constancy in feelings, thoughts, or actions, the only solution short of death is to be transformed into a rock."—Paul G. Quinett

INDEX

ABOUT THE AUTHORS

Meyer Friedman, M.D., is director of the Recurrent Coronary Prevention Project at the Harold Brunn Institute of Mount Zion Hospital and Medical Center in San Francisco. He is an internationally known cardiologist and the author (with Ray H. Rosenman, M.D.) of *Type A Behavior and Your Heart*, as well as hundreds of technical papers and two medical textbooks. From 1939 to 1980, Dr. Friedman served as director of the Harold Brunn Institute for Cardiovascular Research at Mount Zion Hospital. It was there that he discovered, named, and researched the syndrome called Type A Behavior.

Diane Ulmer, R.N., M.S., is supervising director of the Recurrent Coronary Prevention Project.

HERE'S TO YOUR HEALTH!

A compendium of useful titles from Fawcett Books.

15